# THE
# IRON
# CAGE

# THE
# IRON
# CAGE

Nigel Cawthorne

FOURTH ESTATE · London

First published in Great Britain in 1993 by
Fourth Estate Limited
289 Westbourne Grove
London W11 2QA

A catalogue record for this book is available from the
British Library.

ISBN 1–85702–101–0

Typeset by York House Typographic Ltd
Printed in Great Britain by Cambridge University Press

# Contents

# Acknowledgements

I should like to thank Tom Ashworth, John M.G. Brown, Jim Sanders, Mark Sauter, Cort Kirkwood, Tracy Usry and Ted Sampley for all their assistance.

# List of Plates

CHAPTER 1

# Yeltsin Speaks Out

✝

WHEN BORIS YELTSIN visited America in the summer of 1992 he stamped a heavy Russian boot on America's tenderest corn. First in a letter to a US Senate Committee, then in an interview on board his plane, he confirmed what the American people had long believed: that not all the American prisoners of war captured in Vietnam had been returned at the end of that war. Some of them, President Yeltsin said, had been taken into the Soviet Union and might still be alive in the republics of the former USSR even now.

The fate of these missing American prisoners still listed as 'missing in action' (or MIA) at the end of the Vietnam War had long chafed at America. Black MIA flags hang from public buildings on Memorial Day. Twenty-four-hour vigils huddle around the Wall, the black marble Vietnam Memorial in Washington DC. Bamboo cages with pyjama-clad prisoners crouching inside them appear in veterans' parades. 'Bring 'em back alive' bumper stickers have sprouted on the fenders of ageing Chevvies and T-shirts bearing pictures of chained eagles are stretched round the beer-bellies of ponytailed, Harley-riding renegades who once saw action in the paddy fields of Southeast Asia.

While Hollywood has mythologised the MIAs in films like *Rambo* and other muscle-bound epics, the families, friends and former comrades of these missing men have organised themselves into a formidable pressure group. They run veterans' newspapers, collect and collate information, petition congressmen and organise elaborate publicity stunts – anything to bring the fate of their missing loved ones to the public's attention.

Several dedicated individuals have realised that the key to the fate of the missing American prisoners lies not in the re-education camps of Vietnam and Laos or the Soviet Gulag but in Washington. America spends countless billions of dollars on Intelligence every year. If American prisoners were being held in communist countries, the

1

Intelligence services would know about it. Somewhere in the vast forests of Intelligence reports and memos the US government generates every year there must be a smoking gun.

Armed with the Freedom of Information Act, a small band of researchers set about proving their case. One of them, Bill Paul of the *Wall Street Journal*, was advised to set his sights a little wider by a Soviet general who told him that a large number of Allied prisoners of war held by the Germans until 1945 had also ended up in Soviet labour camps. Former cop Jim Sanders, who lived in Virginia near Washington's National Archives, set about investigating this allegation full time.

Another veteran, John M.G. Brown, author of *Rice Paddy Grunt*, was asked by a prominent Washington insider to delve into the historical background of the MIA issue. The handling by the administration of the question of American POWs in enemy hands was not a matter of whim or of haphazard decisions taken by witless bureaucrats. Like anything else in the fields of politics, diplomacy or warfare, it was governed by precedent and policy. Brown began looking for the precedents and the roots of that policy in World War I and the Allied intervention in Russia. Another tenacious researcher, Tom Ashworth, a former marine helicopter pilot from Arkansas, also started down that path.

On that same trip to America, Boris Yeltsin also brought confirmation for Messrs Paul, Sanders, Brown and Ashworth of what their vast, self-funded research project had already told them. It was not just American prisoners from the war in Vietnam who had ended up in the Gulag. Men captured – in some cases kidnapped – during World War II, the war in Korea and the Cold War had also been taken into the Soviet Union and had disappeared in the Gulag. Some of those men might also still be alive in the republics of the former Soviet Union, Yeltsin said.

Cynics suggested that Yeltsin had only spoken out to get money for his country: knowing American sensitivity on the subject of their missing prisoners, perhaps he hoped to wring aid out of them. But that is to misunderstand the politics of the MIA issue.

American MIA activists have long held that the Nixon administration, in its hurry to pull out of Vietnam, abandoned the missing men in communist hands. George Bush and most of the leading members of his government held key junior posts in the Nixon administration where they would have known that prisoners had been left behind. They had gone on to other key government posts where they

2

would have seen Intelligence about these men's continued survival in communist captivity. It could even be said that they had built a career on knowing the big secret. After his time (1974–6) as principal liaison officer with the People's Republic of China – on Vietnam's doorstep, so to speak – George Bush became head of the CIA (1976–7). And as Reagan's vice president (1981–8) he was the White House official assigned to handle the MIA issue.

Bush's response to Yeltsin's revelations can be judged by the way his face fell when Yeltsin mentioned the missing prisoners again during a televised speech at a White House dinner. The Washington rumour machine went into action, putting it around that Yeltsin did not know what he was talking about, he was drunk. And when Yeltsin was safely back in Moscow, the American administration announced that he had 'mis-spoken'. Who knows what that can possibly mean, but it must be as close as you can come to calling the head of a foreign power a liar without starting a war.

Yeltsin's words had not been directed at the Americans. They were for home consumption. More than anything, Yeltsin was afraid of the tanks rolling in on him, as they had on Gorbachev. The American prisoners had been held captive by the military, by the communist old guard. This was one issue he could use to smear them. He could hold them at bay with this shocking allegation, even though it meant treading on the corns of the Western Allies with whom he was now trying to waltz.

Yeltsin's mention of missing American prisoners from World War II, Korea and the Cold War rang few bells in America. The American public knew only of the missing men from Vietnam. However, the fate of missing American prisoners of war from these earlier wars was in fact already under investigation by the US Senate. In 1991 a number of photographs said to be of American airmen still held in Southeast Asia had come to light. Their families appeared on national television and demanded action. As media interest peaked, Senator John Kerry set up a Senate Select Committee, which held its preliminary meetings in October 1991, to investigate. Its remit included prisoners of war missing from World War II, Korea and the Cold War, as well as Vietnam. Shortly after, when reports of an American pilot being held in a camp in Kazakhstan appeared in the Soviet press, a joint US–Russian Commission was set up to look into the fate of any American citizen who might have ended up in the Gulag.

To begin with, Yeltsin's words rang very few bells in Britain either. But the media were soon flabbergasted by the suggestion that British prisoners of war might have disappeared into the Gulag too. By contrast, for some time journalists and writers in France had been investigating the fate of French prisoners of war who had fallen into Soviet hands, though many of them had been from Alsace-Lorraine and had fought for the Nazis. The Italian government had also complained about the huge numbers of Italian prisoners of war taken by the Soviets and never handed back. The Dutch, Belgians, Luxembourgers, Germans and Japanese had all protested about missing prisoners of war at one time or another. But the British, notably, kept quiet about it. After all, Britain and the Soviet Union had been allies during World War II. Who cared if the Soviets had held on to enemy prisoners of war – as reparation or for punishment? Perhaps a few prisoners from friendly nations who had fought on the Allied side had been taken too, mixed up with the others during the general confusion in 1945. But why should the Soviets deliberately take and hold British POWs? President Yeltsin had confirmed that they had taken Americans, though. And America had been an ally of the Soviets too.

Some bells should have rung in Britain. There had been warning signs. In 1990 the work of Sanders, Brown and Ashworth had come to the attention of the US Senate Foreign Relations Committee which was examining US policy regarding POWs and MIAs. During their investigations the committee's staff had discovered that British policy had closely mirrored American policy. The chief of the Senate Foreign Relations committee Republican staff had even been to the British Embassy in Washington with evidence that British prisoners captured during the Korean War had been held in camps in China, and not returned. This, he thought, would make the British government sit up, take notice and do something about the missing British prisoners. They did. The Senate Foreign Relations Committee found that the British government hampered any further investigation.

The Senate Foreign Relations Committee Republican staff produced its report on 23 May 1991. It alleged that 20,000 Americans, who were prisoners of the Germans in 1945 and were 'liberated' by the Red Army, disappeared into Soviet labour camps. It also detailed the numbers of French, Dutch and Belgians who had been taken. The report went on to claim that 20,000 British (which included the Commonwealth) men had been lost into Soviet hands. Sanders, Brown and Ashworth say this is an underestimation. They say that the British forces – which comprised British, Canadian, Indian, Australian, New Zealand, South African and 'Colonial' troops and had nearly 200,000 POWs held in German camps – lost over 30,000 to the Soviets.

4

The report must have come to the British Embassy's attention. It certainly came to mine. In June 1991 I was in Washington when a member of the Senate Foreign Relations Committee staff gave me a copy. I read it on the plane back to England. The G7 conference of the world's richest seven countries was being held in London later that week. Soviet President Mikhail Gorbachev was coming to London to ask for aid. If Britain was going to give the Soviets aid, it could at least ask about the men the US Senate said were missing. I called my MP – Frank Dobson (Labour) – and ran photocopied extracts of the Senate report down to the House of Commons.

The Senate report also mentioned that Frenchmen, Dutchmen and Belgians had been taken. I called their embassies and faxed the appropriate extracts through to them. It did no good. The question of Allied prisoners missing in the Soviet Gulag did not arise at the summit.

Undaunted, I pressed for the British Embassy in Moscow to ask the Russian authorities about the missing British POWs. The allegation had not come from a journalist or an author but from the US Senate. A charge from such an august source demanded an answer. The answer was no. The fate of British prisoners of war was not a matter for the Foreign Office, the British government said. It was the responsibility of the Ministry of Defence.

I was referred to the Army Historical Branch who were 'actively looking into this matter'. However, they told me they had no evidence that British prisoners of war had been taken into the Soviet Union. The report of a US Senate committee whose staff had taken two years to investigate this matter did not count for anything.

Despite a flurry of letters from me and Frank Dobson, it took over a year for the Foreign Office to recognise its responsibility. And that was only after Boris Yeltsin had spoken out and journalists had descended on the site of a camp at Tambov, twenty-five miles southeast of Moscow, searching for missing Americans. Examining the records there, they discovered that the camp commandant had been ordered to prepare the camp for 'foreign prisoners' in May 1945. Some of those prisoners had been British.

This should have come as no surprise. The 1991 Senate Foreign Relations Committee report had mentioned French, Dutch, Belgians, Americans and British being held at Tambov after the end of the war. In France, several books had been published about Tambov and the foreign POWs who had been held there.

According to the *Moscow News* of 10–17 February 1991 other French prisoners who had been at Tambov and had 'lost their French citizenship' were still alive in the then Soviet Union forty-five years after being taken there. If Frenchmen had survived, and if as Yeltsin said some Americans had survived, surely some British men could have survived too. People do survive a long time in captivity, even in the appalling conditions experienced in the Gulag. It is not uncommon for people to complete a twenty-five-year sentence.

Very long sentences are often commuted, but politically sensitive prisoners are rarely allowed to go free. They are forced to settle near the camp or in some other closed area where they have to report to the militia every day.

In 1945 a German mapmaker from the Leipzig Cartographic Institute was captured by the Red Army. His job at the Institute had been to change the names on maps from Russian into German as the German army advanced in 1941. For this he was sentenced to twenty-five years' forced labour in a lead mine near the Arctic Circle in the Bering Straits area. Occasionally, when he was allowed above ground, he could see the lights of Alaska.

The mapmaker knew that, even after twenty-five years, he would not be released. If he stayed, he would die there. In 1951 he escaped, made his way on foot and by train across Siberia and eventually escaped through Iran. On the journey he was helped by a man called Leopold Messmer. When he asked why, Messmer explained that they were fellow countrymen. He was an Austrian who had been captured by the Czarist army in 1914. When the Russian Revolution came, he had been moved from a POW camp into a labour camp. In the mid-1920s he was released – but only after he had been forced to take out Soviet citizenship. There was even a cruel little ceremony. He was handed his repatriation papers, allowing him to go back to Vienna. Then they were taken away again. As a Soviet citizen he could not leave the country. Messmer was a baker by trade, so he opened a bakery in a small town called Abakan in Siberia. He married, raised a family and got on with his life. It is doubtful whether he ever saw Austria again.[1]

British newspapers briefly took up the story of Tambov and the missing British POWs. They questioned the Ministry of Defence who said that the Senate's suggestion of 20,000 British having disappeared in Soviet hands was ludicrous. There were only 2,780 men unaccounted for from the whole of World War II.[2]

Plainly, it is the figure of 2,780 that is ludicrous. World War II involved bombing on a massive scale, shelling, mortars, sea battles and submarine warfare. Huge numbers of ships were sunk and planes downed. Hundreds – if not thousands – of times that number were simply incinerated, vaporised or lost for ever in Davy Jones's locker.

However none of these men is literally 'unaccounted for'. Every missing serviceman from World War II and Korea has been accounted for, otherwise they would still be on the payroll. The salaries of servicemen who are unaccounted for still have to be paid. They are still taking the King's shilling.

I called the Ministry of Defence myself and asked what this figure of 2,780 could possibly mean? They were adamant that this was the number of missing from World War II. So I asked about the accounting procedure. They asked if they could call me back.

The accounting procedure went like this, I was eventually told. When a man goes missing on the battlefield, his name is entered in a column headed 'missing'. But it does not stay there. In a week or two an investigation is held. This decides whether the man has been killed and the body not recovered, or whether he has been taken prisoner. If he is presumed dead, he is moved on to the 'KIA' – the killed in action list – his salary is stopped, any widow's pension due is paid, and all the necessary paperwork is done. If he is *not* deemed to be dead, he is moved on to the POW list and his salary is cut to two-thirds – under the Geneva Convention the detaining power is supposed to pay the other third directly in the prison camp.

Families could delay any declaration of death, if they had good reason to believe that the man was not dead. But they could not delay a finding of death for ever. A finding of death was never made, I was assured by the Ministry of Defence, against the wishes of the family. They all, apparently, came round pretty quickly.

When I pressed the matter, I was told that the figure of 2,780 was the official figure of British missing as of February 1946. But how could anyone – even a man who disappeared on the last day of World War II – still be listed as missing eight months after the end of hostilities? By then, he would surely have to be listed either as dead, or as a prisoner, a few weeks after the fighting had ended.

The MoD seemed at a loss to explain this. They simply repeated that 2,780 was the official figure as of February 1946. I, however, ventured an explanation of this anomaly. Previously I had written a book about the missing prisoners from the Vietnam War and I knew how the Americans had handled similar casualty figures. It was simple. At the end of a war, those who had gone missing on the battlefield and subsequently been listed POW, but who had subsequently not been returned in the prisoner- of-war exchanges, were moved back on to the missing list. Then the procedure simply started all over again. A week or two later, a new investigation would have been made into their fate. Were they dead or were they prisoners? Plainly, if they had not been

7

returned home in the prisoner-of-war exchanges, they were not prisoners. The only other alternative was to move them on into the KIA column.

So why were there 2,780 men *still* unaccounted for in February 1946? Because it takes time to do that much paperwork. People cannot just be written off without due bureaucratic process. Every file must be gone through, each dealt with individually. Relatives would have to be contacted, regiments informed, kit disposed of, pensions paid and orders issued to the pay corps, the adjutant general, the provost marshal. Then the files would have to be sent for archiving. It all takes time – months – especially if you have tens of thousands of files to go through.

Even taking all this into account the figure of 2,780 was contradicted by that given by *The Statistical Digest of the War*, published by Her Majesty's Stationery Office in 1953. This publication said that 6,244 men were still listed missing as of 28 February 1946. And that figure includes only United Kingdom citizens. It leaves out Canadians, Australians, New Zealanders, South Africans, Rhodesians, African Colonials, West Indians, Indians, Gurkhas and other people who had been fighting in British uniform in World War II.

Nevertheless, I was assured, the Army Historical Branch were on the job and the British Embassy had asked the Russian authorities in Moscow for further explanation. Plainly, the government had things in hand. Besides, the story was so fantastical. How could tens of thousands of British prisoners of war have gone missing in 1945 without anyone noticing? And how could it be that the story had never surfaced before? Wasn't the idea of missing British prisoners of war from World War II and Korea as crazy as the crazy stories of America's Rambo fringe? Then, suddenly, the London *Evening Standard* unearthed records in the Soviet archives in Moscow that told of 1,400 British POWs taken into the Gulag. On 7 August 1992 it printed a list of 132 names of Britons who had disappeared in this way. The prisoners, it said, had been taken for their technical expertise. They had specialist Western knowledge badly needed in the Soviet Union as World War II ended and the Cold War got into full swing.

The allegations were now coming from both sides – from the US Senate and the Moscow archives. That gave the story a new veracity. The number of missing British was still debatable. No ageing Siberian peasant had as yet stumbled forward and claimed to be a former British soldier, captured by the Germans, held in a POW camp, 'liberated' by the Red Army and having spent the rest of his life in the Soviet labour system. Yet the story was taking on more and more substance. So why had it never come up before?

But it had. One man, Frank Kelly, a Lewisham lad captured by the Germans at Arnhem and 'liberated' from Stalag 4B, had been returned in 1953 after eight years in a Soviet prison. He was immediately arrested by the British authorities for being absent without leave and his story was quickly dropped.

The story of missing British prisoners of war from World War II and Korea has cropped up repeatedly in the media, in a very disconnected way, over the last forty-seven years, but no one had ever attempted to piece the whole story together, until now.

## CHAPTER 2

# The Geneva Convention

†

THE POSITION OF prisoners of war has always been unenviable. Throughout history they have been used for propaganda purposes and as slave labour, tortured, humiliated and summarily executed. But their role did not end when the war did. Their captors tried to use live prisoners – and even the remains of the dead – as bargaining chips, while their own side often saw little advantage in getting them back. You were an extremely lucky prisoner if you ever saw your homeland again, no matter which side won the war.

The Geneva Convention was established to try to rectify this situation. It began in 1864, when the founder of the Red Cross, Jean Henri Dunant, initiated negotiations establishing the Convention for the Amelioration of the Wounded in War. This was amended and extended by a second Geneva Convention in 1906. The Hague Convention of 1899 and 1907 further extended the provisions of the Geneva Convention to cover maritime warfare.

It was only in 1929 that a third Geneva Convention was negotiated – a Convention Relating to the Treatment of Prisoners of War. This established for the first time what we now think of as the Geneva Convention, which forbids captors putting pressure on prisoners to reveal more than name, rank and number, allows only enlisted men – not officers – to be used as labour, provides for inspection of prison camps and requires the exchange of lists of prisoners' names.

As the Geneva Convention was so widely violated during World War II, the International Red Cross convened another conference in 1948 to reaffirm its provisions. As we know from the situation after the end of the Vietnam War, it did no good.

Indeed, since it was first ratified, the Geneva Convention has been unevenly applied. The West would claim a spotless record, but that is arguable. After World War II many high-ranking German Intelligence officers and technical experts were pressed into service in America.

This was hardly slave labour, but with the threat of standing trial at Nuremberg for war crimes hanging over them, it could be claimed these men were coerced.

Other Germans were starved to death in American and French camps. The French and the British held Germans for labour, long after the end of the war.

In the Korean War, while the British chargé d'affaires in Peking insisted that the North Koreans be forced to abide by the Geneva Convention, United Nations troops tortured communist captives during interrogation and many were summarily executed. Also the United Nations forces in Korea did not return some 34,582 North Korean and 14,277 Chinese prisoners. These men elected not to return to their communist homelands, but that is not how the communists saw it.

In the First Indochina War the French used captured Viet Minh as labourers in the combat zone in Dien Bien Phu – a direct contravention of the Geneva Convention. And in the Vietnam War the Americans were downright careless with their captives. They killed thousands during interrogations which were themselves a contravention of the Convention. They did not return prisoners to the North Vietnamese but gave those they had not killed to the South Vietnamese – who then killed them. Ask any of the POW activists in America, who scream and shout about Americans still being held in Vietnam, whether the US gave its prisoners back at the end of the Vietnam War and they will not be able to tell you. They will never even have thought about it.

Perhaps for ideological reasons, perhaps for cultural ones, the Eastern, communist nations have made a more concerted – and more brutal – effort to wring the maximum advantage from their prisoners of war. They have a coherent, more easily discernible, strategy. They have tortured and humiliated their prisoners for propaganda purposes, summarily executed some captives for revenge and sold others on to third countries in exchange for arms and aid.

Communist countries have also kept prisoners after the end of the conflict, using them as slave labour and bargaining chips. In conflicts where no formal declaration of war has been made, they have denied that the Geneva Convention applied. The Soviet Union signed the Convention only in 1949, so were not obliged to live up to it in World War II. In any case, the Convention applies only to enemy prisoners of war. It makes no mention of how allies turned prisoner should be handled.

Since the inception of the Soviet Union prisoners of war have been used as hostages to force concessions from the Western nations, who have developed their own policy in response. Simply to avoid being perpetually blackmailed by communist nations – who often imprisoned, tortured, slaughtered and brutalised their own citizens – the West found they had to abandon their men and lie about the fact to their own people. Hundreds of thousands of men and women disappeared this way in World War II alone. But this has happened in all the major wars involving the Western powers in the twentieth century. Those abandoned to a life of perpetual servitude include Americans, citizens of the Baltic Republics, Germans, Republican Chinese, South Koreans, Japanese, Filipinos, Thais, French, Poles, Hungarians, Czechs, Ukrainians, Moroccans, Algerians, Australians, New Zealanders, Canadians, Indians, Italians, Belgians, Luxembourgers, Dutchmen and tens of thousands of British.

# CHAPTER 3

# Beginning the Trade

✝

AFTER THE RUSSIAN REVOLUTION in 1917 the new Soviet state made peace with Germany in the Treaty of Brest-Litovsk. In exchange for peace the Bolsheviks gave up Finland, the Baltic States, the Ukraine, 26 per cent of Russia's population, 27 per cent of the area they controlled, three quarters of their iron and steel production, and 3,000 million roubles.

However, Russia's peace with Germany did not suit the Western Allies. It allowed Germany to concentrate its forces on the Western front. British, French and American troops were sent to Russia, ostensibly to guard the huge amount of military stores provided to Czarist armies by the Western Allies; but Winston Churchill – returned to the Cabinet as Minister of Munitions in July 1917 after the disaster at Gallipoli – saw them as the nucleus of an anti-Bolshevik army. This stance led Lloyd George to call Churchill 'the most formidable and irrepressible protagonist of an anti-Bolshevik war'. The Soviets thought so too. They would long remember Churchill as one of the earliest and most implacable enemies of communism.

Under British command – and, later, Secretary of War Winston Churchill – the Allied Expeditionary Force fought the Bolsheviks around Archangel in northern Russia. Churchill even suggested building up the defeated German army as a bulwark against Bolshevism.

The Bolsheviks also sought to utilise German manpower in the International Battalions recruited from among their prisoners of war – the Czechoslovak, Hungarian, Rumanian and South Slav battalions alone numbered 50,000. Another 10,000 Chinese served with labour units.

The Allied Expeditionary Force scored a few victories during the spring and summer of 1918, but by the summer of 1919 they were forced to withdraw from Archangel and, by the spring of 1920, were forced out of Russia altogether.

According to eyewitness accounts, hundreds of Allied troops were captured during this withdrawal. Many of them were not returned, even though the British troops themselves took hundreds of Russian Bolsheviks hostage in the hope of bargaining for the missing men.[1]

The Americans tried to exchange 500 Russian prisoners of war for 7 Americans they knew the Soviets held. But their military position was impossible. They got back only 2 of the 7 men for the whole 500 Russians – and they 'had to toss in a round of cigarettes to seal the bargain', according to the two Company I officers, First Lieutenants Dwight Fistler and Albert May, who negotiated the exchange. They never did learn what became of the other five men.[2]

The Soviets had long realised that these men were valuable. Lenin's Intelligence commissar, Felix Dzerzhinsky, had specifically targeted the men of the Allied Expeditionary Force for capture and had assigned Aleksandr Eiduk, a chief Cheka agent, to the job. White Russian – anti-Bolshevik – prisoners were of little use to them. But foreign prisoners of war were a powerful diplomatic lever.

The Allied governments quickly cottoned on to the Soviets' game and sought to minimise their advantage. While the Allied Expedition was reporting that there were 'hundreds missing from our ranks' the US Military Attaché in Archangel, Colonel J.A. Ruggles, reported only seventy MIA, excluding British and French personnel.

Haggling failed. Colonel Ruggles cabled the War Department in Washington: 'Negotiations for the exchange of prisoners have been terminated by orders from General Pershing, after having been delayed, although under discussion from both sides, through failure of the Bolshevik commander to obtain authority from Moscow.'[3]

The Bolshevik commander could not get authority from Moscow because, by this time, the Soviets were demanding diplomatic recognition in return for the release of Allied POWs. But negotiating for the return of prisoners of war does itself implicitly give some sort of recognition. On 12 May 1919, at the suggestion of the Secretary of State, the Secretary of War reminded Colonel Ruggles in a letter that 'the United States has not recognised the Bolshevik regime as a government either *de facto* or *de jure*'.[4]

Negotiations never resumed.

The official US War Department casualty lists show 137 killed in action (including 28 presumed dead). But according to a telegram from Archangel to US Military Intelligence on 4 February 1919, this figure included 70 missing in action and 57 listed 'killed in action – body not recovered'[5] – leaving only 10 known dead.

However, it was clear that some of the missing had survived long into captivity. In April 1921 *The New York Times* reported the Bolsheviks as telling their American captives that they were being held because the United States government had not made sufficiently vigorous demands for their release.[6]

The Soviet government had tried to barter the prisoners for diplomatic recognition and trade relations. These had been refused even though the Soviets at one time threatened that 'the Americans held by the Soviet would be put to death', according to *The New York Times*.

Nevertheless, the US government held hard to the line spelt out by President Harding's Secretary of State, Charles Evans Hughs: that the US would not consider diplomatic and trading relations with the Soviet Union 'until the Americans now held as prisoners are permitted to leave the country'.

This stance seems to have paid off. When, a few months later, on 20 August 1921, the Riga Agreement promising aid to starving Russian children was signed, 100 American soldiers and civilians were released,[7] though only twenty civilians had been expected. The others, both soldiers and civilians, had been written off earlier by the American authorities.

In December 1920 the British claimed that all their men had been returned, after long months of wrangling. At one point the Bolsheviks insisted on sending a commission to London to enquire about Russians who had been 'forcibly and illegally enlisted in British Army and labour battalions, now probably without any protection, at the mercy of British policy, military authorities and the reactionary former officials of the Czar.'[8] This is the first use of a tactic practised by the Soviets again after World War II and by China and North Korea after the Korean War. When asked about British prisoners of war in communist hands, the immediate response is a complaint about the treatment of communist prisoners in British hands.

But the Soviets were not wrong. After World War I the Western Allies were just as cavalier with Russian prisoners as the Russians were with ours. According to a War Department cable of 17 December 1918 Russian prisoners liberated from German prisoner-of-war camps would be separated into those who could be recruited to fight the Bolsheviks and those who were sympathetic to the communist cause. Two months were set aside for the task. 'The former would then be sent to the Ukraine and the latter left in concentration camps' according to Military Intelligence.[9] The danger was, of course, that Bolshevik prisoners who were sent home might join the Red Army and fight against the Allies.

Freed Russian prisoners who did not want to return to their newly communist homeland posed a threat. Some fifty thousand of them decided not to head east and 'found their way to France. They were expecting a warm welcome from their former allies.' The War Department noted: 'They were interned without delay.'

The Soviets had a great shopping list of demands to be met before the return of British prisoners. The original agreement on the exchange of prisoners was made in February, during discussions on trade. The quid pro quo was implicit. But as trade talks continued there was no sign of the missing men, and on 15 September 1920 the Cabinet decided to halt further talks until the Bolsheviks made some show of good faith. British prisoners began returning on 5 November 1920.

By the middle of November, while the prisoner-of-war exchanges were still going on, talk in the Cabinet turned back to trade, the settlement of the former Russian government's debt and whether it would be possible to get gold out of the new Soviet regime. There was even talk of recognising the new Soviet state. Churchill threatened to resign but was persuaded out of it.

On 18 November 1920 the Cabinet decided by a considerable majority to conclude a trade agreement with the Soviets. A week later a draft of the treaty was approved. Not long after, the return of British prisoners came to an end. The British government maintains that all their men were returned. But as Americans certainly were still being held later, it is likely that British were held too.

The Anglo–Soviet trade pact was not signed until the following March, when it had been altered further in favour of the Soviets. By signing it, the British government had given *de facto* recognition to the USSR.

While in old and secretive societies like Britain's the disposal of troublesome MIA cases could be handled with some tact, the Americans, unused to foreign wars, lacked the necessary bureaucratic finesse. In 1929 those Americans still listed MIA in the Soviet Union were arbitrarily declared dead on the day they went missing.[10] There was a huge public outcry. This forced the establishment of the Veterans of Foreign Wars/US Graves Registration Expedition which was supposed to determine the fate of all American servicemen missing abroad.

Even after the rest of the missing men had been declared dead, there were live sightings. One Intelligence document, dated 20 November 1930, cites an affidavit taken by the US Justice Department from Alexander Grube, a Latvian-American, identified in the affidavit as a 'Russian seaman'. He had been held prisoner in the Lubianka prison in

Moscow and in the Soviet Gulag. In Lubianka he saw 4 American army officers and 15 soldiers; at Solovetz Island prison he met many Allied soldiers and civilians. These included a Mr Martin or Marten and Mr G. Heinainkruk, who he thought were Allied army officers, and a Roy Molner who was a US army sergeant from Archangel.[11] An Alfred Lindsay was also mentioned.[12]

When army records were checked they found that a William J. Martin had been listed as missing on 3 February 1919. But in 1921 he had been declared killed in action on 19 January 1919, two weeks before he had gone missing. It was thought that he was Grube's 'Mr Martin or Marten'. 'Alfred Lindsay' was thought to be Lindsay Retherford who had also been listed as missing and later 'killed in action – body not returned'.

The US government did nothing with this information. Grube warned that if the government asked the Soviets about specific individuals, they would be killed. The prisoners could only be bargained for as a block. But without knowing who was alive and who was not the Allies could never be sure they got them all back, so they could always be blackmailed into new negotiations.

In November 1933 the US recognised the Soviet government, and in 1934 nineteen sets of remains were returned. In all the VFW/Graves Registration Expedition claimed to have 'identified' eighty-six sets of remains – though, given the primitive state of forensic science at the time, it is difficult to know how positive these identifications could have been.

The policy on both sides, however, had been established. The Soviets knew that the Allies had a sentimental attachment to their prisoners and would bargain for them. Britain and America learnt that they were vulnerable to this tactic – and the only way to counter it was to deny the existence of any prisoners the Soviets were holding.

## CHAPTER 4

# Hostile Intent

IN 1945 THE ALLIES were victorious in Europe. The German army was utterly defeated. The British, American and Soviet armies – and a small contingency of French – occupied the whole of Germany. The Russians were allies, not enemies. Every prison camp was 'liberated', but this did not mean that every liberated man or woman was returned home.

This should not have come as a surprise to the British government as the Soviet Union had shown its hostile intent to British prisoners from the beginning of the war. Britons who had escaped from German prisoner-of-war camps and made it into the (at that time) neutral Soviet Union were not interned as they should have been, but jailed. Even when the Soviets came into the war on the side of Great Britain they did not simply hand over the men to the British authorities.

There were at least fifteen of them, and there are fifteen secret files in the Ministry of Defence relating to the men involved – who were ordered to forget about what had happened to them during their time in Russia.

They were all taken prisoner by the Germans during the early months of World War II. Corporal Robert Bainbridge was captured near Arras, France, in May 1940, when a pincer movement by a German tank group cut his company off from the coast. Military Policeman James Allan, formerly with the Scots Guards, was captured in hospital after being wounded in the leg on his way to Dunkirk. Both were sent to Stalag 20A at Thorn, Poland. Bainbridge recalls that conditions in the camp were terrible. The place was full of lice and cockroaches.

Inmates soon began to receive parcels through the Red Cross and their families were informed of what had happened to them. Nevertheless, captivity became intolerable. Bainbridge and Allan were consumed with a single thought – escape.

The Molotov–Ribbentrop Pact of 1939, which had kept the Soviet Union out of the early part of the war, divided Poland between Germany and the USSR. As any attempt to escape across Germany to Switzerland or Spain was out of the question, all escape plans focused on reaching the Soviet zone of Poland and the neutral Soviet Union itself. There, the worst they expected was to be interned for the duration of the war.[1]

On 21 September 1940 Robert Bainbridge, Joseph Waller and William Roberts broke a window and slipped past the German guards. Shortly after they were spotted by policemen, but again managed to escape. Friendly Poles gave them civilian jackets and helped them to cross the Vistula. There they managed to establish contact with the underground, who gave the runaways money and clothes. They were moved from one secret underground address to another until they reached the Soviet frontier.

Although they helped the British, the Poles did not understand why they wanted to get to the Soviet Union. It's foolish to flee there, they were told repeatedly. But the British insisted that they would be safe once they crossed the Soviet border. The Poles, still sceptical, made them learn two Russian phrases: 'I'm an Englishman. Don't shoot.'

These two phrases were not enough to save the life of Petty Officer Maurice Barnes of the British submarine HMS *Seal*. He crossed the Soviet border on the night of 9 September 1940 with Sergeant Major George Briggs of the 15/19 Hussars. The letter that the Polish underground had written for them in Russian did not help either.

'We were separated and a soldier stood behind us,' Briggs would later tell investigators from the British Ministry of Defence. 'I heard the soldiers load their rifles. Then we were made to run and they shot at us. Barnes fell down almost immediately and I heard him moaning. When the soldier who fired at me had emptied his ammunition cartridge he ran up to me and knocked me down, pointing his rifle's bayonet at me. I thought – why wasn't I killed in Belgium?'

A year later Soviet Foreign Minister Molotov told the British Embassy in Moscow that Petty Officer Maurice Barnes was wounded during an illegal crossing of the border and had died on his way to hospital.

Early in October 1940, at night, James Allan swam across the Bug River, after being separated from his Canadian companion, Royal Artilleryman Henry Clark. Allan surrendered to the border guards on the Soviet bank and said, in Russian: 'I am English, don't shoot.' Wet and freezing cold, he was stripped naked and ridiculed by the soldiers while officials decided what to do with him.

Allan was moved through a series of camps at Bialystok, Minsk and Smolensk that made the German POW camp seem to him like the Ritz. At Bialystok he saw the name 'Captain Richardson' scrawled on the wall of the primitive washroom. After he added his own – 'James Allan, English soldier' – he had a response from a French soldier who spoke English. He also met, briefly, two Welch Fusiliers, Bill Bateman and Eddie Boughton. But the inmates were mainly Poles, who were thrown into prisons operated by the NKVD – then in charge of internal security – after the invasion of Poland. Around 200,000 people who allegedly belonged to 'hostile classes' were captured by the Red Army at the time.

William Roberts also recalled the conditions when he spoke to a Russian journalist in 1990: 'In Smolensk I was thrown into a cell 3.5 metres long and 3.5 metres wide. Twenty-four people had been packed into it. Even so, it was terribly cold. The walls were covered with a thick layer of ice. I licked it when I wanted a drink.'[2]

At that time more than 15,000 Poles had been shot in Kalinin, Kharkov and Smolensk. Robert Bainbridge, who was in the same cell with William Roberts, recalled the death of one of the Polish officers who shared the cell with them. 'Before leaving for his interrogation, the colonel told us that he would throw his handkerchief into our cell if he were sentenced to be shot. Some time later we saw a handkerchief falling down. We fell to our knees and began to pray.' The British could not be sure that they were not going to be next.

Bainbridge said that he saw an expectant mother among the Russian inmates. This shocked the British, but not the Russians and Poles. In Smolensk, he also recalled, one of the guards brought children to look at an Englishman.

'I felt annoyed,' Bainbridge said, 'because I had grown terribly thin and was dressed in rags.'

Five Englishmen – James Allan, Private Hubert Lovegrove of the Royal Army Service Corps, George Briggs, Kenneth 'Bill' Bateman and Edward Boughton – found themselves in cell 97 of Moscow's Butyrka prison with seven Frenchmen, who had also escaped from Nazi prisoner-of-war camps. Poles were kept in cell 94, Finns in cell 95, and Czechs in cell 96.

The British complained that they were not allowed to contact the British Embassy or write home. Some of the French in the cell were communists and the British complaints caused a great deal of tension.

On the prison's 'international corridor' there were two other Englishmen. One of them, James Allan recalled, was Harold Walkins, from Rochdale. The two of them had been fighting for the Finns against the

Soviets. When Finland became pro-German at the beginning of World War II, they tried to escape across the Baltic to Sweden, but were picked up off the coast of Lithuania by a Soviet destroyer.

Allan and the other Britons were interrogated regularly. 'There is proof that you are a spy,' they were told. 'You have been smuggled into Russia by Scotland Yard. What were your instructions?'

For some reason the interrogators wanted very much to know whether Britain had secret police. And they wanted to know everything about the Polish underground. The Englishmen, fearing for the safety of those who had helped them, kept silent.

As a protest against their conditions the five British prisoners went on hunger strike. Allan, who was thought to be the organiser, spent five days of the strike alone in a punishment cell. But after ten days, they were reunited and the hunger strike was broken.

Bateman, Boughton, Briggs and Lovegrove were transferred to the NKVD's Kozelsk camp, where Roberts and Bainbridge were being held after a stretch in jail in Minsk. Several dozen Frenchmen were also held at Kozelsk.

Allan was taken to Moscow's notorious Lubianka jail, where he was interrogated for hours on end. The NKVD were particularly suspicious of him. Allan, a natural linguist, had picked up a few phrases of Russian during his time in jail. The Soviet interrogators demanded that he reply to their questions in Russian. When he was unable to, they beat him with rubber truncheons.

'They beat me, threw me on to the stone floor and kept saying, "He understands Russian",' James Allan recalled in his memoirs. 'I realised only later what they expected of me. They wanted me to cry for mercy in Russian and thus betray myself as a spy.'

During these beatings he lost five teeth, and his leg, wounded in France, was badly injured again. Meanwhile his dossier, which he saw on his interrogator's desk, grew thicker and thicker.

Finally, Allan was taken to a well-furnished room where a senior NKVD officer told him he would be exiled to Siberia, for ever, if he did not confess to being a spy. He would never see England or his wife and family again.

He was offered a confession to sign, but the text was covered. Allan refused. Back in his cell, he feared he was going mad. During a later interrogation he became hysterical and thought of committing suicide.

During his time in the Lubianka he wrote repeatedly to the British Embassy, but none of his letters was ever delivered. The embassy was nearby in Moscow, he recalled, but it might as well have been in Australia.

At Lubianka, Allan was held with a number of Russians. One was a famous Soviet airman, called Abramov, who was treated with some respect by the guards. Abramov had been the commander of an airfield in 1939 when a plane carrying German Foreign Minister von Ribbentrop flew over. Abramov had not been notified and ordered his men to open fire. The injured German plane made an emergency landing. Ribbentrop flew into a rage and Abramov was sent to jail.

Allan also met Selivanov, a producer from Leningrad; Kilparisov, a noted sportsman; and Mahomet Robadanov, an inhabitant of Samarkand. Robadanov had killed an NKVD man who had trumped up charges against Robadanov, planning to take his wife while he was in prison.

Three or four times a week, at night, condemned prisoners were shot in the washroom opposite Allan's cell. One morning he saw dead bodies, their faces covered with blood. The warders had not had time to remove the bodies – and got a dressing down from Abramov.

On 22 June 1941 Allan heard the sounds of an air raid from his cell in the Lubianka. The Germans were attacking Russia, he realised. The Soviets would be forced to fight on the British side, which meant that he would soon be released – or so he thought.

But instead of being taken from his cell and handed over to the British authorities, Allan was put on a crowded prison train and taken to a camp at Saratov, hundreds of miles from Moscow. On the forced march from Saratov station to the camp, he stumbled and was bayoneted in the leg by a guard.

Months later he was returned to the Lubianka in Moscow. And in October 1941 James Allan was put in a car and dropped off not 300 yards from the British Embassy. Seeing the Union Jack, he ran towards the building. He stumbled – his prison shoes had no laces. But he kept on going. Behind him was the black NKVD car. Until the last moment he expected to be shot in the back – killed while trying to escape.

In the embassy Allan met Henry Clark, his fellow escapee from Thorn. Clark had been working in the embassy since the Soviets had released him, the staff having persuaded him not to go home. 'They're afraid we might blow the gaff about Uncle Joe,' Clark told Allan.

Allan was asked to stay and work in the embassy too, but he insisted on going home. He sailed back to England from Archangel on HMS *London*, with a high-ranking Allied delegation including Averell Harriman, Lord Ismay, General MacCreedy and Lord Beaverbrook. Allan told Beaverbrook, a prominent member of Churchill's War Cabinet, of his experiences in Soviet hands.

Back in Britain, Allan wrote a long account of his time in Russia, but under wartime security regulations he was forbidden to publish it. He was awarded the Distinguished Conduct Medal – the highest award after the VC that other ranks can receive. His medal, though, came with no citation.

# CHAPTER 5

# Uneasy Allies

DESPITE CHURCHILL'S LONG-ESTABLISHED antipathy to the Soviet Union, the British people were fed with wartime propaganda singing the praises of Uncle Joe Stalin. The USSR was our ally and its system of government not so unlike our own, as intellectuals like George Bernard Shaw, who had been given a glossy guided tour of Russia in the 1930s, had long been saying.

Germany having broken its pact and attacked the USSR in June 1941, Britain was more than glad to form the Anglo–Russian Alliance in July of that year. But after Japan's attack on Pearl Harbor and America's entry into the war in December, the British government's attitude began to change. Churchill returned to his former posture as the scourge of the Soviets and in 1944, behind closed doors, the British Chiefs of Staff decided that after the fall of Hitler war with the Soviet Union was inevitable.

With the war in Europe still raging, the British began to lay plans. SIS agents were infiltrated into the Baltic States and the Soviet Union. The man put in charge of this operation was Kim Philby, later revealed as a Soviet spy. The Soviets knew all about it even before the agents were sent – they were rounded up and shot. And Stalin knew of his British ally's real intentions.[1]

Meanwhile, the Allies began an intricate little dance over all the POWs, assuring each other of their very best intentions, then doing exactly the opposite. On 14 October 1944, for example, General Antonov gave an assurance to the British Chief of the Imperial General Staff that measures would be taken to return released Allied prisoners of war to their countries as quickly as possible.

However, around that same time, Alex Masterton, a Canadian serving with the Argyll and Sutherland Highlanders, was getting a real taste of what the Soviet assurances meant. Captured at Dunkirk in 1940, Masterton survived four years of captivity. In July 1944, as the

Germans were falling back before the Soviet onslaught, he escaped from Stalag 20B and joined up with the Polish underground.

'We had been sort of liberated, but the Russians didn't know where to tell us to go,' he said later.

Masterton and two other Canadian soldiers – Edward Dick from Prince Edward Island and Eugene Racine from Quebec city – headed for Moscow with hopes of being taken in by a Western embassy. On the way they met at least forty Americans wandering around trying to survive by eating dog meat (lightly singed) and uncooked pig fat. The three Canadians got to within about thirty kilometres of Moscow, but the Russians wouldn't let foreigners into the city. So they jumped freight trains and headed for Odessa on the Black Sea – about 2,000 kilometres away – where, they had heard, Allied forces were being shipped home. In Odessa they were arrested by their gallant Soviet Allies.

With the help of some friendly female cooks, the three Canadians managed to escape again and hid on board an American ship. Russian tracker dogs sniffed them out and they were led back to jail. But the captain of the ship told a British ship's captain what had happened. Three days later he managed to get them out.

When Masterton got back to Britain and told his story a British army captain and a man from M16 swore him to secrecy on his honour as a British soldier.

In jail in Odessa, Masterton had met American B-17 bomber crews who limped into the Soviet Union after bombing oil refineries in Rumania and had been arrested immediately. Masterton did not think the B-17 crews ever got out. He had their addresses in the United States and tried to contact them later, but he never got any reply.[2]

On 1 November 1944 General Makarov gave Colonel Brinckman from the British Military Mission in Moscow a detailed list of assurances. These included

> that individual PW falling into the hands of the Red Army will be allowed to communicate with their next of kin . . . that permission would be granted for officers of the British Military Mission to visit PW camps . . . that the Soviet High Command would take care of British PW . . . that individual PW will be brought to Moscow for identification by British officers . . . [and] that the Red Army would report immediately the discovery of isolated graves of British PW who had died, or airmen who had crashed.[3]

During this meeting, General Makarov also said that 'he might be handing over a British officer shortly'. Colonel Brinckman asked where he was and why he could be handed over immediately. Makarov replied that the information was not official.

'If this officer has been detained unduly, I intend to make strong protest verbally and in writing and get Embassy to do the same,' Brinckman wrote to the War Office.[4]

Strong protests did nothing to help Warrant Officer Scotty Young, whom the Soviets were not only holding but made every effort to keep – permanently. Young had been with RAF Bomber Command on a 700-plane bombing raid on the Chemnitz railway sidings near Leipzig. Bomber Command advised aircrew that if they were hit and could not make it home, they should head east towards the Soviet lines – the Soviets had been told to look out for British aircraft.

Young and the other airmen were issued with special identification flags and were warned: 'Don't try any funny stuff with the Russians. Just ask to be put in contact with the nearest British Mission as soon as possible and you'll be back here in a few days.'

He wasn't.

Shot up over the target, Young's plane headed east as instructed, and the crew bailed out behind Soviet lines. After a few days wandering about in the snow, Young managed to find a Soviet patrol. They showed no interest in his special identification flags and arrested him. Their superiors denied Young's claim that he was a British officer. They claimed he was a spy and he was held in the most appalling conditions, with the minimum of food, no sanitation and no medical attention for his wounds.

One morning he was taken out, with another man, and stood in front of a firing squad. The soldiers took aim and pulled their triggers, but they had no bullets in their rifles. These mock executions took place every morning for seven days, until Young was almost driven mad with anxiety.

On the final morning some of the soldiers were issued with real bullets and Young's companion was shot. Young was told by a senior officer that perhaps he was a British officer after all. Mistakes had been made, the officer admitted and Young was questioned closely about Nixon, the Canadian navigator with his aircrew.

When Young complained about his treatment, the Soviets simply denied that anything untoward had happened.

'My friend,' he was told in a menacing tone, 'if you go on like this, your mind will become so deranged that it will be impossible to send you back to your own country.'

The implication was clear. Young held his tongue.

He was sent to the political prison at Pless in Poland where members of the French Communist Party had been detained. Stalin had never been keen on members of Western communist parties which were not directly under his control. Any who fell into his hands – as voluntary defectors to Russia or liberated from POW or concentration camps – could expect the harshest treatment.

When Young asked why he was still being confined, he was told that it was for his own protection. The local people were violently anti-British, blaming Britain for starting the war. However, his conditions improved. He was held in the hospital wing and tended by a beautiful young woman doctor, who sang the praises of the communist system and offered to marry him if he would stay.

During further interrogation Young was told that when peace returned the Soviet Union would be looking for skilled men. He was invited to join the Red Air force, with double his current RAF pay and a commission. He would live a life of luxury. There would be parties, women.

'Do not think that you will be alone in joining us,' he was told. 'There will be many English and Americans who will become members of our air force after the war.'

Young was not impressed with his interrogators' talk of peace and socialism as, clearly, they were more interested in his military skills. 'You are a skilled radar operator,' he was told. 'We need men like you to train more men.'

When he turned down the Soviets' proposal he was denied more medical treatment. Later he found himself in a camp with Nixon and a number of American aircrew. They were repeatedly told that they would be repatriated shortly, but nothing ever happened. Even after the end of the war, no effort was made to send them home.

After months of waiting they escaped and managed to make contact with a British official newly arrived in Warsaw. The Soviets returned them to custody and their treatment took a drastic turn for the worse. But word of their captivity was out, and the British official eventually forced their release.[5]

## CHAPTER 6

# Not Marked PW

✝

THE PROBLEM OF the repatriation of Soviet citizens liberated by the Western Allies presented itself before D-day and the invasion of the European mainland. In North Africa and elsewhere the Allied forces had already captured some Soviet nationals serving in the German army. Many of them had been pressed into service and put up no resistance when captured.

Although the Nazis were no respecters of human rights – especially when it came to what they considered 'inferior races' like Slavs – Germany was a signatory to the Geneva Convention. After their surprise attack on the USSR they found they had huge numbers of Soviet prisoners on their hands, and duly reported the prisoners' names to the Soviets, via the Swiss, in the normal way. There was no response. The Soviets had not signed the Geneva Convention and were only too happy to beat, starve, torture and execute any German soldier who came into their hands. The Soviets were not concerned about the conditions of imprisonment of their own men either. Stalin considered any of his people who had been taken prisoner by the Germans as traitors. In fact, they did not exist. All true Soviet citizens would gladly fight to their last drop of blood for socialism.

The Soviet attitude towards prisoners of war, the Germans believed, freed them from any obligation under the Geneva Convention. The conditions in the Soviet compounds of prisoner-of-war camps were particularly grim. Rations were slashed to starvation point and, with no food parcels from home, the mortality rates were astronomical.

Simply to survive, many Soviet prisoners volunteered for work groups and were given better rations. Later, these groups were armed and given German uniforms. Anyone who objected to this forceable induction into the German army was shot.

Other Soviet nationals, it must be said, volunteered gladly to fight for the Germans. They saw the Germans as their saviours. Mistakenly, they thought that Hitler could be no worse than Stalin and the German invasion was their one chance to throw off the yoke of communism.

The Allied governments were in a quandary: what should they do with these men when they captured them? They asked the Soviet government, who replied that the question did not arise since there were no Soviet nationals serving with the German armed forces.

Nevertheless, the Allied forces continued to capture Soviet nationals in German uniforms and serving with the enemy forces. By the autumn of 1944 the number in US and British custody had reached 28,000. Some 4,000 of those were evacuated to the United States as part of the normal processing of enemy prisoners of war. The others were held in camps in the United Kingdom and France. And their numbers were growing rapidly.

Alerted to Britain's hostile intentions, Stalin realised the danger of large numbers of Soviet nationals in Allied hands. Re-armed, they would make a very powerful force in any Allied attack on Russia. As Soviet nationals they would be seen as an army of liberation, legitimising an Allied invasion of the Soviet Union.

In the autumn of 1944 General Vasilov, then head of the Soviet Mission to the Allies' Supreme Headquarters of the Allied Expeditionary Force (SHAEF), requested that the Soviet citizens being held as enemy prisoners of war be segregated from German prisoners and given preferential treatment. In consequence verbal instructions were issued by Supreme Headquarters, and the provost marshals of the Normandy, Brittany and Loire Base Sections concentrated all Soviet citizens then classified as enemy prisoners of war in a single enclosure within each Base Section.

SHAEF already had detailed regulations covering the handling of liberated prisoners of war. British and American POWs would be treated identically, whichever nationality liberated them. This meant, in fact, that British ex-prisoners would usually be better off, as preferential treatment was given to those who had been imprisoned longest. The huge numbers of British prisoners who had been captured at Dunkirk and in the early battles in North Africa, before the Americans entered the war, benefited most.

Clothing and rations were not quite so good for the ex-POWs belonging to other friendly nations – France, Holland, Belgium, Luxembourg, Norway. And the treatment for enemy prisoners of war – Italians, Germans and the Soviet nationals fighting for them – was, naturally, worst of all.

On 18 October 1944 SHAEF issued new written orders, saying that the Soviet government had asked that its citizens captured while serving with the enemy forces should not be treated as enemy prisoners of war but as liberated Soviet citizens – that is, nationals of a friendly nation. The new orders laid out a set of rules to be followed in the Allies' communications zone. All Soviet nationals would be segregated in their own camps and given a considerable degree of control over their own affairs. They were to be fed and clothed as the subjects of a friendly nation, whatever their uniform. The prisoners themselves would be in charge of the internal administration of the camps, but Allied officers would still be in command and units of Soviet prisoners would be used as labour under the direction of Allied officers.

Supreme Headquarters did not take the responsibility of actually changing the legal status of these Soviet citizens. However, regulations prescribed that the personnel forms and records of liberated Soviet citizens could not in any circumstances be marked 'prisoner of war' or 'PW' and that all entries of this sort found in the records should be crossed out. It was permissible, however, to mention in narrative accounts that Soviet prisoners had been captured in German uniforms so, technically, had prisoner-of-war status.[1]

Record-keeping was difficult because of the language barrier. Soviet officers were called in to help compile rolls of their liberated citizens, which gave the Soviet authorities a good deal of power over the prisoners. Those expressing anti-communist views could be identified and coerced. And the Soviets quickly had an idea of how many Soviet citizens were in Allied hands.

In the autumn of 1944 Supreme Headquarters estimated that, as of 1 March 1945, the Soviet forces would have found 124,000 British and American prisoners of war in German POW camps, along with 425,000 nationals of other friendly nations. Naturally, the Allies were concerned for the welfare of these men. The British Military Mission in Moscow were determined that as POWs moved out of German hands into the Soviets' their treatment should show a marked difference. In October 1944 considerable quantities of supplies such as cigarettes, chocolate, soap, rations and clothing, were shipped to Moscow to be used for the relief of liberated prisoners. Efforts were made by the Allied military missions at the Soviet capital to obtain an advance agreement on the handling and repatriation of their nationals. They were anxious to arrange for the appointment of Allied officers to accompany the Soviet field force so that they could contact and identify liberated prisoners at the earliest possible moment and arrange for repatriation. The only result of the negotiations was that the Soviet authorities were informed of probable locations and numbers of Allied prisoners of war likely to be found by the Soviet forces.[2]

With these facts at their fingertips, the Soviet authorities started demanding the return of all their citizens in Allied hands. This caused immense problems. Technically, anyone captured in German uniform was a prisoner of war and under the Geneva Convention should be held until the end of the war, then repatriated – to Germany. Handing them over to the Soviets was probably illegal.

The Americans particularly were adamant on this point. A large number of naturalised immigrants served in the US army. A man's uniform defined his nationality, the Americans insisted, otherwise a German immigrant – or even the son of a German immigrant – serving in the US army and captured by the Germans could be treated as a traitor and shot. This was less of a problem for Britain, but the British, too, feared that if they did not live up to the letter of the Geneva Convention, the Germans would not either.

Many Soviet nationals captured in German uniform had already expressed the fear that if they were sent back to the Soviet Union they would be punished – executed or sent to the labour camps – for treason. The Allied authorities thought they were probably right. Although some of these men had willingly enlisted in the German army and deserved to be punished as traitors, most had not put up much resistance – and were often eager to be captured. If word got out that even men who surrendered were being sent back to the Soviet Union, it might stiffen resistance, and this would cost Allied lives.

But the Soviets were insistent, so a compromise was worked out: if the men were willing to return to the Soviet Union, they should be sent. If not, they would continue to be held as prisoners of war. This gave the Allies considerable latitude.

The British allowed Soviet repatriation officers into the camps to urge the men to volunteer to return. Many reluctantly went, believing that if they did not volunteer they would be sent anyway – and if they were not seen to rejoice at the prospect of returning to Stalin and their homeland they would suffer all the more. It was not pointed out to these men that, by volunteering to return, they were forfeiting the protection of the Geneva Convention. If they had insisted that, by dint of being captured in German uniform they *were* German, they would have escaped the terrible fate that awaited them.

The reasoning behind the Allied decision was outlined in a memo to the American Secretary of War, Henry Stimson. It pointed out that the Allies had a responsibility under the Convention not to hand these men over if they believed that they would be executed or otherwise punished, but 'the Russians have already threatened to refuse to turn

31

over to us American prisoners of war whom they may get possession of in German internment camps'.

The Soviet government was claiming that this was a parallel situation.

'Of course it is not and the Russians have no earthly basis for withholding them from us. I do not believe that we should allow such a claim to interfere with our judgment in not giving up the Russians,' the memo said.

The memo foresaw that this problem would get worse when the Western Allies and the Soviets began invading Germany itself. However, the War Department did not seem to take the Soviet threat seriously and it advised that America stick to its time-honoured custom of offering asylum, even to people regarded as traitors or political criminals in their own country.[3]

CHAPTER 7

# The Hostages of Yalta

✝

THE SOVIETS WERE deadly serious about their threat to withhold Allied prisoners of war. In a letter sent from Czestochowa in Poland to the British representative in Lublin, dated 4 February 1945, an RAF Flying Officer wrote:

> In Czestochowa there are more than a hundred British and Dominion troops . . . The Russians say that the British authorities have been informed of our presence here, but some of us have been here a week and have received no communication at all. We feel that we shall be here indefinitely unless the British government does something.

Something was about to be done, far to the south of Czestochowa, in the Crimea. An agreement would be signed that would lead to the deaths of hundreds of thousands of Soviets and leave tens of thousands of Allied prisoners in Soviet hands.

In February 1945, almost three months before the end of the war in Europe, Churchill, Roosevelt and Stalin had met at Yalta to discuss the shape of the postwar world. In anticipation of the hundreds of thousands of prisoners of war and displaced persons who would be liberated after the defeat of Nazi Germany, the Western Allies and the Soviets also discussed ways to expedite their repatriation.

On 11 February 1945 the Yalta Agreement was signed. Under its provisions, military officers of the Big Three were allowed into the territories under each other's control at various collection points across each country in Europe. They would process the liberated prisoners and arrange for their transportation home. These liaison officers would assist the liberating power's registration officers in the repatriation process.

However, a secret addendum to the Yalta Agreement said that all British and American subjects held by the Soviets would be returned in exchange for all Soviet citizens whether they wanted to return to the Soviet Union or not.

At Yalta, British Foreign Minister Anthony Eden calculated that the Soviets had overrun German prisoner-of-war camps containing 50,983 British POWs (though because of losses during forced marches as the retreating Germans took their prisoners westwards, the true figure must have been closer to 40,000). These men were still in Soviet hands. Yet by 1 September 1945, with the exchanges in Europe supposedly over, Soviet General Golikov stated officially that a total of 23,744 British POWs had been freed. This fact alone indicates that at least 16,256 British prisoners remained in Soviet captivity. But the real number may be even higher.

Documents unearthed in the US National Archives show that in early 1945 the British listed some 199,500 men as POWs, but after repatriation only 168,476 came back. Nearly all the outstanding 31,000 disappeared in the Soviet zone.

Even at the Yalta Conference, British and American officials feared that there might be problems in getting back their men from the Soviets when they learnt that Beria's infamous security police the NKVD – later renamed the KGB – had been put in charge of repatriations. The British and American negotiators also began discussing raising the possibility of the Western Allies using forcible repatriation of Soviet citizens who were not eager to return to Mother Russia.

American diplomat Charles E. 'Chip' Bohlen, a translator at Yalta, later spoke of the difficulties:

> Another agreement at Yalta that was certainly open to question and perhaps caused the United States and Britain more moral anguish than any other was the one made by our military representatives and signed by Roosevelt for the return of the citizens of one country in the territories overrun by the armies of another. Our military leaders believed that, without some such arrangement, the Soviet Union might find a pretext to retain the thousands of American prisoners who had been sent to camps in a part of Poland and East Germany subsequently captured by the Soviet armies if we did not force reluctant Russian prisoners of war to return to the Soviet Union. It was regarded as prudent to deprive the Soviets of any pretext for holding off the release of American prisoners.

The controlling paragraph of the agreement said:

All Soviet citizens liberated by the forces operating under United States command and all the United States citizens liberated by forces operating under Soviet command will without delay after their liberation be separated from enemy prisoners of war and will be maintained separately from them in camps or point of concentration until they have been handed over to the United States or Soviet authorities, as the case may be, at places agreed up between the authorities.

This wording was repeated – with the substitution of 'Great Britain' for 'the United States' – in the copy signed by Eden.

Bohlen maintains that there was nothing in the agreement that required the forcible repatriation. He continues in his memoirs:

Yet this is exactly what happened in Germany; and for six months or so after the surrender, train loads of Soviet citizens – men, women, and children – were sent back to the Soviet Union against their sometimes physically resisting efforts. The execution of the repatriations was entirely determined by the American and British military. In the spring of 1946, the forcible repatriation was stopped. By that time, all American POWs were out of Soviet-held areas, and there was little Molotov could do about it.[1]

This is not true. The forced repatriations did not stop until 1947.

Roosevelt's Chief of Staff William Leahy also spoke of effects of this part of the Yalta Agreement in his memoirs. On returning from Yalta Roosevelt explained the provisions of the agreement to a combined session of the Senate and House.

Even as he spoke [Leahy wrote] a crisis was in the making in our relations with Soviet Russia that was to reach dangerous proportions and require his best attention up to the actual day of his death.

The swift advance of the Russians through Poland was overrunning many Nazi prison camps where Americans were incarcerated. By the end of February there was a sharp criticism of the Russian handling of American prisoners found in Polish territory. We asked Stalin for an explanation.[2]

In an effort to ease the situation, President Roosevelt and his Secretary of State Edward Reilly Stettinius Jr ordered the Office of Strategic Services – the US behind-the-lines espionage and sabotage unit – to return the secret Russian military and diplomatic codes which the OSS under General William 'Wild Bill' Donovan had just acquired clandestinely.

The US quickly organised an airlift to Rumania and Bulgaria to rescue 1,000 Allied POWs there before the Red Army arrived. British and American observers were left behind, but were ordered to leave as soon as the Soviets got there.

But for the large numbers of Allied prisoners held in Poland there was no such chance of rescue. Many had been taken by the Red Army before the Yalta Agreement was signed. The US Ambassador in Moscow, Averell Harriman, and his number two, Chargé d'Affaires George Kennan, demanded information from the Soviets about the Allied prisoners in Poland. None was forthcoming.

Kennan soon discovered that Allied POWs were being held incommunicado by the Red Army, and he demanded contact with the prisoners. When access was denied, Kennan suggested the US send a stiff protest to Soviet Foreign Minister Molotov.

Concern deepened over the fate of both British and American POWs when a worrying note arrived at the embassy. Dated 14 February 1945, it was signed by one F.H. Brooks and read:

> Here in Nowy Sacz are eight officers and twelve NCOs, all of whom are mostly Americans and British airmen. At the moment we are with the Russian Army in Nowy Sacz for over three weeks and no responsible parties have been notified of our presence and whereabouts. We have no freedom and have been told we are internees.[3]

British concern for prisoners of war 'liberated' by the Soviets reached the House of Commons. On 13 February 1945 Secretary of State for War Sir James Grigg told the House:

> Twelve camps [Stalags 2B, 2D, 3B, 3C, 344, 8B, 8C, 20A, 20B and Stalag Luft 3, 4 and 7] have either been overrun by the Soviet Forces or are in their direct path. There were about 60,000 prisoners from the British Commonwealth in these camps. It is clear that the Germans intended to move the prisoners from these camps to Central Germany and considerable transfers have taken place. The men are apparently moved on foot by daily stages of between 12 and 18 miles. It is likely, however, that many have been overtaken by the Soviet Forces . . . Scores of names of British ex-prisoners have so far been picked up from Lublin Radio.

Although the Germans were moving Allied POWs westwards in front of the Soviet advance, the Allied governments and the Red Cross had not lost track of them. A cable from Geneva to the US Secretary of State details the camps that were being evacuated, the numbers moving westwards, the conditions they were suffering, the stops they were making, who was suffering from dysentery, who had foot injuries and the numbers being abandoned at the roadside.[4]

The conditions were generally appalling. Some 350 wounded Allied prisoners of war were being transported in coal barges. They had no light, no heat, and just two blankets per man in temperatures of 20 to 25 degrees below zero. The routes of forced marches through the Sudetenland were known and the Red Cross even had details of the men's meagre diets. Food parcels were sent to the marching prisoner-of-war columns.[5]

There were other sources of information: former POWs who had escaped turned up in Moscow. Sergeant George Lukashewitz, for example, said that all 2,000 men in Stalag 3C had been liberated by the Soviets and were making their way to Warsaw. He, and others, gave the names of escapees and men left behind in hospitals.[6]

By 1 March men were turning up at Odessa – 163 British and 252 Americans – bringing with them more information about liberated prisoners. There were 28 sick at Wollstein, some 700 had been liberated from Oflag 64 in Szubin, 1,900 from Stalag 30 in Kustrin and 2,000 from Stalag 2B in Hammerstein.[7]

On the same day that Sir James Grigg spoke of '60,000 prisoners from the British Commonwealth . . . many . . . overtaken by the Soviet Forces' the Allies announced comprehensive agreement about repatriation of prisoners of war still in German hands. The Germans agreed to leave POWs where they were, provided the Allies agreed not to send those men back into combat.

On 19 February 1945 Major General John R. Deane, commanding the US Military Mission in Moscow, had a long talk with Lieutenant General K.D. Golubev, the Soviet general charged with implementing the Yalta Agreement signed just one week before. Golubev claimed that there were about 450 liberated American prisoners in Russian hands. Deane believed the figure to be closer to 1,000.

'Through the International Red Cross we had a fairly accurate idea of where the American camps were situated and of the numbers in each,' General Deane later wrote in his memoirs.[8]

Deane complained of the Soviet slowness both in notifying the Military Mission of liberated American POWs and of authorising visits to liberated prisoners. Golubev responded by complaining of the treatment of Soviet citizens in the United States and France.[9]

The British also complained of the slowness of Soviet reporting. 'No official information has yet been received from the Soviet authorities,' Sir James Grigg told the House of Commons on 20 February 1945. 'An unconfirmed report has, however, been received that 1,400 of our men have been liberated from camps in Poland.'[10]

Two days later the War Office told the British Military Mission in Moscow that they had received word that the 'Russians are sending 70 officers and 2,591 other ranks British prisoners of war to Odessa by rail [and that a] transit camp for 5,000 is to be completed at Odessa.'[11] It was clear that these British repatriations were being made in exchange for 7,500 Soviet POWs repatriated from the UK.[12]

Despite these repatriations the numbers of Allied personnel registered as prisoners of war continued to climb. Rearguard actions by the Germans and downed aircrew swelled the numbers, even during the final onslaught. On 26 February 1945 there were still some 257,000 British and US men known to be in German hands.[13] This number continued to climb until the end of March. Despite the Germans' meticulous record-keeping, there was a lag of around seven weeks while prisoners' details were collected, collated and sent to their home countries via the Red Cross and the Swiss protecting power.

# CHAPTER 8

# The Black Hole of Poland

†

By the end of February 1945 detailed reports of the movements and numbers of POWs in advance of the Red Army were flooding in. Two thousand British prisoners liberated from a camp at Gleiwitz were being assisted by the Poles and a great number of British officers and other ranks were said to be in Cracow. The existence of these prisoners had not been reported to the British authorities and no Allied officer was allowed into Poland to see for themselves. Contrary to the Yalta Agreement, the Soviets were attempting to hide their possession of these and other Allied POWs.

More handwritten notes arrived at the US and British embassies. Three escaped American prisoners managed to find their way to Moscow. They were debriefed at the US Military Mission by General Deane. Thousands of other Allied prisoners were still being held, they said.

The withholding of prisoners became so blatant that US Ambassador Averell Harriman prevailed upon President Roosevelt to make a personal appeal to Stalin. On 4 March 1945 Roosevelt cabled Stalin:

> I have reliable information regarding the difficulties which are being encountered in collecting, supplying, and evacuating American ex-prisoners of war and American aircraft crew who are stranded east of the Russian lines. It is urgently requested that instructions be issued authorising ten American aircraft with American aircrew to operate between Poltava and places in Poland where American ex-prisoners of war and stranded airmen may be located . . .

Roosevelt went on to stress the 'intense interest of the American public in the welfare of our ex-prisoners of war and stranded aircraft crew'. Then he urged Marshal Stalin: 'On the general matter of prisoners of war in Germany I feel that we ought to do something quickly. The number of these prisoners of war, Russian, British and US, is very large. In view of your disapproval of the plan we submitted what do you suggest in place of it?'[1]

On 5 March 1945, Stalin cabled:

> There is now no accumulation of US prisoners of war on Polish territory or in other areas liberated by the Red Army, because all of them, with the exception of individual sick men who are in hospital, have been sent to Odessa, where 1,200 US prisoners of war have arrived so far and the arrival of the remainder is expected shortly. Hence there is no need at the moment for US planes to fly from Poltava to Polish territory in connection with US prisoners of war.

Stalin added that, at the moment, he had no proposals to make concerning the status of Allied prisoners of war in German hands.[2]

If Allied prisoners who had been 'liberated' by the Red Army were not in Poland, they must be on their way to Odessa, the Black Sea port that had been designated as the USSR's only repatriation point. There, Allied ships brought in repatriated Soviets from the West. Many were machine gunned on the dockside. The rest were herded into cattle trucks and transported directly to labour camps. Meanwhile, British, American, French, Dutch and Belgian men endured appalling privation, waiting to board the empty Allied ships which would take them to transit camps in southern Italy or, if they were lucky, directly home.

However, as Allied officers were not allowed into forward positions with the Red Army when the German POW camps were being overrun, the Allied authorities could not be sure that the men who turned up at Odessa were all there were. In fact, they soon became convinced – and taking understandable delays into account – that the men who were getting through to Odessa were only a fraction of the Allied POWs the Red Army were uncovering. On 8 March 1945 Averell Harriman urgently cabled President Roosevelt: '. . . information received from our liberated prisoners indicates that there have been four or five thousand officers and enlisted men. The Russians claim there are only 2,100 . . .'[3]

After months of negotiations the Soviet authorities finally allowed British repatriation officers into Poland. Major D.P. Costello of the New Zealand legation to the Soviet Union, Flying Officer D. Floyd and Sergeant K.H. Macallister left Moscow on 1 March. However, the permits they had been issued allowed them to visit only Lublin, and expired on 15 March.

The first contact they made with ex-POWs happened by chance at Brest-Litovsk where their train was halted from 4 p.m. on 3 March to 8 a.m. on the 4th. There they found a train with some 400 British and American ex-POWs on board in the charge of Major Dufus of the Royal Army Medical Corps. History does not say whether they were returned.

When the repatriation team arrived at Lublin on 6 March they found that there was no direct communication with Moscow. The Red Army officer who accompanied them, Major Gurev, offered them little assistance. All messages were to be given *en clair* – that is, uncoded – to Major Sigulya who undertook to pass them to Colonel Vlasov in Praga. And from Praga they were telephoned to Moscow.

The American repatriation team who reached Lublin at around the same time had tried this method of communication, but soon found they were getting no replies from General Deane in Moscow.[4]

The British team soon discovered that there had been large numbers of ex-POWs in Lublin, but they had already been evacuated. There were also large posters in English, French and Russian instructing all POWs to report to 'camps of recollection' at Wrzesnia, Lodz, Praga and Lublin. Under the Yalta Agreement repatriation officers should be allowed into all camps where ex-POWs were concentrated. Two copies of the poster were sent back to the British Military Mission in Moscow. They showed one to General Golubev and gave him a photograph of it, along with a stiff protest.[5]

The contact team at Lublin complained that it was too far behind the front line and had never really functioned as a collecting point. The officers pushed to be allowed to move forward to visit the main collecting points and reported: 'Impression gained was that the Russian intention was to hold the team in Lublin until Poland was clear of recovered POWs and to take care that too many prisoners of war did not go to Lublin. They wanted to evacuate the men in their own way without interference or observation from British contact teams.'[6]

The British repatriation team at Lublin also interrogated two French sergeants who said they had left Ciechocienek on 5 March and that there were some 250 British ex-POWs there. Again, no report of their existence had been made to the British authorities, and no repatriation officers were allowed to visit them.

British POWs who managed to make it to Moscow reported 'thousands of our liberated prisoners still in Poland'. The British Military Mission were, naturally, concerned for their welfare, but they reported to the War Office in London 'enquiries have shown that there is little hope of sending Red Cross stores and military supplies through Red

Cross to Poland. The Americans have tried to send stores both from Moscow and from Odessa; they have even offered to provide their own aircraft but they have been turned down in all cases.' Both the British and the Americans had argued the toss with the Soviets, to no avail. 'Approach which you suggest will I think therefore lead to no result,' cabled the British Ambassador. 'United States Ambassador tells me he exhausted all his arguments with Molotov, and that he made no progress.'[7]

Communication with the repatriation teams in Poland was so bad that the only way for the Allied contact teams to get their reports back from Lublin was to send four ex-POWs – two British and two Americans – to hitch-hike to Moscow. The journey took ten days.

The report they brought said there was reason to believe concentrations of British and American POWs existed at Czestochowa, Ostrow and Cracow and were also 'reliably reported' to be at Ciechocienek and Szubin, while the sick were left at Kustrin, Marienburg and Deutsch-Eylau. There were also huge numbers of stragglers. 'All available evidence indicates large numbers of PW wandering about Poland,' the report said. It was estimated that about 900 British POWs from Stalag 20B alone were out on working parties when the camp was overrun.

At the same time, pitifully small numbers of liberated POWs were arriving at Odessa.

'The arrival of 14 officers and 464 other ranks at the transit camp at Odessa has been reported by our Military Mission in Moscow,' Sir James Grigg told the House of Commons on 6 March 1945. 'We have otherwise received no further information about British Commonwealth prisoners liberated by the Red Army.' He also admitted the presence of thirty to forty British prisoners of war in Bulgaria.[8]

On 7 March the British repatriation team at Lublin succeeded in opening another line of communication. A letter was carried via ex-POWs to Odessa, then forwarded to Rear Admiral Archer, head of the British Military Mission in Moscow:

> The Russian story is that no direct telegraph line exists between Moscow and Lublin. There are known to be [a] considerable number of British at Deutsch-Eylau, Ciechocienek, Szubin, Krakow and Czestochowa. It is essential to get British officers to these places as well as to those named in the Russian poster, as all the ex-PW are agreed that the attractive power of such British officers over the stragglers would be very great. Future parties

from Moscow must come by air. It took us five full days to reach Lublin by rail.[9]

But future parties would not come by air, nor by rail. There would be no further parties to Deutsch-Eylau, Ciechocienek, Szubin, Cracow, Czestochowa, or anywhere else. Even the Allied repatriation teams at Lublin would soon be forced out. The Yalta Agreement would be in tatters and Poland would turn into a black hole for Allied POWs.

On 8 March 1945, less than one month after the Yalta Agreement was signed, Averell Harriman in Moscow sent an 'urgent, top secret, personal message' to President Roosevelt which eloquently spelt out the situation:

> Since the Yalta Conference General Deane and I have been making constant efforts to get the Soviets to carry out this agreement in full. We have been baffled by promises which have not been fulfilled. I am outraged that the Soviet Government has declined to carry out the agreement signed at Yalta in its other aspects, namely, that our contact officers be permitted to go immediately to points where our prisoners are first collected, to evaluate our prisoners, particularly the sick, in our own airplanes, or to send our supplies to points other than Odessa, which is 1,000 miles from point of liberation, where they are urgently needed . . .
>
> For the past ten days the Soviets have made the same statement that Stalin has made to you [FDR], namely, that all prisoners are in Odessa or entrained thereto, whereas I have now positive proof that this was not repeat not true on February 26, the date on which the statement was first made. This supports my belief that Stalin's statement to you is inaccurate.
>
> . . . there appear to be hundreds of our prisoners wandering about Poland trying to locate American contact officers for protection. I am told that our men don't like the idea of getting into a Russian camp. The Polish people and the Polish Red Cross are being extremely hospitable, whereas food and living conditions in Russian camps are poor. In addition we have reports that there are a number of sick or wounded who are too ill to move. These Stalin does not mention in his cable. Only a small percentage of those reported sick or wounded arrive at Odessa.[10]

The Soviets responded to Allied queries by accusing the British and Americans of perfidy over the handling of Soviet prisoners liberated by Allied forces in the West. At the same time Moscow was asking the

Americans for $6 billion in postwar credits and for both Britain and America to recognise the new communist regime the Soviets had installed in Poland.

American aid to the Soviet Union did not resume until August. Meanwhile, thousands of British and American POWs from the German Stalags 2-B, 3-C, 8-A, 8-B, 8-C and 20-A and Oflag 64 – among others – were being withheld by the Soviets.

The Allies were not above paying ransom for their POWs. It had been discussed. On 20 July 1945 the idea was mooted that the Allies pay the Japanese government a ransom for the POWs in their hands. The British were happy to go along with it – they had more prisoners suffering hardship in Japanese hands. But the Americans – who presumably would have had to stump up the ransom if it was to be paid – considered that the money might help the Japanese to resist. That would prolong the war, so was unacceptable from the military point of view. The idea was shelved.[11]

## CHAPTER 9

# More Harm than Good

✝

ON 10 MARCH 1945 General John Deane wrote from Moscow to Lieutenant Colonel James D. Wilmeth of the American Prisoner of War Contact Team in Lublin, Poland:

> There is no use of my going over the difficulties I have had in Moscow in attempting to help your situation. Needless to say, our efforts would fill a book, but the results are nil despite the fact that we not only have gone to the Ambassador level but to the Presidential level.
>
> I was informed that your pass for Lublin is good until March 15th. However, I want you to remain there beyond that date and not leave unless they threaten to forcibly make you. I have been trying for two weeks to get authority for a trip to Poland and get first hand information on the situation . . .
>
> The ten prisoner of war contact teams arrived at Poltava [in Southern Russia between Khakov and Odessa] today and at least four officers and non-commissioned officers will go to Odessa to relieve Hall. Thus far we have had no authority to establish contact teams in Poland and I am constantly told your work is finished, which I know is not true.[1]

Despite difficulties in communications, Deane had received a telegram from Wilmeth on 8 March indicating that there were 28 British and 10 American prisoners of war at the hospital in Lublin.

The British repatriation team was also up against the 15 March deadline. But they noted:

> There was a change of policy on 12 March. It seems that the idea was to keep us in Lublin while the evacuation of ex-PW was pushed forward in those parts of Poland which we were not allowed to see. By an odd coincidence, communications between

Lublin and the outside world grew rapidly worse about this time; on the evening of the 9th the telephone line to Praga broke down, and on the following day, there was no communication even with Lukow.[2]

They concluded that 'the Russians' intention was to hold us in Lublin until Poland was clear of ex-PW and to take care that too many did not come there'. And as there were also collection points at Praga, Lodz and Wrzesnia: 'We have thus no idea of the total numbers or names of the men concerned.'[3]

At the same time the British Mission in Odessa reported that until the middle of March the Russians had no organisation for the evacuation of British and American personnel in the Bromberg area of Poland.

On 13 March 1945 Colonel Vlasov stated that Lublin was no longer a collecting point. So now there were no collecting points for liberated Allied prisoners in Poland, or for that matter in East Prussia, the Soviet zone of Germany or Austria. Odessa was the only official collecting point, even though it was hundreds of kilometres from the POW camps the Red Army were overrunning. The Soviet authorities refused to extend the Allied repatriation officers' permits to visit Lvov and Lublin. And in newly liberated Bulgaria, repatriation officers from the British Military Mission found their movements severely restricted too.[4]

Churchill complained directly to Stalin by cable, though Eden urged caution. 'I believe that we shall do more harm than good by taking a strong line with the Russians,' he said.

But Averell Harriman was not much of a man for caution. On 14 March 1945 he sent another cable from Moscow to Washington, this time to the Secretary of State, Edward R. Stettinius Jr, which was also read by Roosevelt. Harriman expressed his growing disquiet:

I assume the [State] Department has been informed by the War Department of the great difficulties General Deane and I have been having with the Soviet Government in regard to the care and repatriation of our liberated prisoners of war. In the beginning it appeared that the Soviet authorities were going to interpret our agreement substantially as we did, namely that we be allowed to send our contact officers to several points within Poland to which our prisoners first find their way, to fly in emergency supplies and to evacuate our wounded on the returning trips of the planes, although in Soviet planes rather than United States planes. We obtained authority for one contact team of an officer and doctor to go to Lublin with one plane load of supplies and they have done extremely useful work there. No other teams or supplies have since been permitted and authority for the Lublin team to remain has recently been withdrawn. The Soviets have now contended that Odessa is the only present 'camps and points of concentration' referred to in the [Yalta] agreement to which our contact officers are to be permitted.

. . . Our prisoners have suffered serious hardship from lack of food, clothing, medical attention, et cetera, in finding their way to concentration points in Poland and on the long rail trip to Odessa because we have been stopped from sending in our contact teams and emergency supplies. A considerable number of sick and wounded are still hospitalized in Olan. I have been urging for the last two weeks General Deane be permitted to survey the situation with a Red Army officer. This was first approved in writing with the qualification that arrangements must be made with the Polish authorities. An officer of our military mission informally approached the Polish Embassy here and was advised that no Polish authorization was necessary as it was entirely within the competence of the Red Army. We have been unable, however, to get authorization for Deane's trip.

It seems clear that the Soviets have changed their point of view during the last several weeks and are now rigidly determined that none of our officers shall be permitted in Poland.

I saw Molotov again today about the situation. He maintained that the Soviet Government was fulfilling its obligation under the agreement and both the Red Army authorities and the Polish Provisional Government objected to the presence of our officers in Poland. When I pressed him on what valid objection the Red Army could possibly have, he pointed out that we had no agreement with the Polish Provisional Government. In spite of my contention that this was a Soviet responsibility he kept reverting to the above fact. I then directly asked him if he was implying that we should make such an arrangement with the Poles and if so, whether the Red Army would remove its objections. He did not answer this question directly but left me with the impression that he wished me to draw that deduction.

I am satisfied that the objection comes from the Soviet Government and not the Provisional Polish Government as our military mission had been in informal contact with the Polish Embassy here who have been extremely cooperative as have all Polish authorities including the Polish Red Cross to our prisoners in Poland.

I feel that the Soviet Government is trying to use our liberated prisoners of war as a club to induce us to give increased prestige to the Provisional Polish Government by dealing with it in this connection as the Soviets are doing in other cases. General Deane and I have not (repeat not) been able to find a way to force the Soviet authorities to live up to our interpretation of our agreement. Unless some steps be taken to bring direct pressure on the Soviets, our liberated prisoners will continue to suffer hardships, particularly the wounded and the sick.

. . . It is the opinion of General Deane and myself that no arguments will induce the Soviets to live up to our interpretation of the [Yalta] agreement except retaliatory measures which affect their interests unless another direct appeal from the President should prove effective. We therefore recommend that the first step be a second request from the President to Marshal Stalin . . . In the meantime, however, we recommend further that the [State] Department and War Department come to an agreement on what retaliatory measures we can immediately apply in the event an unfavourable answer is received by the President from Marshal Stalin.

Consideration might be given to such action as, or combination thereof: (One) That General Eisenhower issue orders to restrict the movements of Soviet contact officers in France to several camps or points of concentration of their citizens far removed from the points of liberation, comparable to Lvov and Odessa; (Two) That Lend-Lease refuse to consider requests of Soviet Government additional to our fourth protocol commitments for such items as sugar, industrial equipment or other items that are not immediately essential for the Red Army and the Russian war effort; (Three) That consideration be given to allowing our prisoners of war en route to Naples to give stories to the newspapers of the hardships they have been subjected to between point of liberation and arrival at Odessa and that in answer to questions of correspondents, the War Department explain the provisions of our agreement and the Soviet Government's failure to carry out the provisions of our agreement according to any reasonable interpretation.

I request urgent consideration of this question and the Department's preliminary reaction. General Deane requests that this cable be shown to General Marshall.[5]

While Averell Harriman set out his stall, the British Ambassador in Moscow was more guarded. On 15 March 1945 Sir Archibald Clark Kerr reported:

> The indications are . . . that our liberated prisoners are gradually being collected, although often in conditions of some hardship, and that they will eventually be sent to camps. When they get there repatriation officers will no doubt be granted facilities to look after them as at Odessa. It is also clear that the Soviet Government take Article 2 of the Prisoner of War Agreement to refer to camps where our men have been concentrated and not merely where they happen to be in large numbers.

However, in his quiet way Sir Archibald recognised clearly the game that was being played. 'In spite of assurances given,' he wrote, 'Molotov has either been unable to overcome the objections of the Soviet military authorities or is using this question as blackmail to force us into some relationship with the Polish Provisional Government.'

In the face of this blackmail Clark Kerr recommended a personal message to Molotov or for Churchill to make a personal approach to Stalin. However, he qualified his advice by saying: 'I think . . . that it would be a mistake to take action now at the highest level which might be interpreted as a charge of bad faith and so lead to even greater difficulties in the execution of the Agreement.'

Despite the Foreign Office cabling Moscow about the 'large numbers of our men scattered in various parts of Silesia and Poland' which Molotov refused to allow the British Military Mission to visit,[6] the British Embassy in Moscow were beginning to take another tack. If the Soviets would not respond to general questions about huge numbers of missing men, perhaps they would answer specific questions about named individuals.

On 15 March 1946 the British military attaché in Moscow asked the Soviet repatriation authorities about two missing British POWs – one called Matthews and another called Otto Hanson. The Soviets replied that they could not trace them, though three men named Matthews had passed through Soviet repatriation camps. Four separate enquiries were made about Matthews before the military attaché gave up.[7]

CHAPTER 10

# On the Ground

✝

THE DIPLOMATIC GAME being fought over numbers and names was having dire consequences on the ground. On 16 March 1945, about noon, a British ex-POW was walking through the village of Reda in Poland. He had no cap but was still wearing his khaki uniform. Four Soviet soldiers stopped him and accused him of being a German spy. The British POW replied in broken German: 'I am an English soldier.'

The Russians did not listen to him or ask him any more questions. Instead, they beat him to death with their rifle butts.

Polish villagers showed the corpse to another British ex-POW passing through the village. He recognised the dead man as Lance-Corporal R.E. Livett of the 15/19 Hussars. Livett had been reported missing on 18 May 1940. Later, the British government was notified that he was a prisoner. The two men had escaped together from Stalag 20B in January 1945. The second man confirmed that Livett had been beaten to death and reported that all identification had been removed from the body, along with his trousers and boots.

The villagers buried Lance-Corporal Livett. Later an eyewitness to the incident reported to the British consulate on 11 January 1946 that the grave had been defiled twice, once by the Soviets and once by a member of the Polish communist regime's secret service. The eye-witness also compared the treatment of the dead British prisoner of war with that given to two members of his family. One of his sons had been conscripted into the Germany army, captured by the British and subsequently released, while the villager's brother had been taken by the Soviets in 1945 because he was unemployed, and died of hunger and maltreatment in a labour camp.[1]

While men died haphazardly in Poland, the great game was still under way in Moscow. On 16 March 1945 Sir Archibald Clark Kerr reported the state of play to the War Cabinet:

The Americans are experiencing the same difficulties as regards their own liberation of prisoners of war. The United States Ambassador told me yesterday he had taken the matter up personally with Molotov on March 14th but without success. Molotov trotted out the alternative objections of the Soviet military authorities and necessity for securing agreement with Polish provisional authorities. The United States Ambassador told he knew from his own military people and the American Red Cross, both of whom have some direct contacts in Poland, that the Polish authorities are in fact only too anxious to help. He therefore regarded Molotov's attitude as a sort of blackmail to force us into some sign of recognition of Polish provisional government.

However, Averell Harriman was not about to sit still for this blackmail. Sir Archibald's wire went on: 'The United States Ambassador has reported to Washington that he cannot make any further progress here and has suggested the time has come to consider retaliation either by preventing Russian officers visiting Russian camps in the west except in a few specified rear areas or by cutting down on further lend-lease supplies.'

These were soon to be cut off so precipitously that American ships carrying equipment to the USSR were turned around at sea.

The American repatriation officers were having no better time of it in Poland than the British. Clark Kerr wrote: 'Meanwhile American liaison officers in Lublin who have been told by Soviet military authorities to leave on the expiration of their 15 days permit have been instructed by General Deane to stay at Lublin unless actually removed by force.'

He also warned that the 'United States Ambassador expects some severe criticism of the Russians from the American prisoners now on their way home'.[2] For the British, this would not be so much of a problem – British ex-POWs were simply given a leaflet entitled 'Information for Repatriated Prisoners of War Proceeding on Leave' warning them to keep quiet about what they have seen. The section headed Security says: 'We must ask you *not* to give interviews to the Press or the BBC.'

Another British booklet named 'To All British Commonwealth Ex-Prisoners of War' and labelled Restricted, was published by the Director of Prisoners of War, February 1945. It warned that 'the information given in this document is not to be communicated, either directly or indirectly, to the Press or any person not authorised to receive it'. In provision 25, headed Security, it said: 'You must not grant interviews to press, newsreel or broadcasting representatives unless permission is given.' The RAF produced a similar booklet, which, in provision 59, specified that this 'permission' could only be given 'by a representative of the Director of Public Relations, Air Ministry'.

In fact, there was little to fear. The handful of British correspondents who made it into the Eastern zone agreed to clear all stories from Odessa through the British Military Mission in Moscow. In fact, it seems none were filed. But the Military Mission itself was reporting: 'The repatriation of British Commonwealth prisoners of war is proceeding *un*satisfactorily.'[3]

At Harriman's prompting, the American government seemed to be taking the situation much more seriously. On 18 March 1945 President Roosevelt sent the following 'personal' and 'secret' cable to Marshal Stalin:

> In the matter of evacuation of American ex-prisoners of war from Poland I have been informed that the approval for General Deane to survey the United States prisoners of war situation in Poland has been withdrawn. You stated in your last message to me that there was no need to accede to my request that American aircraft be allowed to carry supplies to Poland and to evacuate the sick. I have information that I consider positive and reliable that there are still a considerable number of sick and injured Americans in hospitals in Poland and also that there have been, certainly up to the last few days and possibly still are, large numbers of other liberated American prisoners either at Soviet assembly points or wandering about in small groups not in contact with Soviet authorities looking for American contact officers.
>
> I cannot, in all frankness, understand your reluctance to permit American contact officers, with the necessary means, to assist their own people in this matter. The Government has done everything to meet each of your requests. I now request you meet mine in this particular matter. Please call Ambassador Harriman to explain to you in detail my desires.[4]

But Harriman did not get a call from Stalin, who again rejected requests for American contact officers and stores to be sent to the collection points in Poland on the ground 'that there were no more American prisoners of war in Poland'.

Clark Kerr was reporting the same thing as Harriman. Three liberated British POWs from Lublin arrived in Moscow and reported that thousands of other liberated British were still in Poland. Men arriving at Odessa were reporting many sick and wounded there. The

Military Mission had pressed repeatedly to send officers and stores to these hospitals, and to evacuate the casualties by air. 'We have obtained no satisfaction, since the Russians continue to deny that there are any of our men in Poland,' the British Embassy reported. As Roosevelt had already sent a 'rough' personal message to Stalin, Clark Kerr recommended that Churchill do the same. In his cable to the Foreign Office, Clark Kerr mentioned that his dominion colleagues in Moscow, particularly the New Zealand minister, were seriously worried about 'what they feel is the deliberate failure of the Russians to fulfil their agreement'. But they decided to wait for Stalin's reply to Roosevelt before making their own complaints.[5]

Following General Deane's example, the British decided to tough it out in Poland. On 21 March 1945 Eden cabled the British Military Mission in Moscow instructing the British contact team at Lublin to stay put and, along with their American counterparts, resist any effort to make them leave.[6]

Eden wanted Churchill to follow Roosevelt's example and telegraph a protest to Stalin. He even drafted one for the Prime Minister. But Churchill thought both the timing and the tone were wrong.

'I do not wish to send this telegram,' he minuted to Eden on 21 March, 'as it would only make a row between us after a month's silence.'

But Churchill was eventually persuaded to draft his own telegram to Stalin. It used language, he told Eden, that 'gives no excuse for a rough answer'.[7] It read:

> There is no subject on which the British nation is more sensitive than on the fate of our prisoners in German hands and their speedy deliverance from captivity and restoration to their own country. I should be very much obliged if you would give this matter your personal attention, as I am sure that you would wish to do the best for our men, as I can promise you we are doing for your men as they come into our control along the Rhine.
>
>    We seem to have a lot of difficulties now, [Churchill added] since we parted at Yalta, but I am sure that all these would soon be swept away if we could only meet together.[8, 9]

Eden took a harder line in a telegram to Molotov that same day, 21 March 1945:

> I am surprised to hear that the agreement reached about our prisoners at Yalta is not being satisfactorily carried out. We have had no information since February 17th when your authorities

told us that 2,611 of our men had been collected and were being sent to Odessa. Only 1,847 of these have arrived in time to be embarked on the ship sent to collect them. Yet we know that there are a very large number still in your hands.

More seriously still, difficulties are continually being made about visits of British officers and furnishing of supplies to hospitals and other places (such as Praga, Lodz and Wrzesnia) where British subjects are collected on their way to embarkation points. We have thus no idea of the total numbers of the men concerned, of the condition in which they are, or of their needs.

The only places to which visits have been permitted (viz: Volkovysk, Lublin, Lvov and Bronnitz) are not sufficient as they are not first collection points.

Planned capacity of Odessa was 7,000. Lvov was supposed to hold 5,000 and Volkovysk 5,000. If those camps reached capacity a possible fourth camp at Bronnitz would be used that could hold 7,000. However, though Allied repatriation officers had been allowed into Odessa, the nearest they had got to the front line where POWs were being liberated was Lublin in eastern Poland, hundreds of kilometres behind the Soviet lines.

Eden asked for immediate access by British officers to forward areas 'where we know from reliable reports that our prisoners are being collected'. He complained, diplomatically, of 'serious delays', rejected the excuses made by the Soviet military and the Polish authorities, and demanded that the Yalta Agreement be carried out.[10]

On 22 March 1945 President Roosevelt received Marshal Stalin's reply:

I am in receipt of your message about the evacuation of former US prisoners of war from Poland. With regard to your information about allegedly large numbers of sick and injured Americans in Poland or awaiting evacuation to Odessa, or who have not contacted the Soviet authorities, I must say that information is inaccurate. Actually, apart from a certain number who are on their way to Polish soil as of March 16, I have today received a report which says that the 17 men [an unknown group not mentioned in other correspondence] will be flown to Odessa in a few days.

With reference to the request contained in your message I must say that if it concerned me personally I would be ready to give way even to the detriment of my own interests. But in the given instance the matter concerns the interest of Soviet armies at the front and of Soviet commanders who do not want to have around odd officers who, while having no relation to the military operations, need looking after, want all kinds of meetings and contacts, protection against possible acts of sabotage by German agents not yet ferreted out, and other things that divert the attention of the commanders and their subordinates from their direct duties. Our commanders bear full responsibility for the state of affairs at the front and in the immediate rear, and I do not see how I can restrict their rights to any extent.

I must also say that US ex-prisoners of war liberated by the Red Army have been treated to good conditions in Soviet camps – better conditions than those afforded Soviet ex-prisoners of war in US camps, where some of them were lodged with German war prisoners and were subjected to unfair treatment and unlawful persecutions, including beating, as has been communicated to the US Government on more than one occasion.[11]

President Roosevelt apparently accepted Marshal Stalin's explanation. And the retaliatory measures suggested by Harriman and Deane were rejected.

Despite Stalin's protests, the British were still reporting Americans, along with their own men, in Poland. The British Military Mission sent evidence to the Foreign Office which 'shows conclusively that there are numbers of British (and United States) prisoners of war at various points to the west of Lublin and Warsaw'.[12] In Churchill's name Clark Kerr demanded them back, but Stalin refused. Later Clark Kerr was to become one of the foremost proponents of the forced repatriation of Soviet citizens.

On 23 March 1945 Stalin got round to replying to Churchill's telegram:

So far as concerns British prisoners of war, you have no grounds for anxiety. They are living in better conditions than was the case with Soviet prisoners of war in English camps, where the latter in a number of cases have suffered persecution and even blows. Moreover, there are no longer any English prisoners in our camps – they are en route for Odessa and the voyage home.

Stalin's riposte that Soviet prisoners had been maltreated in Allied hands is breathtaking – when they were returned, he himself ordered them to be shot. Churchill sent a copy of this cable to the King.[13]

On the same day Molotov replied to the protest from Foreign Secretary Eden:

I cannot agree with your assertion that this agreement has been unsatisfactorily carried out so far as the Soviet side is concerned. Moreover I cannot regard as justified the exaggerated claims which do not follow from the agreement. I can assure [you] that British prisoners of war are in good conditions. We will continue to take care of British prisoners of war in future.

Odessa was rapidly filling up. Already, on 12 March, General Golubev had informed Admiral Archer at the British Military Mission in Moscow that Odessa had accommodation for 5,000 French and 5,000 British, Commonwealth and Americans.[14] But the Americans soon concluded: 'If Russians continue to evacuate other Allied nationals to Odessa in large numbers there is an obvious danger that many British and Americans may have to be held elsewhere.'[15]

Planned to hold 7,000, Odessa rapidly became overcrowded. But the Russians claimed that no other camp was being used – even though they were. This is all part of the Soviet wonderland, which the British and Americans found impossible to deal with.

The pressure of cables from Roosevelt, Churchill and Eden began to tell. On 21 March contact teams two and three left Moscow for Lvov and Volkovysk, the agreed points of concentration for recovered British Commonwealth prisoners of war, with permits that ended on 5 April. These camps were not even in Poland, but on the Russian side of the border, at least 110 kilometres east of Lublin. The British Military Mission in Moscow also pointed out that sixteen days simply did not give them long enough to do their job,[16] and made repeated representations to the Soviet authorities, who refused to extend the permits as there were no British prisoners of war in the camps. This statement, as the British government so delicately put it later, 'has been proved incorrect'.[17]

While the Soviet authorities were allowing Allied teams up to Lvov and Volkovysk, the British contact team in Lublin pushed to visit the other concentration points where they knew British POWs were gathering. Their Red Army chaperon, Colonel Vlasov, said these questions could be settled only in Moscow, and advised them to return there. He repeated that Lublin, as of 13 March 1945, was no longer a collecting point for Allied ex-POWs. The collecting points in future would be Cracow, Lodz and Rembertow, Vlasov said. He agreed to give the team a signed statement to that effect later that day. In fact, he left Lublin without doing so.

This cavalier attitude forced the British repatriation team to several unpleasant conclusions:

The Soviet Authorities have broken the Agreement of 11th February, by which British representatives were given the right to visit collecting points where British PW are concentrated. Apart from other points (Czestochowa, Ciechocienek) where we definitely knew that large numbers of British ex-PW were organised under Russian supervision, the Russian poster . . . specifically mentions several camps to which neither we nor any other British representatives were admitted. [It] is impossible to estimate accurately the numbers of British ex-PW still in Poland . . .

Lamely, the British team in Lublin commented: 'Outside the Russian camps stragglers appear to number several hundreds.'[18]

Passing this information on to the government in London, the British Military Mission in Moscow (30 Military Mission) added:

In so far as the Soviet Government appear to have made any attempt to justify their actions, it is based on a two-fold denial that – a) there are no 'points of concentrations' or camps; b) there are no British ex-prisoners of war in Poland; both of which are flagrantly contrary to facts within the knowledge of 30 Military Mission.

However, the war is still going on. In January 1945 the Swiss had arranged for the Allies and Germans to exchange around 5,000 seriously sick and wounded prisoners of war.[19] In March the Foreign Office was cabling Berne asking what had happened to the large number of sick and wounded prisoners passed by German doctors for repatriation who had still not been returned.[20] The fear was that they too might have fallen into Soviet hands.

# CHAPTER 11

# The Numbers Game

✝

ON 24 MARCH 1945 SHAEF's POW Department circulated its regular 'Strengths of Prisoners of War in Germany' memo. It carried the last coherent listing of registered prisoners from the war. The figures were not estimates; they gave a detailed breakdown of POWs by nationality, by camps, by German war zone and by Allied theatre. These were registered prisoners of war, men whose presences had been reported by the Detaining Power – Germany, and the Germans were meticulous in their record-keeping – and often confirmed by the Protecting Power – Switzerland. The British prisoners' names were then reported by the International Committee of the Red Cross to London, and the British Red Cross, the Order of St John and the families of the men themselves were informed. This reporting process took six to seven weeks.

The total of registered British prisoners of war had climbed steadily throughout the war. On 1 February 1945 it was 185,631. On 24 March 1945, the last reported figure, it reached a peak of 199,592. Although men were being liberated, this number may well have gone on climbing. During the last battles of the war – and the continuing air raids – men were still being captured. But they would have been listed as 'missing' or 'missing believed prisoner'. Of the 199,592 confirmed prisoners of war, only 168,746 returned.[1]

It was already clear to the Allies that prisoners of war had been detained by the Soviets for the purposes of blackmail. When Averell Harriman estimated several thousand, Stalin replied that he had seventeen. Plainly, confrontation was not the way to handle the matter. So the Western Allies tried a new tack – appeasement.

On 26 March 1945 Roosevelt began moves to recognise the new Polish regime. Churchill was eventually forced to go along. Meanwhile, on the same day the US Chief of Staff, General George C. Marshall, issued an order on a 'revised policy' to the US Military Mission in Moscow and other Allied European Commands: '. . . revised policy liberated prisoners: Individual interviews authorized provided personnel briefed beforehand against disclosure camp intelligence activities, evasion and escape briefings, equipment. Censor all stories. Delete criticism Russian treatment . . .'[2] Although the war against Hitler was almost won, the public perception was still to be that the Soviet Union was a stout ally of the United States.

Denied access to the forward areas where British prisoners were being liberated by the Soviets, the British Military Mission in Moscow also came up with a new tactic. They suggested asking the Russian Red Cross to seek permission for Major General J.E.T. Younger of the British Red Cross to visit Belgard and Stargard in Pomerania, Obrzycko in Poland, Landsberg in northeast Silesia and the Katowice area where there were 'eight hospitals, one camp and thousands of British POWs working in mines and on farms', as well as Lvov, Volkovysk and Odessa. Plans were made for the BBC to broadcast details of this trip, so that the British ex-POWs at large in those areas would contact him.

But this new plan did not run smoothly. General Younger rejected Colonel Brinckman's suggestion that he go right forward into Germany and visit the POW camps directly after they had been liberated by the Red Army.

'I feel that this is too ambitious and might jeopardise the entire trip,' Younger wrote.[3] He scrawled on the bottom of the secret memo outlining his trip that, as well as an interpreter and local transport, he would need an 'assured method of sending back information'. And he suggested that the British Military Mission 'point out that I am not in the Army, I am not a government official, but an independent representative of the British Red Cross exclusively concerned with the care of the sick, wounded and prisoners of war'.[4]

Despite these assurances General Younger and the Red Cross failed to get into the forward areas in Russia, Poland and Germany.

Even though the British and Americans had extremely restricted access behind Soviet lines, the Western Allies had numerous agents behind German lines. It is ironic that, while the British could not find out what was happening in areas held by an ally's army, copious information was coming out of hostile territory.

By 3 April 1945 the Allies were getting a clear picture of the movements of POWs as they were carried westwards ahead of the Russian advance. The arrangements made for quartering, the rations, the incidence of frostbite, the number who died and where and when they perished were all well documented.[5]

Hugely detailed reports of the conditions in camps and the numbers of men being liberated in the Western theatre were being returned to SHAEF. On 3 April 1945 for example, 3,247 US, 1,890 British and Dominion, 54 South African, 261 Indian, 16 Iraqi, 448 French, 448 Russian and 210 Yugoslavs were liberated at Bad Orb.[6] Liberated men were quickly logged and provided with passes. These were shown at each stage as they were passed back through the lines, to prevent men from being accounted for twice.

But the numbers of POWs being released – and still held – staggered the imagination. On 4 April 1945 a secret SHAEF memo entitled 'Evacuation of British and American Released Prisoners of War' informed the appropriate departments to prepare for the return of, in round numbers, 280,000 Allied prisoners of war – 80,000 Americans and 200,000 British.[7] This figure closely approximates the 199,592 registered prisoners of 24 March and the 199,500 figure mentioned in SHAEF Eclipse memo number 8 of 25 March 1945. Despite the Ministry of Defence's equivocations ever since, there seems no doubt about how many prisoners were in the camps at the time.

Despite the huge numbers of prisoners of war still expected to be liberated, especially in the east, General Golubev wrote to the British Military Mission in Moscow on 4 April 1945 saying that, as there were no more prisoners at Lvov and Volkovysk, there was no need to extend the British contact teams' permits.[8] These were to expire the next day. Given the large number of men who passed through Lvov – a camp that turned out to consist of a casino and a converted warehouse – and the number still expected, the British Military Mission told the contact team at Lvov to 'remain there unless removed by force'. The repatriation team reported that they were promptly 'confined to their hotel and can only take exercise under escort'. Their stores and vehicles were confiscated by the Russians for 'safe keeping'.[9]

The British Military Mission in Moscow also wanted the team at Volkovysk to stay put, but could not contact them.

On 6 April 1945 Major Gibson at Lvov managed to phone the British Military Mission in Moscow. Soviet officers at Lvov had told him that Cracow was the best place for British officers to be, though the Soviet authorities had not offered, or permitted, the repatriation teams to visit there. Major Gibson had been told that many British prisoners of war had gone to Cracow, but on finding no British contact officers there, they had returned to their temporary Polish homes where they were still 'lying up'.

Gibson was convinced that a considerable number of these men would be rounded up in Poland and passed back through Lvov. He continued to insist on seeing all former POWs passing through Lvov, but despite his protests he remained confined to his hotel.[10]

On 6 April 1945 Colonel Brinckman wrote to General Younger of the Red Cross saying that there were 'meant to be 1,581 British in hospitals to be visited, so far only 40 hospital cases had been accounted for'.

Brinckman also sent a revised itinerary for Younger's visit, restricting the tour to Lvov, Volkovysk, Wollstein – where 139 British prisoners were reported on 15 January – and the hospitals in the Hindenburg and Katowice areas where there were 1,425 on 15 January. Then he would go on to Odessa. This truncated tour, they hoped, might receive the approval of the Soviet authorities.

Meanwhile, a new area of the POW problem had opened up. Under Field Marshal Alexander the Allied armies had fought their way up to Italy and were now nearing the Soviet lines in Austria, where more camps had been liberated. On 6 April 1945 the War Office cabled AFHQ – Alexander's headquarters – that they did not expect having the same difficulties in obtaining visas for British contact officers to enter Soviet-occupied Austria 'as occurred over Russia and Poland'.[11] They were soon to be proved tragically wrong.

On 14 April the British Ambassador in Moscow reminded the Foreign Office that the Soviets had insisted that visas for contact teams going into Austria had to be obtained in Moscow. However, the Soviets had not yet agreed, even in principle, to allow British officers into Austria; so no applications had been made.

In his cable, Sir Archibald Clark Kerr also recommended that the team going into Austria should not be sent via Moscow. Judging by past form, they would meet with endless delays. As the Soviets had consistently refused to allow contact teams into forward areas in Poland and Germany, he did not 'expect therefore that facilities elsewhere denied us will be granted to us in Austria and I fear we shall be told . . . that there are no collecting points in Austria and that all our liberated prisoners of war are already on their way to Odessa'.

Clark Kerr did not expect that they would get any satisfaction from the Soviets until an Allied Control Commission was set up in Austria.[12]

CHAPTER 12

# Blackmail

✝

GENERAL YOUNGER CABLED Field Marshal Sir Philip Chetwode, the head of the Red Cross in London, saying he was still

> seeking permission to venture to Central, SW Poland and Silesia from Russian Red Cross. British sick in Silesia . . . the Military Mission say there are fifteen hundred British sick, some camps, and where reports, both American and British, indicate that there are a lot of our men scattered round the country in villages, mining districts and so forth, where they were employed by the Germans in working parties and on farms.

The British authorities in Moscow were also getting deeply concerned about the situation in Poland. No British contact teams had been allowed into Poland since the one at Lublin, and now the Soviet authorities were putting renewed pressure on the British Military Mission in Moscow to remove its only two forward contact teams at Lvov and Volkovysk, even though they were well on the Russian side of the Polish border.

On 8 April 1945 the British Embassy in Moscow summed up the situation in a report to the Foreign Office:

> Soviet authorities at Lvov have refused to extend permits of our officers beyond April 5th [stating] . . . that the camp at Lvov had been cleared . . . Owing to lack of communication with Volkovysk we do not know whether the same has happened there but it seems likely. [He] . . . had written to M. Molotov . . . pointing out . . . that the British public would never understand withdrawal of our officers until all our missing prisoners had been accounted for, particularly because a great number must have been liberated by recent operations of the Red Army or would shortly be . . . There is I am sure great opposition to allowing our people to have

62

access to Poland and also some inclination to blackmail us into dealing with the Warsaw authorities.[1]

From 8 April to late May 1945, well after cessation of hostilities in Europe, many other cables concerning the handling of Allied prisoners of war use the word blackmail. The object of this extortion, a series of diplomats and high-ranking military men suggest, was the recognition of the new regime in Poland and Allied acquiescence in the establishment of a communist government in Austria.

The Soviets, complete masters of the game, were blackmailing the West with something they said they didn't have. But still it worked. This particular gambit depended on restricting the flow of information in and out of Poland. The Soviets, like the Germans before them, banned the possession of private radio receivers in Poland so that the locals – and liberated POWs hiding there – could not listen to the BBC.[2]

The British contact team ordered out of Volkovysk turned up in Moscow on 9 April 1945. They had not resisted the Soviet order expelling them because the British Embassy had been unable to contact them to tell them to stay put.[3] Even while there, they had not been allowed to do their job properly and the Soviet authorities had not lived up to the Yalta Agreement. The British team had no say in the administration of the camp and no access to at least one party of ex-prisoners who were passing through by train. When they were kicked out, there were still twenty-eight British ex-prisoners of war at Volkovysk, though the excuse given in Moscow was that there were none.

The next day Admiral Archer took up the matter with General Golubev and received the bare-faced reply: 'I find quite incomprehensible your insistent demand for your repatriation officers to make an unlimited stay at those places where *none* of your compatriots have been liberated from prison and where, consequently, there is no one to support either in a material or moral sense.'

Golubev contended that the group of Englishmen who turned up at Volkovysk on 5 April had been sent there by mistake. As to Lvov: 'I once again insistently demand that you give the appropriate instructions to Major Gibson for the immediate departure of himself and his group from Lvov to Moscow.'[4]

The British Military Mission cabled London:

Up to the time of the Yalta Agreement there was practically no indication of any desire on the part of the Soviet authorities to co-operate; and following the signature of the agreement, frequent difficulties have been experienced, particularly when the Soviet military authorities denied all knowledge of facts of which the Mission had conclusive evidence.[5]

The British Embassy continued to protest that the Soviets' failure to allow contact teams into these areas constituted a clear breach of the Yalta Agreement and the War Cabinet informed the American government of its protest. This matter was of such sensitivity that the cable outlining the problem carried a note saying: 'This telegram is of particular secrecy and should be retained by the authorised recipient and not passed on.'[6]

Liberated British POWs who, in the confusion of things, had managed to make it through to Odessa continued to insist that, contrary to Soviet reports, more British ex-POWs were still in Poland. Sir Archibald Clark Kerr cabled the Foreign Office that the Soviets should, at least, be pressed to despatch supplies to the Polish Red Cross for distribution to these prisoners. General Younger, the Red Cross man in Moscow, also asked his chief in London to discuss this matter with the Foreign Office.

Six of the liberated POWs had reached Odessa with their Polish wives. Not all prisoners of war were kept in camps; many worked in factories and mines. Under the Geneva Convention prisoners of war are allowed to work, provided the work does not directly aid the war effort. In Poland particularly, many British POWs worked on farms and some found themselves romantically involved with farmers' daughters. When they married, the Polish girls became British subjects. But the Soviets would not recognise this. They separated the Polish wives from their British husbands and put them in a separate camp. The British Military Mission sent a cipher telegram to the War Office, saying they must move quickly 'otherwise these women may be liquidated'.[7]

Following a second formal protest to Soviet Foreign Minister Molotov about restricted access to the forward areas by the British Ambassador on 16 April,[8] General Younger's itinerary was limited further to Lvov, Volkovysk, Odessa and Cracow,[9] though Younger also wanted to visit Thorn, Czestochowa, Lamsdorf and Tost. He never got to visit any of these places.

Ex-prisoners of war were still trickling through to Odessa, but the situation there was not good. Between 8 and 12 April 1945 Colonel Hundall of the British Military Mission prepared a report on the generally appalling conditions in the repatriation camps at Odessa. Much of it is taken up in detailing the overcrowding, shortage of food and clothing, lack of bedding and poor sanitation.

In a paragraph headed 'Control', the report notes this is 'very much in Russian hands'. Under the terms of the Yalta Agreement, of course, control should have been in the hands of Allied repatriation officers.

'No British Officer is permitted to enter the buildings unless accompanied by a Russian officer although British officers hold passes signed by General Golubev,' wrote Colonel Hundall. 'It is most difficult to get anywhere unless accompanied by a Russian. Sentries with fixed bayonets are posted outside the buildings.'[10]

The men in the camps at Odessa were not allowed to write letters[11] and the Soviets would not give their permission for the British to run a weekly air service to Odessa; nor did they give a reason for the refusal.[12]

Even those men who made it to Odessa found that their troubles were not over. Four ex-POWs, eager to get home, boarded a ship bound for Naples without the permission of the Soviets. The sentry who allowed the violation to occur was reportedly executed. AFHQ recommended that an apology be made to the Soviet government. The four POWs made it safely to Italy, where they were reprimanded.[13]

When British officers did get into the camps at Odessa they started debriefing the ex-POWs. Names of other men they had seen in the camps were sent to Moscow. Rear Admiral Archer compiled lists of men known to be still in Soviet hands and passed them to General Golubev with requests for information about the men.

On 12 April 1945 Archer produced a list of thirteen Britons in Russian hospitals and tartly remarked: 'As I am not receiving your reports on these and other parties of sick and wounded, I am relying on the information passed to me from Odessa.'[14]

The Americans were also having problems. On 12 April 1945 Lieutenant Colonel William Fenell reported that 2,687 American prisoners had been shipped out of Odessa – out of a total of 2,858 Americans who eventually left that way – along with 4,400 British POWs. However, both Colonel Fenell and Ambassador Harriman reported that another 2,000 American POWs were still in Poland. These men did not return.

On 13 April 1945 a top-secret cable from Alexander Kirk, US political adviser to Supreme Allied Command Mediterranean (SACMED) and later US Ambassador to Italy, said that another 884 Americans had turned up in Odessa on 2 April, but were being 'held up'. It seems that they did not return home either. Although Odessa had been the third largest city in Russia, it had been heavily damaged by fighting in the war and the conditions there in 1945 were grim.

It is interesting to compare the restricted access to Allied prisoners offered by the Soviets with the facilities provided by the Allies to the Soviets. On 13 April 1945 Soviet repatriation officers were taken to a camp for Soviet soldiers in Italy. A report of their visit was sent to the US Secretary of State:

> Russians were permitted and encouraged to set up their own camp administration. Russians of all categories are accepted at Florence camp, outfitted with clothing, PX supplies and same facilities as for United States personnel. After minimum processing they are flown to Bari to await shipment to Russia. When Soviet military missions representatives were taken to inspect both camps, they expressed pleasure and said treatment was 'too good'.[15]

The problem of the Allied prisoners of war, meanwhile, was certainly reaching the highest levels. While they were with the new President on 16 April – President Harry Truman had taken over after the death of Roosevelt – US Secretary of State Stettinius mentioned to visiting Foreign Secretary Sir Anthony Eden his concern about the difficulty both their countries were having with regard to UK and US servicemen who were prisoners behind the Soviet front lines. His view was that the treatment of American prisoners was quite unsatisfactory, and the US had not been able to contact teams sent into the area to care and provide for their men. The Soviets had promised to do something about this at Yalta, Stettinius complained, but had done nothing. He intended to raise this issue with Molotov.

The British were also having problems. That very day His Majesty's Ambassador in Moscow had written to Molotov again pointing out that the Soviet action amounted to a violation of the Yalta Agreement and pressed for a reply to his request that British officers be allowed once more to visit the camps at Lvov and Volkovysk. This crossed with a letter from Vyshinski, who had taken over the matter at the People's Commissariat for Foreign Affairs. Andrei Yanuaryevich Vyshinski had had dealings with British citizens before. He had been a prosecutor during the show trials of Stalin's Great Purge in the 1930s and the leading advocate of 'socialist law'. The case that first brought him to prominence was the so-called Metro-Vickers trial in 1933, where British engineers were charged with trying to wreck Soviet hydroelectic constructions.

Vyshinski took the standard line that there were, and had been 'no British prisoners in the camps in question; that British officers had only been allowed there on a visit of inspection; and that their presence at the camps was neither necessary nor intended by the Yalta Agreement. When more prisoners arrived we should be informed and our officers would be given facilities to visit the camps'.[16]

While the Soviets remained implacable, the continuing pro-Soviet propaganda in the West undermined the Allies' negotiating position. Sir Archibald Clark Kerr cabled a strong complaint to the Foreign Office about a story in the *Daily Express*, which had said: 'In the Soviet Union everything possible was done for liberated British and American prisoners of war.'

This was irresponsible reporting, Sir Archibald said, and he pointed out:

> We have had to make repeated protests at the failure of the Russians to take proper care of our prisoners and at their refusal to grant adequate facilities to the Repatriation Commission. Publication in the British press of statements such as that of the *Daily Express*, besides being untrue, will not only detract from the effect which our protests have, but will give the Russians a pretext for maintaining the obstructive attitude which they have shown hitherto.[17]

Unable to comprehend the enormity of what was happening, many people in government believed that the Soviets were reluctant to take British and American repatriation officers into the concentration points behind the lines because they were disorganised and the facilities poor. But, on 18 April 1945, Company Sergeant Major MacLennan of the Seaforth Highlanders reported that there was a well-run repatriation camp for British and American prisoners at Schlochau and an efficient reception camp at Kulmsee, near Thorn. The food and accommodation were good. New arrivals were given a medical examination and issued with clean underclothes.[18] But no repatriation officers were allowed to visit these model facilities, and there could be only one reason. The Soviets were excluding Allied repatriation officers so that no one would see what happened to liberated prisoners of war. And when they were spirited away into Soviet labour camps, the authorities could deny they ever existed.

## CHAPTER 13

# No Retaliatory Action

$\dagger$

ON 19 APRIL 1945 the US Secretary of State was preparing to meet Soviet Commissar of Foreign Affairs Molotov at the gathering of foreign ministers in San Francisco that would establish the United Nations. The State Department drew up a list of topics that might be raised. These included the implementation of the Yalta Agreement on the exchange of liberated prisoners of war, a $6 billion loan the Soviets were asking for, and the failure of the Soviet government to allow Red Cross and, later, UNRRA – the United Nations Relief and Rehabilitation Administration – personnel into Poland. It was thought that this last item might provoke Molotov to retort that it was a matter for the Polish Provisional Government.

The Secretary of State was reminded that, despite the President's pleas, contact teams had been denied access into Poland – in violation of the Yalta Agreement. But any mention of Yalta might raise the question of the Americans' refusal to return, at that time, Soviet nationals in German uniform who claimed the protection of the Geneva Convention as German prisoners of war. The State Department feared German retaliations if they returned these men. The US had insisted to the Germans that all men captured in American uniforms should be treated as American citizens, regardless of their nationality. But the Secretary of State should assure Molotov 'that we have no intention of holding Soviet citizens after the collapse of Germany regardless of whether they desire to return to the Soviet Union or not'.

On 19 April 1945 Associated Press reported from Paris:

Germany's complete roster of prisoners of war, including an itemization of all captives from every Allied country taken by the Germans since the outbreak of the war, has been seized by American Third Army troops . . . The captured records contain latest whereabouts of Allied prisoners of war, their dates of capture and other data. They list the prisoners who have died since capture and those wounded when taken.

The capture was made by headquarters personnel, who seized the complete staff of ten German officers and forty enlisted men engaged in keeping the prisoners' cards up to date.[1]

*The New York Times* said it was doubtful that the roster would be published due to its length.[2]

All the captured files were duplicated and shared by the British and Americans – one held the originals, the other held the microfilm copy. So both of the Allies knew exactly how many men were in the camps that were later overrun by the Red Army. The British government now claims that it is not sure exactly how many British prisoners of war were held by the Germans during World War II.

As well as being able to nail down the exact number of missing men, the British government began to receive reports of their treatment by their Soviet 'liberators'. According to one report from the British Military Mission in Moscow: 'Five British prisoners of war were detained by the Russians from 27th Feb to 21st March in a sugar factory near Oels in Silesia. During this period they were forced to work under guard although they were registered several times as British' – a violation of Article 6 of the Yalta Agreement, which limited the employment of ex-POWs.[3]

Although such cases gave the British information to put pressure on Stalin, the Soviet authorities continued to drag their feet. Moscow had to clear the release of every British prisoner held in Red Army territory and they were literally being released one by one.

The legendary General Patton headed the Third Army which had captured the German POW files. He was growing very tired of the Soviet's behaviour, but he was restrained. An order was issued 'that no repeat no retaliatory action will be taken by US forces at this time for Soviet refusal to meet our desires with regard to American contact teams and aid for American personnel liberated by Russian forces'.[4] This order remained in force even after V-E day.

While Secretary of State Stettinius and Foreign Secretary Anthony Eden had discussed bringing up the matter of POWs with Molotov, they were in a quandary about Poland. Britain had gone to war over the German invasion of Poland. A Polish government in exile still sat in London. If Britain was forced to deal with the Polish Provisional Government to get their contact teams in, it would be seen as an appalling betrayal. So British policy over the POWs in Poland went into a holding pattern.

On 20 April 1945 the Foreign Office in London cabled a message for Eden in San Francisco: 'It is clear that Soviet Government will not allow our contact teams into Poland. The Russians deny the existence of any British prisoners of war in Poland but we have evidence that there are prisoners of war concentrated at Cracow and Czestochowa, and in hospitals. This is a clear breach of Yalta Agreement . . .'[5]

Rather than recommending Eden bringing up the matter with Molotov, the Foreign Office reported that they had 'turned to the Red Cross channel'. They had been trying the approach in Moscow for nearly a month through General Younger.[6]

That same day the Foreign Office received a cable from Moscow: 'Although Russians deny there are any of our men in hospitals in Poland, General Younger intends to confront Soviet Red Cross with statements from our liberated prisoners in Odessa and to press them to arrange for despatch of supplies to the Polish Red Cross for distribution amongst our men.'[7]

This did no good. The response was a further trimming of Younger's itinerary. By 6 May he accepted that he would not even reach Lvov and Volkovysk. The only place he would eventually see was Odessa.[8] The Red Cross route was closed as well.

Around 4,000 British POWs had been recovered and repatriated via Odessa, but some hundreds whose names had been compiled on Archer's lists remained unaccounted for. And with the war in Europe coming rapidly to a conclusion it was estimated that 'those of our prisoners who had not previously been moved by German forces from areas now occupied by the Red Army must number close on 100,000'. It was urgent that contact teams be sent to the areas where these men had been liberated, but access was being denied. By now, though, they had practically given up hope. Further protests, the British Embassy noted, would be of more value 'for purposes of record than for obtaining practical redress for our grievances'.

The situation continued to deteriorate. On 21 April 1945 the Americans reported: 'We are informed by General Key that Soviet ACC Hungary now has formally disapproved of entry into Hungary of US repatriation contact team.'[9] The British Military Mission in Hungary soon found that it, too, was denied access to camps where British subjects were being held in Budapest.[10]

On 22 April 1945 the British and American governments accepted the German offer to leave POWs in the camps – and not withdraw them ahead of the advancing Allied forces – provided the liberated POWs were not returned to active service.[11] The French rejected the offer.[12] Just two days later, the Allies heard from the International Committee of the Red Cross in Berne that the Germans were not complying with the standstill agreement and that British, American and French prisoners were being taken into a redoubt where the Allies feared the Nazis would make their last stand.[13]

A band of fanatics holding thousands of Allied prisoners hostage in the mountains of Bavaria would have been difficult, if not impossible, to dislodge. The suicide of Hitler on 30 April 1945 put an end to this plan.

Meanwhile, Stalag 3A at Luckenwalde in Germany had been 'liberated' by the Red Army. Many men, fearing their fate in Soviet hands, ran off. The Soviet POWs were issued with rifles and told to follow the tanks. The same invitation was given to the other nationalities, according to former POW Sergeant H. Wagner of the British army. But he does not think any accepted. The camp continued under Soviet administration, but when nothing happened for a day or so prisoners ignored their instructions to stay put and slipped out of the camp. A large number made their way westwards. Eventually some bumped into American troops who organised transport back to England on Dakotas.

An Australian airman said the Soviets refused to let the 'British types' leave. 'Apparently, we were to be held as hostages, with the exchange rate of three Russian officers for each British, or the same for six Russian privates,' he said. 'Things got so sticky they started to shoot and a couple of our guys were clocked.' The Australian eventually escaped from the camp.

Lengthy reports on the incident were turned in to the military authorities, but it did no good. The Australian airman was told 'POWs come under the diplomatic side'. He believes that the Soviets are still holding some of the POWs. Apart from himself and the bombardier, the other five of his crew have simply vanished.[14]

A New Zealander returnee, a Man of Confidence – the elected representative of the POWs who dealt with the Germans on a day-to-day basis – reported that 800 of the 1,200 New Zealanders in his charge never made it home. Another Australian who had escaped from the Soviets in late June 1945 reported that he had contacted numerous officials about his many mates who had been kidnapped, but nothing was done.

Others who escaped from Luckenwalde got to the Elbe at Magdeburg before they found their way blocked. They were rounded up by the Soviets and marched back deeper into the Soviet-held territory. However, a British Intelligence officer managed to slip his way into one column. He quickly organised an escape plan, and led the men down an alley where a barge took them to the Allied side of the river.[15] These were the lucky ones. Many of their fellow inmates of Stalag 3A were never heard of again.

Private Everrett was liberated from Brandenburg jail by the Red Army. Captured in 1943, he had been put to work on a farm in Poland. But after an attempt to escape through Danzig to Sweden, he was court martialled and imprisoned. After the liberation of Brandenburg he soon got the impression that the Soviets were ready to go to war with the Western Allies. Everrett feared being imprisoned by the Soviets and in the general confusion seized his opportunity. He and a fellow prisoner, a naval petty officer, slipped away and headed for Schöne-beck on the Elbe and the American lines, a distance of some eighty kilometres. They travelled at night, and along the way they picked up a young girl who was fleeing from the Soviets, and a number of Czechs. The journey took almost ten days.

When they reached the Elbe the bridge had been partially destroyed and Soviet soldiers were checking the refugees who were still able to clamber across. Rather than risk the whole party being arrested, Everrett went on his own to the Red Army post. He was told he would not be allowed across to the American lines. He should collect his things and join the other British prisoners the Soviets had collected, ready to be transported east.

Everrett slipped back to his friends, but they could not decide what to do. The petty officer went off with the Czechs to find some other way across the river, while Everrett and the girl went into a nearby village. They struck lucky. The family who put them up kept a canoe in their loft. Later, he and the girl crept back to the river and hid with the canoe in the bushes.

They timed the passing Soviet patrols and when the coast was clear they launched the canoe and started paddling across the Elbe. They had gone about three quarters of the way when a Red Army patrol fired at them, but they made it safely to the far bank where they were picked up by an American artillery battalion.

Everrett never knew whether the petty officer made it home and he fears for the fate of any fellow servicemen who dallied in Brandenburg, waiting to be repatriated. On his return to England he was interrogated by MI5.

Another ex-POW, H.G. McLean, escaped from Muhlberg after the Russians had relieved the camp. When he got back to England, McLean reported: 'The Russians did nothing for us, alternately telling us to go out and forage for ourselves one day, and threatening to shoot anyone who left the camp the next day. After a few days, we got fed up with the shilly-shallying and left. I walked to Wurzen, where I met the Americans, and from then it was plain sailing.'

Owen Roberts was also liberated from Stalag 4B at Muhlberg on 23 April 1945 by Soviets, some of whom were on horseback and were mistaken for Cossacks. 'Early in May, my navigator and an Aussie navigator and an air gunner from London acquired some bikes and rode to the American lines,' Roberts reported.

Ex-POW G.J.W. Simister, another inmate of Muhlberg, marched to the American lines at Riesa after being liberated by soldiers on horseback. 'The Russians promised extra food – their promises were the same as the Jerries'.' He, like others, thought that the Soviets stalled and prevaricated about returning them. When he returned home in July or August 1945, he too was interrogated by MI5 in an office building opposite Marylebone station.

Tom Swallow was at Muhlberg too. But he did as he was ordered and stayed put. The Soviets, he recalls, had many excuses why they could not simply be handed over. They were only eight kilometres from Torgau, where the two armies had met on 27 April, and the American lines were just an hour away. Even so, when the food ran out Swallow and the other POWs who had stayed behind were marched eastwards, away from the Allied lines. After six weeks they were found by a wandering American patrol. Trucks were organised and the Allied POWs were exchanged man for man for Soviet prisoners the Americans had brought up.

Robert Williams, also liberated by Soviet cavalry, was ordered by the senior RAF officer not to leave the camp. Williams reported that, on 26 April:

> the Russians told us they would not feed us, we were to live off the land as they did. We could go as far east as we wished but were not to cross the River Elbe – if we tried we would be shot. Two POWs were shot and wounded trying to cross the bridge near Belgern. Ten days later, Jonesy, Mac and I – all from the 7th Royal Tank Regiment – crossed the River Elbe on the back of a Russian tank and walked for three days until we met an American soldier guarding a bridge at Wurzen on the River Mulde. It was 8 May 1945.

Six British prisoners of war got out of Czechoslovakia because a stranger fluent in Russian helped them to slip past the Red Army checkpoint on the road from Prague to Pilsen. When they looked back, their guardian angel had disappeared into thin air.[16]

Royal Army Service Corps driver William Henry Sadler was a farm worker at Stalag 18 when the Soviets came through in March 1945. He managed to make his way back to Britain, and in 1990 he said: 'I often wondered what happened to all those other blokes.'

It is interesting to note that of the large number of British ex-POWs liberated by the Red Army who were interviewed by David Rolf for his book *Prisoners of the Reich*,[17] the vast majority made it to the British or American lines under their own steam. Even those who were repatriated say that the Soviets were in no hurry to hand them back. Most report being afraid of the Soviets. Some were told by Soviet soldiers that they did not intend to stop in Germany and were on their way to London. Many believed it.

The former POWs say they feared that the Soviets had no intention of giving them back. Unlike the general public in Britain and America, most POWs had not been bombarded for four years with propaganda about kindly Uncle Joe Stalin. They believed that they were going to be shipped off eastwards to slave labour camps in Siberia,[18] and they escaped as soon as they could. Only two or three of Rolf's informants report being returned by the Russians in the proper fashion, while many report being prevented, or even fired upon, when they tried to cross the lines.

CHAPTER 14

# Charge and Counter-Charge

†

ON 25 APRIL 1945 the British Embassy in Moscow presented Deputy Commissar of Foreign Affairs Vyshinski with copies of thirty-seven signed statements by liberated British POWs who had valuables, articles of clothing or food removed from them under force of arms by Soviet soldiers, and two signed statements by British women complaining that they had been raped by Soviet soldiers.

Private Fraser Clough of the Seaforth Highlanders and Private Donald Alexander of the Black Watch both had their wristwatches taken by drunken Russian soldiers. In both cases they explained that they were British soldiers, but it made no difference.[1] It was not uncommon to see Soviet soldiers with arms full of wristwatches.

Rifleman Cecil Miles and Lance Corporal Gordon Lewis of the South African Field Ambulance found themselves working in an oil plant for the Russians. In their statement, which was marked top secret, they say that they were liberated from a POW camp by the Soviets. On 24 March 1945 they received a pass from the Russian commandant at Cosel, Upper Silesia, to proceed to Gleiwitz, together with fifty Frenchmen. As they passed through the village of Reigersfeld they were halted by a band of drunken Soviet soldiers.

The soldiers put them to work dismantling machinery in a synthetic oil plant. After three days the two ex-POWs were sent back to Cosel in a lorry to pick up supplies. There, they managed to speak to the commandant again. He gave them another pass. This time it permitted them to proceed to Katowice. But when they got back to the oil plant and handed it to the officer there, he laughed and said they would go when he had finished with them.

They continued working at the plant until 31 March. Then they managed to escape with four Frenchmen. They ran into the woods while being transferred from the houses where they had been billeted to the former prisoner-of-war camp at the factory. They slept in the woods that night and on 1 April managed to get back to Cosel once again. There, the commandant issued them with yet another pass, allowing the six of them to proceed to Katowice.

This time they took a long way round, avoiding the plant. They were stopped outside another oil plant at Blechammer, but were allowed to proceed. The four Frenchmen remained at Katowice while Miles and Lewis went on to Cracow and, eventually, made it home.

In their statement they describe their week at the factory:

> Our hours were from 0600 hrs to 1945 hrs each day. There was one Russian guard to each ten workmen, and one Russian engineer to forty men. The only food we received was about a litre of thin soup twice a day and a loaf of Russian black bread between three men each morning. We had to do heavy manual labour removing machinery. The guards treated us reasonably well, but the engineers threatened the workers with an extra hour's work a day if they did not work harder. We were accommodated at night in an empty house. There were twelve men in each room. The room in which we slept would have been large enough for three single beds. We had no blankets, and had to sleep on mattresses brought from another house by some of the Frenchmen without the knowledge of the Russians. We had only our greatcoats to cover us. We were both suffering from diarrhoea caused by drinking lake water. We asked a Russian Senior Lieutenant if we could see a doctor. He laughed and said the doctor would come sometime.[2]

The two rape victims were an Englishwoman and her daughter who were visiting Paris in 1939 and found themselves trapped when the Germans overran France. In August 1940 they were taken by the Germans first to Essen and then to Sorau. They worked in a restaurant there and lived freely, though they had to report to the police twice daily. When the Soviets came on 13 February 1945 the two women had no papers to show. The mother was ordered to stay where she was while the daughter was taken to the commandant.

The daughter was taken upstairs. Half an hour later the mother heard a scream and rushed upstairs. She found her daughter unconscious on a bed. She was soaked from head to foot. A Russian had thrown a bucket of water over her. A Russian soldier's revolver lay on the table beside the bed. The girl had been raped.

When the mother complained to a Soviet officer he went through the motions of an investigation. A man was brought and the daughter recognised him as the rapist. Nothing was done.

On 20 February 1945 the two women left Sorau with a party of Frenchmen. On the road they were overtaken by a Soviet motorcyclist. He took the two women to an empty house where, he said, they could stay for the night. He took the mother upstairs and raped her.

The two women remained alone in the house that night, and left in the morning when the occupants returned. There was no one to complain to. Eventually they made their way to Odessa where they told the British Mission of their treatment.[3]

Vyshinski dismissed all the charges brought by British servicemen and civilians. In a letter dated 9 June 1945 he pointed out that 'all the statements were of the same type and contained no concrete data'. The men who were supposed to have perpetrated these heinous deeds had 'no distinguishing insignia' so it was 'impossible to establish whether they were members of the Soviet armed forces'. They could be 'bandit elements' or 'marauders'. Vyshinski commented that it was 'regrettable that His Majesty's Government deemed it possible on basis of such insufficient data to approach the Soviet Government'. He also noted that the statements in question had been taken 'in the absence of representatives of Soviet military authorities'.

In reply to enquiries about British former POWs who might be missing in the Soviet zone, the Soviets complained that there were 1,712 Soviet citizens in three camps in Britain who had not been reported to them. The British had withheld a further 340 Soviet citizens. The British pointed out that the 1,712 were held in camps run exclusively by the American military authorities and it was up to them to inform the Soviets. Indeed, they had done so. The other 340 people referred to had claimed that they were not Soviet citizens at all. They were Poles from east of the Curzon line or nationals from the Baltic states. The British government had accepted this.[4] The Soviets did not. Every time the treatment of British POWs was mentioned, the British were bludgeoned with these counter-charges. Soon they became reluctant to take up cases with the Soviet authorities.

The British IS9 (Intelligence) department sent agents into the areas still occupied by the crumbling German forces with the aim of freeing British prisoners of war and getting them to safety. These agents were often German or Austrian Jews who, having fled to Britain and joined the forces, were then British nationals. One of these rescue missions was called Operation Beagle.[5]

On the night of 20 March 1945 three British agents – Walter Korb, Hans Schmit and Anton Muller – were parachuted into occupied territory. They buried their parachutes and jumping suits and made their way to a safe house. They lay low for three days while the police and Wehrmacht combed the district, then set about their mission.

On 6 April they freed three British POWs and took them to the Soviet lines – only to find themselves treated like common criminals and robbed of their watches and other valuables. When they asked for them back, the commissar said: 'You pigs will not be needing them anymore.' He ordered them to be taken away and shot.

A sergeant and three soldiers took them to the hamlet of Gleichberg, where they were to be executed. There, two of the Soviets went through their pockets again and one of them tried to pull the last ring from one of the POWs' fingers. But the sergeant stopped him.

The sergeant spoke a little German. 'I think you gentlemen understand what my orders are,' he said. The IS9 men and the POWs said they did, and asked why they were to be executed. The sergeant said that, being soldiers themselves, they should understand why they had to be shot. However, he took pity on them and said he would not shoot them if they left the region quickly.

The IS9 men took the POWs back to the safe house. Korb told them that they should stay there until the situation got better, but the POWs wanted to head for Yugoslavia where they hoped to join the partisans. The IS9 men said that they would accompany them, but the POWs insisted they stay behind to assist more British prisoners.

The SS was still active in the area and the three IS9 men dressed themselves as farm workers. Their disguises were actually more useful in dealing with the Soviets. They were picked up several times more, held overnight and even beaten up. But each time local farmers vouched for them and succeeded in getting them free.

At the end of May they ran into two more British POWs who were in hiding. Schmit and Muller stayed with them while Korb made his way to Graz to contact the British authorities, but he could not find any, so headed on. With a great deal of difficulty he managed to cross into the Allied zone at Koflach and was sent on to IS9 at Klagenfurt. There he asked that his report be sent to the proper authorities so that he could send some news back to his colleagues who were anxiously awaiting his return.

Korb also reported that some liberated British POWs who had helped the Soviets to round up Nazis in Austria were themselves shot by the Soviets for no apparent reason.

Although the story of Operation Beagle was sent to the proper authorities, the War Office considered it unwise to ask the British Military Mission to take these matters up with the Soviets in Moscow.

'From previous experience we consider they would probably be met with a flat denial,' the War Office cabled AFHQ. Furthermore, 'the Soviet authorities would have been placed on guard without achieving any useful purpose'. Meanwhile, the forward British contact teams in the east were still hanging on. On 25 April 1945 the British team at Lvov had reported that reliable Red Air force sources had identified about 100 downed British and American aircrews concentrated at Kiev. Naturally, they were not allowed to go there – they were not even allowed to visit the camp at Lvov. But Major Gibson was permitted daily visits to Corporal Heslington who was dying of cancer in Lvov hospital. There he discovered seven other British ex-POWs and one American whom the repatriation teams had not been told about. He reported his discovery to Admiral Archer, who pointed out in a letter to Golubev that the hospital thus constituted a concentration point under the Yalta Agreement and asked that the British contact team be allowed to stay on in Lvov.[6]

As the diplomats seemed to have got nowhere with the POW problem General Deane, head of the US Military Mission in Moscow, tried military channels. On 26 April 1945 he cabled Eisenhower at SHAEF, complaining that British and American contact teams had only been allowed to the concentration points at Odessa, Lvov and Volkovysk, and were permitted to remain only when POWs were actually there. Deane also noted that the 'Soviets do not notify us of POWs found by them except at the points where we have contact officers'.

Even from their brief visit to Lvov and Volkovysk, US contact teams were convinced that the POWs were arriving from an 'Army Group concentration point to which we are not allowed to go'.[7]

Soviet military could be outspoken too. General Filip Golikov, head of the Soviet Repatriation Commission, was interviewed in *Pravda* on 30 April 1945. He claimed that Soviet citizens in British and American prisoner-of-war camps had been mistreated. All liberated British and American prisoners had been repatriated, except for small groups, he said, but there had been unwarranted delays in repatriation of liberated Soviet prisoners of war. And he accused the British and Americans of breaking the Yalta Agreement.[8] He stated:

Since the commencement of the January offensive the Red Army has liberated more than 205,000 war prisoners and civilians from Allied and other foreign states on the territory of Germany it has occupied. Of these in this brief period 64,188 have already been sent back to their homelands; all the British and Americans, apart from a small group of sick, and a few individuals have already been repatriated. The rest will be shipped as soon as transport facilities, of which there is a great shortage, are available.

He contrasted that with the Western Allies' repatriation record. Out of 150,000 released by them – not including those latterly on the territory of Western Germany whose number had not yet been ascertained – only 35,000 had been returned, he claimed.

Many thousands of our people are at the present time in British and American camps on the territory of France and Italy, as well as in Britain and the United States, compelled to wait long months for transportation home.

Soviet repatriation organisations are doing everything possible to improve the material, medical and cultural services to the liberated Soviet citizens. It must be noted, however, that [they] are not everywhere treated as citizens of an Allied power. There are instances when our people are kept in quite unsatisfactory conditions. There have been no few cases when, in violation of the [Yalta] agreement of February 11, 1945, Soviet representatives have not been notified of the presence of liberated Soviet citizens. For example, in England recently representatives of the repatriation department found three camps in which there were 1,712 Soviet citizens. Our representatives had not been notified of the existence of these camps. The camps were controlled by American police. The conditions of the Soviet citizens in these camps were absolutely intolerable. In Camp No. 1 they were kept together with Germans under German administration; Camps No. 35 and 40 were fenced with barbed wire; machine guns stood on watch towers. The men worked on excavation jobs 10 and 12 hours a day. They were very poorly clothed. When a Soviet general came to the camps the men wept with joy and asked to be immediately sent back to the Soviet Union . . .

Eight hundred officers were removed from these camps and taken to the United States, and their whereabouts has not yet been ascertained. The transfer of groups of Soviet citizens to America in a similar manner was effected until quite recently and frequently without the knowledge of our representatives. Some 300 Soviet citizens are still missing on the territory of Great Britain.

It is clear that facts of this order are in violation of the agreements on the question of repatriation concluded during the Crimea Conference in February 1945 between the governments of the USSR, Great Britain and the United States of America.

Some time ago no few intolerable instances occurred in the case of Soviet citizens in Egypt, where attempts were made to persuade Soviet people not to return to the USSR, all kinds of provocative and intimidating methods being frequently used to this end. Particularly zealous in this respect were thugs from Anders' Polish army, who had ample opportunity to conduct provocative activities in the camps for liberated Soviet citizens.

These gentlemen, as a rule, frightened Soviet people with cock-and-bull stories to the effect that war prisoners upon returning to the USSR would be regarded as traitors to their country and that severe punishment was awaiting them. Thanks to the inexplicable connivance of British officials of the transit camp for Russian war prisoners in Suez, this camp was visited for several days by Polish corporals Zelichowski, Malewski and Belowicz, who circulated base anti-Soviet slander and attempted to persuade several persons from the western districts of the Ukraine to escape from the camp and not return to their native land.[9]

The Soviet newswire TASS carried this statement, as did the Soviet English-language paper *Moscow News*. And Moscow Radio also broadcast it to the world.

The Foreign Office were shocked that the Soviets had decided to turn what had hitherto been delicate diplomatic negotiations into a battle of charge and counter-charge in the press. Their reply to Golikov's statement was that His Majesty's Government 'did not consider that Anglo–Soviet relations would benefit in any way from the abandonment of established diplomatic procedure in favour of a campaign of public recriminations'. Meanwhile, the British Embassy in Moscow and the War Office in London were cabling Foreign Secretary Anthony Eden in San Francisco on 5 May 1945 that at least 40,000 British prisoners were still in Soviet hands – although the number was in reality probably considerably higher.

## CHAPTER 15

# End of the Hot War, Start of the Cold

THE WAR IN EUROPE ended on 7 May 1945. But this did not mean that all POWs were released and sent home. Distressing reports of Soviet maltreatment of former POWs continued – not just of British and American prisoners but also Dutch, Belgians, French, Hungarians, Rumanians, Italians and Germans. A US Intelligence report from the OSS–CIG (Office of Strategic Services–Central Intelligence Group) files, dated April–May 1945, outlines their conditions:

1. Informant, a Pole forced to serve in the German Army, was taken prisoner by the Russians in 1944. He was kept for a time in the Transit Camp in KAUNAS, then NINSK until he was deported across SIBERIA to the SEVINSKAYA camp near VLADIVOSTOK. At the end of 1945 – April, he escaped and tried to get to Europe. He was, however, arrested by the NKVD after he got beyond Moscow, and placed in the POW and Internee Camp in TAMBOV, which was occupied by Germans, French, Americans, British, Dutch, Belgians . . . The prisoners numbered, in the informant's estimation, well over 20,000; they were both military and civilian, most likely overrun by the Russians during the offensive.
2. All prisoners were forced to work, and the food they were given was very bad and monotonous. They were housed not in huts but in dug-outs.
3. The monotonous food caused some strange disease which made the legs and arms swell; the swelling spread and the swollen places developed sores and wounds. [These are symptoms of oedema or dropsy caused by malnutrition.] After a time men afflicted with this disease died. Informant was told that more than 23,000 Italians, more than 2,500 French and approximately 10,000 Romanian and Hungarian prisoners had died in this manner. There were also many casualties among Poles and other nationalities.

4. Prisoners in this camp included men of very high culture and learning and great experts in many fields of science. Informant observed that German engineers were employed on a special task – the drawing up of blue-prints for a four-engined aircraft, which would carry about 500 men and achieve a speed – it was alleged – of 1,000 kilometers per hour. The Russians were extremely interested in these blue-prints, and men working on the invention were granted all possible facilities both in work and the conditions of life in the camp.

5. When informant left the camp, there were still numerous French due to be repatriated in the next batch; there were also some Belgians and Dutch, and others, including some English-men and several score of Americans, the presence of whom in this camp is probably unknown to the British and USA authorities. When he was leaving, these Englishmen and Americans asked him urgently (as did the French officers and men) to notify the Allied authorities of their plight. Informant succeeded in reach-ing France and a convoy of Allied nationals.[1]

The American Office of Strategic Services always had good relations with the British secret services and this report would undoubtedly have been passed on to America's closest allies. And though many politicians and diplomats still had a touching belief that Stalin would honour his word on returning Allied POWs, the British security services must have been more cynical. They knew that Britain had taken the first steps towards going to war with the Soviet Union. They knew Stalin's attitude to the prisoners of war, especially any who had contact with the West. They could have had little doubt about the Soviet tyrant's intentions.

On 30 August 1945 another report was made that forty-five Amer-icans were being held at Rada near Tambov, behind barbed wire and under guard. This camp at Tambov is the same place where two French POWs' – who were still alive in the Soviet Union forty-six years later – had once been held, according to *Moscow News*, 12 February 1991. It was also the camp where records discovered in 1992 showed that British and American POWs had been taken in 1945.

The maltreatment, concealment and withholding of Allied ex-POWs seems to have been happening right across the Soviet zone. On 2 May 1945 Admiral Archer complained to General Golubev about the treat-ment of twelve British and South African ex-prisoners of war known to be on a Soviet train on 26 April 1945 at Ploesti. They had been seen by officers from the British Military Mission in Rumania. They were ill, ill-fed and ill-treated. They slept on straw, were denied medicines and had been stripped of their personal belongings.[2] The commandant at the station prevented the British officers speaking to the ex-POWs and the train pulled out before they reached the platform. Fortunately, they were able to catch up at the next station. They also discovered that some 160 British ex-POWs had passed through Ploesti a few days before.[3] The Soviets denied everything.[4]

The British and American contact teams had also been denied access to Hungary, but Alexander Kirk, US political adviser to Supreme Allied Command Mediterranean (SACMED), reported to the State Department:

> Reliable information has been received by British Military Mission Rumania of presence in those liberated parts of Budapest and immediate rear of Russian Army in Hungary of British civilians and British PW escapees . . . Although Soviets have shown good will to British escapees in past, it is not always possible for Soviets' forward troops to identify or maintain British subjects, withholding some.

The War Cabinet knew of the problems the British were encountering. For instance, on 2 May 1945 Mr Roberts at the Prisoner of War Section of the British Embassy in Moscow was complaining that while they knew that there were other concentration points for liberated POWs 'lack of precise information makes it difficult to press for visits by officers even if the Soviet government were willing to agree'.

Roberts also complained that the Yalta Agreement was being interpreted in a 'most unsatisfactory manner' and told Vyshinski that although the Germans had retreated from Poland three months before, some hundreds of British POWs were still to be accounted for there. Some 4,000 had made it back through Odessa. (The Soviets had, in fact, notified the British that, of 3,854 British POWs liberated, 3,639 had passed through Odessa.) Roberts estimated that 'those of our prisoners who had not been . . . moved by the Germans from areas now occupied by the Red Army may be close on 100,000'.

He stressed the importance of getting authority to visit men held in hospitals across eastern Germany and argued: 'Probably the most effective way to secure redress of our grievances would be to threaten a full statement in the House of Commons which might also constitute a reply to General Golikov's recent complaints in *Pravda*.'[5]

No such statement was made, though some MPs sensed that something was going terribly wrong. On 2 May 1945 Miss Ward MP asked in the House of Commons whether the Russians had 'carried out their part of the [Yalta] agreement with regard to British prisoners?'

Lamely, the Minister of State at the Foreign Office, Richard Law, replied: 'There are one or two matters on which we are not satisfied. These matters are being taken up with the Soviet government.'

Sir Herbert Williams MP asked why it was necessary that British prisoners repatriated through Odessa had been 'prohibited from making any statement'?[6]

The awful truth had not percolated through to members of Parliament and the government were certainly not eager to bring up the question of prisoners of war who had not yet returned from the tender hands of Stalin.

Rather than make a fuss in the House of Commons about the whereabouts of British prisoners of war or Golikov's statement and risk alienating the Soviets, the answer was to speed up the overland exchange of prisoners. Although the Soviet and Allied armies had met up some time before, the Soviets had prevented Allied ex-POWs crossing the lines. Instead they insisted that they be repatriated via Odessa, 800 kilometres to the east, even if they were only a matter of miles from their own men.

On 2 May 1945 Vyshinski officially proposed to the British Embassy in Moscow that the repatriation of Soviet and British POWs should be overland at Torgau, rather than via Odessa and Marseilles.[7] A similar proposal had been made to the Americans. It was noted that the Soviet authorities were 'clearly anxious to secure early agreement in principle and we consider the proposal most advantageous'.[8]

The Foreign Office immediately instructed the British Embassy in Moscow to accept the proposal in principle. The embassy should also suggest to the Soviet authorities that details should be settled between Soviet, British and American commanders in the field and arrangements made by them to fix an exchange point on the front. Vyshinski's proposal that the negotiations be done through the British Military Mission in Moscow was rejected because it would entail unnecessary delay.[9] A compromise was reached. Representatives of the Soviet High Command were to meet representatives from SHAEF and AFHQ. And on 5 May the deal was done.[10]

However, the new agreement did not please everyone. Mr Roberts was worried that the Soviets would now start demanding the return of Poles and citizens of the Baltic States, now part of the USSR. He asked Lieutenant Colonel Phillimore at the War Office to tell SHAEF only to return men, whatever their nationality, who wanted to go back. If they disclosed their identity and objected to being sent back, they should be held for the time being, 'pending a decision as to their ultimate disposal'.[11]

During the delicate negotiations on the overland repatriations, Admiral Archer handed General Golubev a list of British prisoners known to be in a camp overrun by the Red Army on 28 April and asked what had happened to them.[12]

Mrs Thorold, a Red Cross worker in Odessa, wrote to General Younger on 4 May, expressing her distress at the disappearance of the wives of British and South African ex-prisoners of war there. The women had accompanied their husbands to Odessa. But lacking the proper papers, they were separated from their husbands and subsequently vanished.

'It seems an appalling thing that the wives of British soldiers who are presumably now British subjects can just disappear like this in an allied country,' wrote Mrs Thorold. 'The matter has a profound effect on the POWs passing through who had faith in the British authorities being able to do something.'

General Younger brought up the matter with the British government.[13] All appeals to the Soviets on humanitarian grounds fell on deaf ears. By June, the women had not reappeared. They were definitely not at Odessa. Mrs Thorold had discovered that they had been removed to an unknown destination on the night of 28–9 April.[14]

Meanwhile, Private F. Hasdell of the Northants Regiment, Fusilier S.J. Wilkins of the Royal Welch Fusiliers and Private H.J. Tripp of the Royal West Kent Regiment turned up on 5 May and complained that they had been forced by Soviet soldiers to construct a fence and collect and bury refuse – another violation of Article 6 of the Yalta Agreement.

On 4 May 1945 the British delegates to the Allied Control Commission in Hungary reported that they too were having problems. Twenty-five British prisoners were being held, with a large number of other Allied personnel, at a repatriation centre in Budapest where the food was insufficient and the sanitation unsatisfactory. The British POWs were not allowed to leave the camp, write letters or listen to the radio. English papers and magazines were censored and the Commission officers were only allowed to speak to the men in the presence of the commandant and an interpreter.

The commandant said that his orders prevented him improving the situation. The Soviet authorities refused permission for the British to evacuate their POWs by air to Italy on the ground that they were the responsibility of the Repatriation Committee in Moscow. But the British authorities in Budapest felt that strong protests about this matter would only result in the Soviets forbidding them to visit the camp at all.

There were other British POWs living with the British Mission in Budapest, but the general permission given earlier to evacuate these and similar American POWs had suddenly been withdrawn. American diplomats with AFHQ at Caserta in Italy decided to take up the matter with the Soviet authorities, but felt that the Soviets would refuse to act on the ground that POWs were not a matter for the Allied Control Commission.[15]

By 6 May the Foreign Office was still talking of at least 40,000 British ex-POWs in Soviet hands and were insisting on the importance of British repatriation officers visiting the camps. They were asking that any spare officers and stores in Moscow be sent forward to help in evacuating liberated POWs. But they were not taking a very firm line: 'We do not want to insist on our [Yalta] agreement about this if it is at all likely to delay the speedy evacuation of as many British subjects as possible.'[16]

General Younger had also given up. On 6 May 1945 he sent a memo to the President of the Union of the Red Cross and Red Crescent, conceding that the new agreement on repatriations overland made the camps at Lvov and Volkovysk obsolete and Odessa necessary as a repatriation point only for the 'odd remnants', which Admiral Archer estimated would be 2,000 at the most. Consequently, Younger finally abandoned his long-delayed visit to Lvov and Volkovysk, though he also minuted for the record that there were still British prisoners of war in Poland – who had neither been visited nor contacted.

General Younger continued in his duties, pressing for news of missing prisoners. On 14 May he wrote to Dr Kolesnikov, President of the Union of Russian Red Cross and Red Crescent Societies: 'Information given to us by our liberated prisoners of war indicates that there are still a considerable number of soldiers of the British Empire at present sick in Soviet hospitals' and asking what was happening to them. The next day, Younger mentioned to Kolesnikov that the camp at Lvov was closed. Then on 30 May 1945 Younger asked Dr Kolesnikov about a Soviet radio report that Gunner A. Wootton of the Royal Artillery, army number 1509679, had been wounded. Gunner Wootton's father had asked the Red Cross to verify the story and Younger asked Kolesnikov to trace the source of the story and give him any information he could find.[17] That same day Admiral Archer asked Major General Basilov, head of the Department for Foreign Relations at the People's Commissariat for Defence, for information about Lance Corporal Chambers, a sick British ex-POW who was in the Jesuitenkloster Maria-Schein Russian hospital near Teplitz-Schonah.

The liberation of Europe meant that other nations were trying to find out what had happened to their POWs. The Belgians had been attempting to get contact teams into Russia for some time. But although they had cut down their numbers from 33 to 4, by 7 May they still had no permission. Forty Belgian prisoners who had been returned via Paris complained that they had been badly treated by the Soviets. They had been force marched, given practically no food, robbed of their possessions, and made to work on roads and clear debris, like convicts. Their conditions had only been alleviated when a Soviet officer who spoke French intervened. One of the Belgians said that he had been a communist before being taken by the Soviets, but now had second thoughts.

Major Acker of the Belgian Military Mission asked a Soviet repatriation officer, Colonel Melnikov, if he could explain the Soviets' behaviour, which appeared contrary to all their interests and ideology. Melnikov said that two Belgian SS brigades with the Germans on the Eastern Front had fought with such fury and distinction that they had left the Soviets with bitter memories. Melnikov also said that their Belgian uniforms might have been mistaken for those of the Todt, the German labour division.[18]

Other Allied ex-prisoners of war were suffering similar harassment on V-E Day. At Stalag 2A at Neubrandenburg which was under Soviet control, drunken soldiers were molesting sick Allied prisoners and robbing them of food supplies, which were running low, making it hard to keep control. There were 1,100 Americans in the camp itself with another 2,600 Americans and 650 British attached to it within a 50-kilometre radius. Two hundred of the Americans were hospitalised, with fifty seriously ill.[19]

With no full statement on the POW situation, the House of Commons became restive. With Soviet contact teams travelling freely in the Allied zone, the government was asked whether the Soviets were reciprocating. Minister of State Richard Law replied that the answer would be too long to make a verbal reply, so the government's response would be published in the Official Report. This read:

> Apart from a few brief visits by British representatives for the purpose of establishing contact with the liberated British prisoners of war in Lublin, Lvov and Volkovysk, no British officials have been permitted to enter Poland or Soviet-occupied areas of Czechoslovakia, and Austria; the question has not yet arisen as regards Germany.

British correspondents had also been denied access.[20]

Captain Duncan MP then asked Mr Law: 'Is the right hon. gentleman aware that British officers are not allowed to see British repatriated prisoners of war until they reach Odessa, and will he make representations that British officers should be allowed to get in contact with these escaped British prisoners of war much further forward?'

Mr Law replied: 'Yes, sir.'[21]

Those two replies were the extent of the government's comments on the POW crisis and the extent of their parliamentary reply to General Golikov's statement.

The Soviets, however, lost no chance to complain about the way their nationals had been handled by the Anglo–American authorities. Over lunch, Ambassador Bogomolov harangued Robert Murphy of the State Department about the shameful way they were treated. The Russian people were shocked at times by the lack of American appreciation of their sensibilities. He repeated the story of Soviet nationals being kept 'in cages, behind barbed wire and guarded by American negro soldiers'.[22]

Bogomolov's contentions would have been true in regard to Soviets captured in German uniform, but he was plainly milking it for propaganda purposes.

On 10 May 1945 a Norwegian, General Ruge, managed to get a message out of Soviet-held Luckenwalde Stalag 3A. It travelled via the American Ninth Army and SHAEF to the Norwegian government in exile in London. He asked them to insist on his release and repatriation via Murmansk.[23]

Three days later a Norwegian general, who did not want his name used even in secret in cable traffic for fear of reprisals against other Norwegian POWs, turned up in Moscow. He reported to General Deane at the American Military Mission that the conditions in Luckenwalde under the Soviets were extremely bad. The camp commandant was usually drunk and the treatment of the British and American prisoners was not good.

'A great many British and American prisoners were flown out in American transports against the Russians' wishes,' he said, referring to men who had escaped, 'and the Russians have vented their resentment on the remainder.'

Deane cabled to Eisenhower at SHAEF, asking him to send supporting data so that he could put pressure on the Soviet repatriation committee. A conference had also been set up at Halle, so that the details of the overland repatriations could be worked out. Deane urged Eisenhower to have the SHAEF representatives at the conference to confront Golubev with 'all actual data possible concerning the mistreatment of our prisoners by the Russians'.[24]

Eisenhower's response was prompt. The next day, 11 May 1945, he and his Assistant Chief of Staff, Major General R.W. Barker, cabled Deane in Moscow giving him the go ahead for action:

> Information received from prisoner of war camps in rear of Russian lines indicates thousands of United States and British prisoners of war held in close confinement under unsatisfactory conditions. We could have evacuated them by air a week or ten days ago if the Russians would agree to cooperate by permitting us to land planes at nearby airfields, as specifically authorized by Article 4 of the Yalta Agreement. Unless this evacuation can be effected promptly, there may well ensue most undesirable consequences. Please express to Russians the urgency of this matter and ask that they direct their Commanders on western front to permit the landing of United States and British planes at fields near camps for evacuation of our prisoners of war.[25]

Deane sent a copy of this cable to General Antonov and General Golubev.[26]

On 10 May 1945 Major Gibson managed to get another message through from Lvov: he was convinced, from information received from liberated POWs, that a considerable number of British ex-POWs were still in Soviet hospitals in forward areas.[27] At that time the British Military Mission estimated that there might still be as many as 3,000 stragglers, sick in Soviet hospitals, and others lying up in Poland and other liberated areas who needed repatriation via Odessa.[28]

But these complaints were not put to the Soviets. Only questions about specific individuals at specific places stood any chance of a reply. On 11 May 1945, Admiral Archer pressed General Golubev on several outstanding matters including the fate of forty British soldiers who had drowned when the ice broke as they were crossing the Vistula; British and Indian ex-POWs gravely ill; and three Britons working in a hospital at Schulitz because they knew of no way of getting home. There were six others in Schulitz. Two of them were living in a former work camp there.[29] The British authorities knew of these men from other British ex-POWs who had turned up at Odessa, but when General Basilov replied to Archer on 2 June he said that the Soviets could find no trace of them.[30]

# CHAPTER 16

# Forced Repatriations

✝

As SOON AS the war in Europe was over on 7 May 1945, the forced repatriations went into high gear. Worries had already been expressed in the West that if Stalin did not get his men back – whether they wanted to return or not – Allied POWs liberated by the Red Army would be withheld. Millions of Soviet citizens – including Cossacks and other White Russians who had left Russia during the Revolution and had never been Soviet nationals – were returned at gunpoint. Even concentration-camp survivors were forcibly repatriated to their certain death. Plainly this was a game for very high stakes.

Five days after victory was announced in Europe, Associated Press reported from Allied Advance Headquarters in Reims:

> Nearly half of the estimated 200,000 British and 76,000 American prisoners of war still in Germany are believed to be within the Russian zone of occupation and Supreme Headquarters has twice requested a meeting or an agreement to arrange their return.
>
> Up to late today, there had been no reply from Marshal Ivan S. Konev, to whom the requests were addressed, one through the 21st Army Group and the other through Moscow. Presumably, the war prisoners still are waiting in the camps.
>
> Col. E.P. Straub of SHAEF's Prisoner of War recovery branch, said there was every reason to hope for a meeting within the next day or two which might permit the direct recovery of the prisoners.

If that were to happen, the report said, the last of these men might be on their way to England and the US within two weeks to a month.[1]

Two days later, AP were still reporting that 133,400 British and American prisoners were still thought to be in the Soviet zone.[2] The Western Allies, armed with Red Cross lists and captured German

91

records, were unlikely to be mistaken about the numbers remaining behind the Soviet lines.

As the Red Army had driven westwards they had not only overrun the prisoner-of-war camps, they had also liberated hundreds of thousands of civilian internees, concentration-camp inmates and slave labourers held in Poland, Germany and Austria. In all, it was estimated, the Soviets held over a million people that the Western nations wanted back.

That was the ante Stalin put up.

The Allies had liberated or captured almost two million Soviets. Almost a million of them had been forced to serve the Nazi regime in one way or another just to survive and could be considered traitors – though just to have surrendered to the Nazis was to betray Mother Russia in Stalin's view. Along with them were many thousands of anti-communists who had either served in the Revolution against the Reds or more recently in the German army under Soviet dissident General Vlasov. These were a danger to Stalin. In any forthcoming confrontation between East and West, they could form the core of a powerful anti-Soviet army. All were lumped together to be delivered to the NKVD by the British and American armies.

The forced repatriations began even before the end of the war. The commander of the US First Army, Lieutenant General Courtney H. Hodges, enquired of Eisenhower's staff at Supreme Headquarters on 13 April 1945 'as to how much force an Army Commander should use in control of displaced Russians . . . Talking with Judge McCloy today, he agreed that of course an Army Commander could use any force necessary to insure the success of his operations.'

Broadly, that became the position for both British and American commanders. The results were harrowing, not least for the Allied soldiers who had to enforce it.

No one was under any illusion about why the forced repatriations were taking place. 'Stalin had told Eden that he regarded the exchange of prisoners purely as one of reciprocity,' wrote historian Lord Bethell. 'If the West kept Soviet citizens back on the grounds, unacceptable to Stalin, that they did not want to return, the Soviet authorities would keep British and American prisoners as hostage.'

In 1974 Bethell tried to talk to Eden – then Lord Avon – about the forced repatriations, as he was 'the one person who could fill in the gaps on how the policy was settled'. Lord Avon refused to speak to him. But in 1944, he had written on the POW issue that 'in war we cannot afford to be sentimental' while Sir James Grigg, the War Minister, said that 'if the choice is between hardship to our men and death to Russians the choice is plain'.[3]

On 13 May 1945, 222 Soviet citizens from a camp at Plattling in Germany were returned to the Soviet lines. One man succeeded in committing suicide despite the most elaborate precautions. The Russians insisted on receiving the dead bodies of suicides as well as live prisoners during the repatriations.

Allied soldiers had even more problems when they repatriated 399 former Soviet soldiers by train. A report of the operation reads:

> All of these men refused to entrain. They begged to be shot. They resisted entrainment by taking off their clothing and refusing to leave their quarters. It was necessary to use tear gas and some force to drive them out. Tear gas forced them out of the building into the snow where those who had cut themselves fell exhausted and bleeding in the snow. Nine men hanged themselves and one has stabbed himself to death and one other who had stabbed himself subsequently died; while 20 others are in the hospital for self inflicted wounds. The entrainment was finally effected of 368 men who were sent off accompanied by a Russian liaison officer on a train carrying American guards. Six men escaped enroute. A number of men in the group claimed they were not Russians.[4]

Walter Bedell Smith, Eisenhower's Chief of Staff in 1945 and American Ambassador to Moscow from 1946 to 1949 wrote:

> Our most serious problem with the Soviet government while I was in Germany concerned the implementation of an Allied agreement made at Yalta and reaffirmed at Potsdam, looking towards the return of displaced persons – prisoners of war, slave laborers and others – to their country of origin . . .
>
> I found on one occasion that an American unit, somewhat overzealous in carrying out its responsibilities, actually had begun forcibly to load on a train some of these Russian displaced persons who had refused to return voluntarily to the Soviet Union. Some of them had taken refuge in a church and pleaded with the Americans not to send them back to the Soviet Union. When their pleas seemed unavailing, one or two actually committed suicide.[5]

Many senior politicians blamed the junior officers, but no one was ever punished for the forced repatriations. They continued until 1947 and it is also clear from the documents that have been released that forced repatriations were government policy.[6] This policy, the Allies hoped, would result in the repatriation of all of their soldiers and citizens. To that end, hundreds of thousands of entirely innocent Soviet citizens – as well as those who had fought for the Germans – were forcibly returned to Soviet control.

Many of the British soldiers involved still cannot fully understand such barbarity. One individual, who was with POW and displaced-persons recovery teams at Dachau, remembers watching – despairingly – a particular train packed with crying children heading from Germany to the Soviet labour camps. Another, who was involved in repatriations of Soviet citizens from the concentration camp at Bergen-Belsen, claimed that the Soviets did not even wait until they were out of hearing before they shot all the returnees. Still the British soldiers dutifully went back and collected another batch of women and children to be taken at bayonet point to their deaths. When interviewed in 1990, that former soldier said that he had not spoken about the forced repatriations since 1946. When he returned to England then and told people what was going on, no one would believe him.

These forced repatriations were of course secret. The book *Forced Labour in the Soviet Union* spells it out:

> In 1944, the Soviet government began diplomatic negotiations with the aim of compelling its allies to send home all Soviet citizens in their zones, regardless of their wishes. At first, this desire met with some reluctance on the part of the Western Allies, but they gave in. These proceedings were not revealed in the official communiqués, since the American and British authorities apparently wished to avoid public discussion of a measure that actually condemned to great hardship not only persons guilty of treason but also thousands of innocent men and women.[7]

Years after they were completed they remained a highly sensitive matter. The official, classified, 1947 study on repatriations – entitled 'RAMPs: The Recovery and Repatriation of Liberated Prisoners of War', compiled at European Command in Frankfurt on orders from General Lucius Clay, under the direction of the US War Department – naturally mentions the forced repatriations. A note attached to the report, dated 1 August 1955, says: 'This document is to be handled for official use only. The term Forcible Repatriation cannot be used for dissemination to the public per Security Review Section, TAGO [The Adjutant General's Office].'

CHAPTER 17

# Conference at Halle

†

SHAEF AND THE Soviet High Command agreed to hold a conference at the former Luftwaffe School west of Halle, near Leipzig in Germany, 'for the purpose of conferring . . . on the matter of repatriation of prisoners of war and displaced persons'. The Soviet and US/UK delegates were to work out the details of the overland exchange that had been agreed in principle on 5 May. The Western Allies hoped that one result would be the immediate evacuation by air of 40,000 US and UK POWs being held behind Soviet lines.[1] The Russians had other plans.

The six-day conference began on 16 May 1945. The joint Anglo–American delegation was led by General Barker, USA, of SHAEF. The Soviet delegation was led by General Golubev, Soviet Assistant Administrator for Repatriation.

Both Golubev and Barker had a good grounding in the POW issue. Golubev had been fielding British and American questions for some time and Barker had a good knowledge of the numbers involved. He had just completed a report for the Chief of Staff on United Nations (at the time 'United Nations' referred to the anti-Axis nations) Prisoners of War in Germany:

> By the middle of March 1945, there were approximately 2,173,000 United Nations prisoners of war located in over 70 prisoner of war camps in Germany, including 199,500 British; 76,850 US; 754,600 French; 784,300 Russians; 122,100 Yugoslav; 65,700 Belgian; 69,300 Polish; 10,200 Dutch; 87,100 Italian and some Norwegian and other prisoners of war. These figures, representing military personnel registered as prisoners of war, are not to be confused with the estimated 2,500,000 to 4,500,000 displaced persons.[2]

Like everyone else at that time, Barker used the 199,500 figure for British prisoners of war.

Barker was also of the opinion that the Yalta Agreement worked very much in the Soviets' favour. As the conference opened he wrote:

> We must avoid anything which will commit us to an exchange on a man-for-man basis. The tenor of the agreement should be such that each Government will proceed with the repatriation of liberated personnel in their custody and that the rate and numbers of transfer will be based solely on the capability of each party to move and/or receive that personnel.

But it was never going to be that easy. For the Allies it was a difficult meeting from the very beginning. The Anglo–American delegation comprised Barker and two British officers, with the minimum of support. When the Soviet mission was finally assembled it numbered some forty officers and forty to fifty enlisted men. Among the officers were one lieutenant general and six major generals. They arrived in requisitioned German vehicles of all makes, an American-type armoured car (fully armed) and a radio truck, which was in operation most of the time. All male personnel were heavily armed with pistols, sub-machine guns and rifles.[3]

The meeting began with the Soviets refusing to allow repatriation of Allied soldiers by air transport, which made the entire repatriation process much more cumbersome and logistically difficult.

> After opening statements [Barker wrote in his post-conference report] I proposed the immediate initiation of steps looking toward prompt release and return to Allied control of all British and American prisoners of war then in Russian custody, using air and motor transport. This proposal was firmly resisted by General Golubev, who cited all manner of local administrative difficulties which precluded the operation. He stated that serviceable airfields did not exist, which was known by myself to be not the case and I so informed him. The Russian position was very clear that neither now, nor at any time in the future, would they permit Allied airplanes to be used for the movement into or out of their territory of prisoners of war or displaced persons, except 'Distinguished persons, sick and wounded'.

This was the first of many sticking points. After the first four-hour session the Allied negotiators were left with few illusions. On 17 May 1945 Barker wrote to SHAEF complaining that 'British and American prisoners of war, now in Russian custody, are being used as a bartering point in order to force our hand. Hence, these men are, in effect "hostages".'

Barker's words echo those of his diplomatic colleagues.

After the initial meetings with the Soviets, the idea was to carry on lower-level discussions in an attempt to work out mutually acceptable arrangements. However, these meetings soon proved futile. And the decision was made that all discussions were to be carried on directly between the heads of the delegations, with certain members of their respective parties in attendance.

'On the Russian side, those present numbered normally from twenty to twenty-five, including several general officers,' Barker wrote. 'The SHAEF representatives in attendance normally were myself, General Michelsen, Brigadier Venables and two to four representatives of the technical services.'

One of the discussion points was the failure of the Soviets to provide British and American liaison officers permission to visit Allied POWs held by the Red Army. After six days of bitter wrangling, a formula was finally agreed for the direct overland exchange of prisoners across the lines on a reciprocal basis.[4]

The results of the meeting were detailed in a memo sent to the US Secretary of State, dated 1 June, affirming that a repatriation plan had been 'agreed to by representatives of Supreme Headquarters, Allied Expeditionary Force, and Supreme Command Red Army, at Halle, Germany, May 22, 1945, for the most expeditious overland delivery of Allied and Soviet ex-prisoners of war and displaced persons liberated by the Allied Expeditionary Force and the Red Army'.

It also noted that the Red Army still refused to permit the Allies

to fly transport aircraft into Soviet-occupied territory . . . Although General Golubev would not agree to . . . first priority delivery of US and UK ex-prisoners of war he gave his most solemn personal assurances that all US and UK ex-prisoners of war would, in fact, be given preferential treatment. A request for second priority for Western European ex-political deportees, in accordance with the desires of the Western European governments that such persons be repatriated before their respective ex-prisoners of war and other displaced persons, was countered by the flat assertion that all political prisoners held in German concentration camps overrun by the Red Army had been released and that there were, accordingly, no more political prisoners in Soviet-occupied territory. With respect to this category of displaced persons, not even verbal assurances were to be had.[5]

So there were no political prisoners. As to prisoners of war – in a separate 'secret' report to SHAEF, General Barker, along with British Brigadier Venables and SHAEF G-5 General Michelsen, said: 'The SHAEF representatives came to the firm conviction that British and American prisoners of war were, in effect, being held hostage by the Russians until deemed expedient by them to permit their release.'[6]

Although it was signed on 22 May 1945, the Leipzig Agreement – as the result of the Halle Conference was called – actually went into effect on the afternoon of the 20th when some 2,200 British and American prisoners still being held by the Russians were released. And, in another gesture of good faith, on the afternoon of 22 May General Golubev allowed two groups of SHAEF officers to go on a tour of camps in the Soviet area where British and American prisoners were thought to be located. 'This is the first instance of either American or British officers being permitted to visit such camps in the forward Russian areas,' Barker commented.[7] It would also be the last.

In his post-conference report, Barker wrote:

There is every indication that the Russians intend to make a big show of rapid repatriation of our men, although . . . we may find a reluctance to return them all, for an appreciable time to come, since these men constitute a valuable bargaining point. It will be necessary for us, therefore, to arrange for constant liaison and visits of inspection to 'uncover' our men.

General Barker's predictions proved highly accurate. After that single, showy exchange of 2,200 Allied prisoners – followed by the forced repatriation of large numbers of Soviets who had survived by serving the Germans in uniform[8] – and a single visit by one Allied officer to one camp in the Soviet forward area, the tap was turned off again. The Soviet zone of Germany, Austria and Poland was again closed to Allied contact officers, making it impossible to 'uncover' their prisoners of war.

The postwar report of the repatriation of Allied personnel – RAMPs – put a different gloss on the conference at Halle:

The Leipzig Agreement initiated what has been called the greatest mass movement of population in history. Effective, under its own terms, twenty-four hours after signature, on 23 May 1945 [it] was brought into operation on 20 May to recover promptly 2,200 United States and British prisoners of war who had been assembled by the Soviet forces at Luckenwalde. The first shipments from west to east also consisted of liberated prisoners of war. After the first exchanges, liberated prisoners of war were mingled, on both sides, with the great masses of displaced persons. Up to 1 July 1945, a total of about 1,390,000 Soviet citizens had been delivered to the Soviet forces, and about 300,000 repatriates had been received from them. For some weeks after that date, deliveries were slowed up, except for some 300,000 Soviet citizens who were left in place when our armies withdrew from the areas occupied by the Soviet forces. The redrawing of the zonal boundaries necessitated the establishment of new reception–delivery points. There was some delay in opening these, and for a time during July the Soviet authorities did not accept deliveries. Movements to the east were also slowed up because of the emptying of the camps near the zonal borders, making longer journeys necessary and transportation by truck less practicable. There was some delay in opening the exchange points in Austria, but Soviet camps at Passen and Linz were brought into operation on 21 July. By September 1945, more than 2,000,000 Soviet citizens had been moved out of the area formerly under the control of the Supreme Headquarters, and the mass repatriation of Soviet citizens was complete.[9]

The problem is that not 300,000, but an estimated 3,000,000 displaced persons were expected by the Allies. And although returning POWs may well have been mingled with those returnees, everyone crossing the lines went through detailed identification procedures. POWs were segregated. Detailed nominal rolls were prepared, and copies distributed through the relevant channels, before a man was repatriated. The military authorities and the Allied governments would have known exactly how many men were returning during these exchanges. The RAMPs report does not say.

CHAPTER 18

# One-Way Traffic

THE ALLIES HAD high hopes for the Halle Conference. They expected the POW problem to be sorted out there, once and for all. On 16 May 1945 Admiral Archer in Moscow relented to the Soviet pressure and ordered the British contact team at Lvov to return to Moscow. Then he tried another tack. British army and Red Cross stores had been sent to Volkovysk and he requested permission to send three officers to retrieve them.[1] On 18 May General Basilov replied that the stores would be despatched by the Soviet personnel there, so there would be no need to send British officers.[2]

On 20 May Archer again requested permission to send representatives to Volkovysk to take charge. He also asked for the return of three British vehicles the British had provided for the use of their repatriation officers there. Finally he asked that the British officers at Odessa be able to live inside the camp with the ex-POWs.[3] Under the Yalta Agreement, Archer pointed out, the internal administration of a liberated prisoner-of-war camp is the responsibility of the repatriation officers concerned. The Russians rejected this proposal – it was 'without purpose and inconvenient'.[4]

The American Military Mission in Moscow was also on the case. On 18 May General Deane was still sending lists to the Soviet authorities of American prisoners who had been seen alive in Poland but had never appeared in the evacuations. He was also urging the evacuation of 'every American still remaining in Poland'.

Meanwhile, Soviet repatriation officers still had the run of the Western Front. On 17 May 1945 Colonel Melnikov used the Second Army and SHAEF to forward a message to Major General Dragun, who was then at the Russian Mission for Repatriation in Paris. Melnikov reported that by 16 May the British had handed over 16,000 Russians at Grabau and the Americans had handed over 10,000.

'Conditions satisfactory,' he said. 'Transportation done by cars. 20 officers arrived, do not send more.'

The message continued cheekily: 'British authorities would like to receive indications about the location of British and US PW camps. Would like to send aircraft to fetch their people. Would also like to send a repatriation team.'[5]

So while 26,000 Soviet POWs had been handed over, the Soviets had not even given any indication of how many Allied prisoners they were holding. And while the British allowed twenty Russian officers to oversee the handover of prisoners, the Soviet zone was closed to the British.

Allied ex-POWs in the Soviet zone who had obeyed the 'stay put' order were now surrounded by armed guards. Some later reported that security was tighter under the 'protection' of their Soviet allies than the custody of their German foes.

British ex-POWs were also becoming deeply suspicious of Soviet moves to take them east. A cable from the British Military Mission to Hungary dated 17 May 1945 said that it saw 'No reason for movement accelerating Odessa on the contrary PW themselves would prefer to wait here . . .' And the next day the British Mission–Rumania reported: 'Hope authority is given and Russians here informed earliest of fact of route being closed down. At present they insist on all PWs going to Odessa.'

Allied command continued to receive intelligence from the field that British and US POWs were seen 'moved to the east' or 'towards Odessa' for weeks after.

That same day, 18 May 1945, a cable from the Ninth United States Army to the Supreme Allied Headquarters described the deteriorating conditions in Stalag 4-B at Muhlberg, a German POW camp that had been overrun by a Red Army tank battalion:

Reports received that 7,000 United States and British ex-PWs formerly in Mulburg [sic] (Stalag 4-B) and NOE REISA 8715-E need medical supplies, additional medical attention and food. Many have left because of conditions. Reports indicate camp leader doing all in his power to enforce stay put order. Russians alleged to have threatened to use force to prevent escape.

The immediate evacuation of both the camp and the hospital was suggested by VII Corps, who also requested SHAEF to liaise with the Soviets 'with a view to negotiating the return of these United States and British ex-PWs to Ninth Army'.[6]

However, two GIs who had escaped from Stalag 4-B and reached the Allied lines after a considerable adventure, confirmed exactly what British and American diplomats in Moscow, and the Allied negotiators at Halle, had been saying – Allied prisoners of war were being held hostage in an attempt to blackmail the West.

One of the escapees from Stalag 4-B, Martin Siegel, had been the US POWs' intermediary and translator with Major Vasilli Vershenko, the officer in command of the Red Army tank battalion that had overrun the camp.

The first question Siegel had asked Major Vershenko was: When were the US POWs to be repatriated?

Vershenko had replied that he was primarily concerned with the 'Russian prisoners held in a separate compound at Stalag 4-B [as] they had to be interviewed individually since they felt that there were many "cowards, traitors and deserters amongst them and they had to be dealt with expeditiously",' Siegel reported.

The repatriation of Allied POWs, Vershenko told him, was a 'complex logistical matter'.

This response and Vershenko's officious tone had worried Siegel.

'That night, my bunkmate, Cpl. William Smith of the 9th Division shared our mutual concerns and we decided to take off on our own,' Siegel later reported. 'The next evening, we "liberated" two Russian bicycles, got through a gap in the wire where a Russian tank was parked and took off West to where we thought the American Army would be.'

Siegel and Smith then had what they described as a 'two-week adventure', which included making another escape from a band of fanatical Hitler Youth who were still at large in Soviet-occupied Germany.

Having reached safety himself, Siegel was naturally concerned for the Allied prisoners left behind at Stalag 4-B. He was sure that they were being held hostage for ransom because Major Vershenko had told him that 'the Russians and the Americans had agreed to a pact whereby the Russians would receive "credits" for each American POW returned'.

Siegel later told the US Senate that his worries 'were treated with initial scepticism, then annoyance at my persistence, and finally with assurances that the matter "would be investigated" '.[7]

The Soviets were indeed asking for 'credits' – Molotov's request of the month before to the US Secretary of State for a $6 billion line of credit. That would be equivalent to $60 billion at today's prices, or more than the entire cost of the Gulf War. The Vietnamese, who have been repeatedly accused of withholding American prisoners after the

Vietnam War, continue to demand repatriations from the United States.

While the Halle Conference was going on, *The Times* reported from Paris on 18 May the progress of the negotiations to return British and American prisoners to the West – and the far larger number of French prisoners – from camps liberated by the Soviets. The newspaper hoped for an early solution 'whatever difficulties exist . . . It is, indeed, surprising that there should be any problem about the movement of Allied prisoners in the Russian zone.'

There had been local instances of exchanges being organised, but *The Times* drew attention to the situation at Luckenwalde where a large number of Allied prisoners had been collected in anticipation of the Halle Conference.[8] A convoy of lorries sent to pick them up had been returned empty. The Soviets did not want to be robbed of their showy exchange of prisoners until after the Leipzig Agreement was signed.

'It is understood that there are still some 30,000 British and American prisoners of war in eastern Germany and another 30,000 in Austria and Czechoslovakia,'[9] *The Times* said.

SHAEF were also bandying around figures. On 19 May a cable signed by Eisenhower at the Allied Supreme Headquarters stated that: 'Numbers of US prisoners estimated in Russian control 25,000.'

In a secret cable to American Chief of Staff General George Marshall, on 21 May 1945, General Eisenhower estimated at least 105,000 live US prisoners in Europe, including 25,000 still in Soviet hands. The official figure given later by the United States government for all known US POWs in the European theatre in World War II is only 78,000.[10]

The situation now gravely troubled Marshall who cabled Eisenhower the same day: 'Concerned over report . . . that 25,000 US prisoners still in Russian hands. Request completest details and when transfer to US control expected.'

It could be that these men, too, were on their way east. In late May, many British and US Intelligence reports still talked of continued shipments of Allied prisoners to Odessa, sometimes with German prisoners – even though the Soviets had already told Deane in Moscow that Odessa was closed as a POW repatriation point.

The repatriations following the Halle Conference caused some relief. Air Marshal Tedder at SHAEF cabled Churchill on 22 May:

Yesterday I was pleasantly surprised to hear from a number of men that, some days ago, a large party of them had been sent by the Russians by train, from Brux to Pilsen and there handed over to the Americans. I hope one is not unduly optimistic in thinking this may be a promising sign. Knowing your concern for our ex-POWs I thought these sidelights might be of some interest to you.[11]

On 22 May 1945 *The New York Times* also found these returns exciting. In a wireless report sent from Paris, it said that 62,960 American prisoners had been evacuated by air and that some 7,000 Americans still remained in the Soviet zone; 1,500 transports and bombers were being used for the airlift and as many as 36,000 prisoners had been evacuated by air in one day.

> The number of British and French soldiers held by the enemy was, of course, far higher than the number of Americans [the report went on]. The figures for the middle of March, when Gen. Dwight D. Eisenhower launched his assault into the Reich, showed 75,850 Americans, 199,500 British and 734,600 French prisoners of war in Germany. In all there were approximately 2,173,000 United Nations prisoners of war in seventy camps in Germany.[12]

Again the 199,500 figure is used for British POWs in German hands, a figure that the Ministry of Defence now denies.

On 25 May Eisenhower cabled AGWAR and the Twelfth Army Group: 'We expect to have all US ex-prisoners of war recovered from Russians within seven days. The greatest part of those held by the Russians have been returned to our custody during the past three days.'[13]

Amid all this jubilation, one sour note was sounded. On 25 May the Foreign Office received information that Flight Lieutenant Hubert, Sergeant John Oaks and Captain Samborski had been arrested by the NKVD in Nowy Sacz and taken to Cracow. They also received an enquiry from Mark Lawrence, service number 623878, who had taken an active part in the Warsaw uprising. He wanted to know whether he should stay in Poland.

He could supply valuable information and reported that the fate of British prisoners liberated from the German camps raised 'very grave anxiety.

'They have been put in barracks and are not allowed to circulate in the town and meet or contact Poles.' Lawrence also reported that Soviet anti-British propaganda was very strong. Hitler was being compared to Chamberlain and the Nazi hangman to the British treatment of the Boers.[14]

CHAPTER 19

# Exchanges in Austria

†

THE MOST NOTORIOUSLY bloody forced repatriation was the return of the Cossacks. Some 38,000 Cossacks in Austria, old enemies of Bolshevism who had served as whole formations in the German army, were soon to be forcibly repatriated by Field Marshal Alexander's command. There were mass suicides of women and children and many of those returned were shot. Alexander resisted his orders to repatriate these men, but eventually complied in the hopes of rescuing British and American prisoners from the Soviets.

Although it led to the deaths of tens of thousands of men, women and children, at the time the British and Americans thought this was a small price to pay to resolve the situation in Austria. The Red Army under Marshal Tolbukhin had overrun much of the country by mid-to-late March, 'liberating' not only the POWs already in Austrian camps such as Stalags 17-A and -B near Wiener Neustadt but also tens of thousands more in temporary camps who had been force marched through the Czechoslovakian mountains with the retreating Germans from as far east as Poland. Earlier secret plans had been drawn up to rescue these men but, by the middle of May, it was too late.

Alexander already knew about the growing POW problem in the other European theatres of war through reports of POWs who were being shipped home from Odessa, via Italy. On 13 May 1945 he sent a message to the Adjutant General of the War Office (AGWAR) in London: '. . . understand however from British ex-POW returning from Odessa that there are a number of British escapees from POW camps in East Prussia and Poland still hiding in Poland owing to being unwilling to surrender themselves to the Russians.'[1]

That same day Harold Macmillan, Minister of State, Mediterranean, and political adviser to Alexander, recorded in his diary:

Among the surrendered Germans are about 40,000 Cossacks and 'White' Russians, with their wives and children. To hand them over to the Russians is condemning them to slavery, torture and probably death. To refuse, is deeply to offend the Russians, and incidentally break the Yalta Agreement. We have decided to hand them over (General Keighley is in touch and on good terms with the Russian general on his right), but I suggested that the Russians should at the same time give us any British prisoners or wounded who may be in this area. The formal procedure is that they should go back through Odessa (which I understand means great hardship). I hope we can persuade the local Russian commander to hand them over direct (we think he has 1,500–2,000) and save them all this suffering, in exchange for the scrupulous adherence to the agreement in handing back Russian subjects.

We have already found a good number (I think over 1,000) British prisoners (many of them sick and wounded) in the Klagenfurt area. I watched the ambulances bringing them to the airfield. They are flown straight away in Dakotas to Naples or other hospitals and camps in southern Italy.[2]

Alexander notified the War Office on 16 May that an exchange of liberated POWs had been agreed between the Eighth Army and the Soviets. He cabled:

Understand exchange . . . 14 May at Graz from 2,000 [fit] and 250 sick Russians immediately available from Wolfsberg. Movement of others dependent on local commanders ability to loan transport. Area of operational roads congested. Large numbers surrendered personnel supposedly of Russian origin ex-German Cossack Division were in Volkersmarkt Area on 12 May. Rumoured that 500 to 1,000 British PW are inside the Russian lines near Graz. If and when freed will evacuate by air from Klagenfurt.[3]

Clearly this 'exchange' is one-way traffic. Not only are no British prisoners reported to be returning from behind Soviet lines, they have not been contacted or returned as their presence there is still only 'rumoured'.

On 22 May 1945 Alexander cabled London and Eisenhower at SHAEF:

Agreement reached with Major Skvortzoff Repatriation Staff Tolbukhin's Hq. and General Grazdekin 57 army GRAZ for handover to them all Soviet ex PW in British zone. 2,874 transferred 17/18 May. Permission obtained from local Soviet commander for repatriation detachment to enter Russian zone but difficulty experienced in tracing BR/US PW. Approx. 300 have exfiltrated [escaped] into Klagenfurt. Unconfirmed reports suggest BR/US PW still being evacuated Odessa by rail in boxcars with German PW. Many instances of theft of clothing and personal effects.[4]

Again Alexander came up empty handed, returning all the Soviet POWs for none of ours. Indeed he cannot even trace them. These 'unconfirmed reports' of British and American prisoners being sent east came from the 300 prisoners who had escaped from the Soviets to Klagenfurt. And they were being shipped east in boxcars with German POWs who were on their way to Soviet labour camps.

The day after the Halle Conference another important meeting took place. The Chief of Staff of Patton's Third Army, Major General H.R. Gay, met Soviet General Derevenko at Linz to discuss the return of POWs from Austria. Derevenko complained that the transfer should have begun on 20 May, and pushed for it to begin that day, the 23rd. It was agreed that Russian returnees should be sent by train to Melk, where the same trains would be filled with Western Europeans for the return journey.

'Do you have British and American prisoners of war on hand at Melk now?' asked General Gay.

'The British and American prisoners of war are not in the vicinity of Melk,' replied General Derevenko. 'They are further down [south] – they are in the vicinity of Wiener Neustadt, but they will be brought up immediately.'[5]

General Gay admitted to having 20,000 displaced Russians and 16,000 displaced Poles, while at Wiener Neustadt in Austria deep in the Soviet zone south of Vienna and west of Bratislava, Czechoslovakia, the Soviets had concentrated 60,000 former prisoners of war.

Having agreed to return all the liberated Soviet POWs in the British zone on 22 May, the British had nothing left to bargain with. So, on 24 May, the handover of 38,000 Cossacks was ordered.

'It had to be done. We had no power to stop it. And not to do it would have meant they would have not sent back our British prisoners,' Macmillan told TV interviewer Ludovic Kennedy in 1984.[6]

In his account of the repatriation of the Cossacks, *The Minister and the Massacres*, Nikolai Tolstoy says that Macmillan could not have believed that the Cossacks had to be sent back under the Yalta Agreement. He was familiar with the screening instructions received only a week before – which were designed to ensure that only Soviet citizens were returned to Stalin's mercy. Many of the Cossacks had French or Yugoslav citizenship, or were stateless, because they had left Russia during the Revolution, before the establishment of the Soviet state, so had never been Soviet citizens.[7]

Tolstoy also says he doubts that 'Macmillan effected an agreement with the Soviets which resulted in the speedy return of British prisoners of war'. This 'exchange', Tolstoy says, did not take place.

Clearly, the exchange had not taken place by 26 May when Alexander cabled the War Office again:

> Agreement with Russians at Graz only applies to handing over Soviet citizens in British zone Austria. No repeat no reciprocal guarantees in respect of British PWs obtained except half-hearted promises which so far have not been honoured. Evacuation to Odessa still continuing from this area.
>
> Premature to plan on overland exchange on a local contact basis till Moscow issues directive to Graz commander.
>
> Considered essential Moscow be asked to announce their agreement to local overland exchange, as there are 15,597 USA account, 8,462 British account awaiting repatriation in this theatre.[8]

Unusually, Alexander also sent this cable to Deane at the US Mission in Moscow, to Eisenhower via the prisoner-of-war section at SHAEF, to the Australian, Canadian and New Zealand governments and to the British ACC (Allied Control Commission) delegations in Hungary and Rumania where other Allied POWs were in the process of disappearing. One motive for such a wide distribution of this message could have been to make it more difficult to ignore, or 'weed', later.

In an urgent reply on 28 May the Chiefs of Staff urged Alexander to demand reciprocity from Marshal Tolbukhin. And on the 29th they informed the Americans of the exchange. A top-secret cable from Britain's Air Ministry Special Signals Office to the Joint Staff Mission in Washington tied the forced repatriation of the Cossacks to the return of Allied POWs:

> Following from Chiefs of Staff.
> 1. We agree Cossacks should be dealt with in accordance with the Yalta Agreement. There are still [a] number of British and American PW in Soviet hands including 15,597 Americans and 8,462 British released by Marshal Tolbukhin. Although exchange

points at Graz had been fixed between Eighth Army and local Soviet commander for their exchange with liberated Soviet civilians AFHQ report that Marshal Tolbukhin is merely accepting Soviet citizens and intends to continue to evacuate British and Americans to Odessa. This is contrary to understanding with Eighth Army and to agreement with USSR that further exchanges should be overland . . .

2. Information received from 15 Army Group shows that 5 Corps have in fact to hand over Cossacks to Russians. We consider that Combined Chiefs of Staff should inform SACMED repeated to SCAEF [Supreme Commander Allied Expeditionary Forces] that action of 5 Corps is approved and that all should be exchanged under Yalta Agreement but that Marshal Tolbukhin should be pressed to exchange the British and Americans . . . at the same time.

3. We consider that Soviet Government should be informed of Marshal Tolbukhin's action . . . and pressed to issue immediate instructions to him for exchange of British and American PW overland . . . As no further shipping is scheduled after end of May for evacuation from Odessa issue of necessary instruction to Marshal Tolbukhin is of extreme urgency.[9]

The American Fifteenth Army Group also informed the British Eighth Army on 29 May: 'It is proposed to move 23,000 Russian nationals from various areas to Graz at rate maximum 2,200 per day to be handed over to Russian forces. Date of commencement move . . . likely to be about 5 June.'

The 23,000 'Russian nationals' to be exchanged were prisoners of war and slave labourers held by the US Fifth Army in Italy, plus 14,000 of the same categories in Eighth Army custody.[10,11]

However, just one day after Alexander and Marshall had cabled SHAEF, Deane, the War Office and others that there were '15,597 United States and 8,462 British POWs in Marshal Tolbukhin's hands', General McNarney, senior American general at Alexander's headquarters, cabled Washington saying that there had been a misunderstanding. The figures quoted were 'not United States/British prisoners of war held by the Soviets [but] Soviets held by United States and British in AFHQ'.

American researchers claim that McNarney's cable is the beginning of a cover-up. The British Ministry of Defence and the American Department of Defense deny this. However, Alexander had already agreed to hand back all Soviets in British hands on 22 May. The transfer of the Cossacks – if they counted as Soviet citizens – was under way. There were 38,000 when the repatriation of the Cossacks had started and it would be difficult to give such an accurate count of the numbers left at this point. Outside McNarney's cable to Washington and a similar cable from AFHQ to London, the idea that these 15,597 Soviet POWs in American hands and 8,462 in British hands is never mentioned. And throughout the continuing cable traffic, official communications, and parliamentary and press statements the numbers 15,597 and 8,462 continue to be given as the number of American and British POWs held by Tolbukhin. Later, the Soviets would even make a tacit admission that they held these men.

## CHAPTER 20

# The Closing of Odessa

†

As WELL AS writing off 15,597 American and 8,462 British POWs in Soviet hands, McNarney's cable also mentioned that it was 'informally understood here Russians *no* longer evacuating United States/British to Odessa'.[1] Overland exchanges had been agreed in principle on 5 May and even before the Halle Conference had convened, General Golubev had told General Deane in Moscow that after 12 May 1945 no more POWs would be sent to Odessa.

Meanwhile, however, a row had blown up between the British and the Soviets at Odessa. *The Staffordshire* had been forced to sail empty, after a disagreement over whether it should carry French POWs. On 21 May 2,000 French prisoners, including women and children, were embarking on *The Staffordshire* when they were turned back by the Soviets. There were some 16,000 French prisoners held in Odessa at the time, in awful conditions, many sleeping in the open without adequate covering.[2]

It was not until 27 May that Admiral Archer, head of the British Military Mission in Moscow, was formally 'informed by Soviet Repatriation Committee . . . that instruction would be issued to stop sending British officers, soldiers and civilians to Odessa also that henceforth those Allied PWs liberated in Southern Regions would be despatched to Graz to be handed over to Eighth Army'.[3]

But there had been some understanding on the matter earlier. On 24 May Admiral Archer and General Basilov has discussed the problem of POW stragglers after Odessa had been closed. They also mentioned the possibility of arranging for British ex-POWs arriving in Rumania or Hungary to be air-lifted home or repatriated across the lines at Graz.

Following Alexander's telegram outlining the situation in Austria, on 29 May, Admiral Archer told General Basilov that, in view of these new arrangements to exchange prisoners of war at Graz, it was essential that the 15,597 liberated American and 8,462 British POWs in Austria were *not* sent to Odessa and requested that the Soviet army authorities in Austria be so informed.

This matter was urgent as already on the 24th, Archer had discussed the imminent departure of the last ship from Odessa to the UK. In his message on the 29th he reminded Basilov of the necessity of getting a Corporal Clayton, who was in Cracow, to Odessa before the last ship sailed.

On 29 May General Younger of the Red Cross confirmed that Odessa was closing on 31 May and the Soviet authorities had been requested to send no more ex-POWs there. Red Cross workers Mrs Veale and Miss MacRae were to embark on one of the last ships from Odessa. Mrs Thorold was to stay on to look after the stragglers.[4] But Veale and MacRae had difficulty obtaining exit permits and Younger, afraid that they might miss the last ship to England, wrote to Dr Kolesnikov of the Soviet Red Cross/Red Crescent for help.

The Americans were just as conscious of the problem of the continuing shipment of ex-POWs eastwards. On 30 May 1945 the Pentagon Chief of Staff General Marshall sent a top-secret cable from Washington to the senior American general in Alexander's headquarters, McNarney, to Deane in Moscow and to Eisenhower:

> Information received from British indicates that 15,597 US and 8,462 British now in Marshal Tolbukhin's hands. Understood further that Soviet Commander proposes to continue the evacuation of these POWs to ODESSA rather than repatriate them overland as had been proposed by Soviet Government and accepted by UNITED STATES and British. Request fullest information urgently.[5]

According to US government documents, the Soviets stopped repatriating US personnel through Odessa on 28 May 1945, two days before this message was written. The last British ship seems to have sailed on 31 May 1945, though there still appears to have been some non-Soviet shipping sailing from Odessa in the first week in June. By 31 May, 4,377 British and Commonwealth personnel had been repatriated through Odessa. No more came later. Interestingly, the lists show a large percentage of those returned through Odessa were 'missing', not reported POW.[6] They could have been aircrew who downed behind Soviet lines and, hence, never made it on to German or Red Cross lists, in which case they would not have been part of the 199,500 registered prisoners of war in German hands reported to the British government.

CHAPTER 21

# The Day They All
# Went Missing

✝

THERE WERE SOON other indications that the Leipzig Agreement had
started to break down. One of the five designated exchange points for
liberated POWs was Ludwigslust in Germany.[1] Five days after the
agreement was signed, on 27 May, an urgent message reached SHAEF
saying that the appropriate orders had still not reached Ludwigslust
and POW exchanges there had consequently been held up.[2]

There was also concern about the large number of ex-POWs in
Czechoslovakia. On 28 May 1945 the War Office's daily report on
POWs said: 'According to a member of the SHAEF Political Warfare
Executive, who has recently returned from a journey to Prague, there
were about 1,900 British and US prisoners of war in that city, the great
majority being British.'[3]

Questions were being asked in Parliament. But although Solicitor
General Sir Walter Monckton had been despatched to Moscow to
attend a long-planned meeting of the Repatriations Commission, the
Commission still had not met. And the Prime Minister told the House
of Commons on 29 May that there would be 'no statement in advance
of that meeting'.

The same day Sir James Grigg told the House of Commons:

The overall position now is that 156,000 British Commonwealth
prisoners have been repatriated, over 140,000 of them by air.
About 10,000 are awaiting repatriation either in General Eisenhower's or Field Marshal Alexander's zone and about 400 in
Odessa. It is known that about 8,500 are in the part of Austria
controlled by the Red Army, and it is hoped that arrangements
will soon be made for their transfer to the British or American
Forces. There must be a number of stragglers on the continent
whose collection and repatriation will take some time, and it is
therefore impossible at the moment to estimate how many

prisoners cannot be accounted for. The number is not likely to be large.[4]

The figures he quoted totalled 174,900. So the numbers were progressively being eroded. Only two weeks before, on 15 May, Sir James told the House of Commons that 'it was estimated at the beginning of this year that 180,000 British Commonwealth prisoners were in German hands'[5] (though in March 199,500 were in German hands).

Sir James Grigg's 29 May total − 174,900 − would have included a number of men listed 'missing', who were not registered prisoners, so the shortfall is more than 24,600. However, the 174,900 figure is still larger than the 168,000 ex-POWs who did return home.

On 30 May a letter arrived at the British Consulate in Moscow from Lance Corporal R.S. Mackay, a military policeman in the Soviet hospital in Bromberg, suffering from frostbitten feet. He asked the consulate if something could be done to get him repatriated as the Soviet authorities did not appear to know what to do with him. Admiral Archer made a formal protest to General Basilov: 'Although this British soldier has been in your charge for a considerable period and is in a Russian hospital, no official notification of this fact has at any time been forwarded to me.'[6]

The British government made another protest to the Soviets on 30 May 1945, this time with a special 'political' cable from the Foreign Office. It came in reaction to a memorandum given to Foreign Secretary Anthony Eden by the Soviet Ambassador in Washington, which dismissed the British government's anxieties over their liberated prisoners of war as 'groundless pretensions'. The Foreign Office protested that they would be unable to dispel these anxieties as long as the Soviet government persisted in refusing to allow

> the British repatriation officers to perform the tasks for which they were sent out and which were clearly laid down in the Yalta Agreement.
>
> As regards the treatment of Soviet citizens liberated by British armies, His Majesty's Government cannot conceal their astonishment at the tone and content of the Soviet communication. His Majesty's Government very much resent that such a statement should have been made. In addition, His Majesty's Government wish the Soviet Government to know that they are at a loss to understand why it has been found necessary to protest, often in very offensive terms, about matters in regard to which complete and conclusive explanations have already been given either to the Soviet Embassy or to the Soviet repatriation officers.

The Soviet accusations, the stiffly worded cable concluded, were 'a deliberate distortion of the facts'.[7]

One of the Halle negotiators, Brigadier Venables, was forced to admit a serious flaw in the Leipzig Agreement. On 30 May 1945 he pointed out in a cable that no arrangements were made with the Russians at the Halle Conference for visits by British or American repatriation officers to camps in the Soviet zone. Such arrangements, he said, were not considered necessary as they were already fully covered by paragraph two of the Yalta Agreement which read: 'Soviet and British repatriation representatives will have the right of immediate access into the camps and points of concentration where their citizens were located.'[8] But after allowing one Allied repatriation officer to visit one camp, the Soviets reverted to their pre-Halle stance and completely excluded Allied officers from the Soviet zone.

If there were any remaining doubts about the Soviet intentions they were cleared up in the following cable dated 30 May from the SHAEF Mission to France sent to the SHAEF G-5 Displaced Persons branch:

> . . . Report of LT D HAVERNAS according to confirmed reports, Russians still do not release thousands of French ex-PWs and civilians, forcing them to work. Many transferred eastwards to unknown destination. Please inform high authority.[9]

On 30 May 1945 a top-secret meeting was held in Moscow between Stalin and Truman's envoy, Harry Hopkins, who had also been a confidant of Roosevelt. The subject of prisoners of war came up. Hopkins asked Stalin how many prisoners the Red Army had taken. Stalin claimed that the Soviets were holding about 2,500,000 of whom about 800,000 were non-Germans.

After the meeting Hopkins cabled Truman: 'You can be sure that at your next meeting [at Potsdam] Stalin will have some pretty specific proposals to make about prisoners of war, and more particularly, I believe, about war criminals. He did not, as we anticipated, express any criticism of our handling of war prisoners.'

Only a month before Soviet General Golikov, while insisting that 'all liberated British and American prisoners have been repatriated', had been haranguing the American chargé d'affaires in Moscow, George Kennan, over the 'mistreatment of Soviet citizens in British and American prisoner of war camps'. Clearly the Allies' forced-repatriation programme was now paying dividends.

The day of Hopkins' meeting with Stalin a cable from SHAEF

headquarters again reiterated the connection between the repatriation of Soviet citizens and the release of Allied prisoners: 'The airlift for Soviet citizens from France and Belgium and the Ruhr is dependent on their being sufficient US/British PWs and Western European repatriates available at the Russian border zone for the return lift. Daily bid must be made by armies for this return lift.'[10]

That same day General Kenner, Eisenhower's Surgeon General at SHAEF headquarters, received a memorandum from a British officer, Lieutenant K.H. Clark of the RAMC. It was headed 'Displaced Persons, Allied ex-PW and German PW'. Clark's memorandum tabled the number of Allied ex-POWs and displaced persons being held captive in Red Army territory on 30 May 1945:

### Russian Sphere

|         | PW      | DP      |
|---------|---------|---------|
| Belgian | 50,000  | 115,000 |
| Dutch   | 4,000   | 140,000 |
| British | 20,000  |         |
| US      | 20,000  |         |
| French  | 250,000 | 850,000 |

The figures are staggering. Clark suggested these Western nationals should be exchanged for Soviet nationals across the tactical line at a rate of 35,000 a day.[11]

The next day, 31 May 1945, a cable detailing the magnitude of the masses of allied prisoners of war and displaced citizens held in Soviet territory, signed by Eisenhower, was sent from Supreme Allied Headquarters to the US Military Mission in Moscow. Eisenhower wanted an explanation from the Soviets for the slow pace of repatriation. The 'discrepancies' between the Allies' most up-to-date figures of Allied POWs and displaced Western Europeans known to be in Soviet-occupied territory and the number actually repatriated by the Soviets were outlined by Eisenhower:

Latest available displaced persons and prisoners of war figures show almost 1,600,000 Western European (French, Belgian, Dutch and Luxembourgers) either repatriated from or at present held in SHAEF area. Soviet delegates at LEIPZIG conference stated

118

only 300,000 Western Europeans in their area. Combined working party on European food supplies, composed of representatives from UNRRA, SHAEF, USSR, UK and USA, including Soviet delegate LIUSHENKO estimated approximately 3,000,000 displaced Western Europeans in enemy-held territory at beginning 1944. This discrepancy of over 1,000,000 Western Europeans is causing the Dutch and French Governments considerable anxiety.

Then, on 1 June, Eisenhower made a surprising turn around. He cabled from SHAEF in Reims to, it is believed, the War Office in London:

> It is now estimated that only small numbers of US prisoners of war still remain in Russian hands. These no doubt are scattered singly and in small groups as no information is available of any large numbers in specific camps. They are being received now only in small driblets and being reported as received.
>
> Everything possible is being done to recover US personnel and to render accurate and prompt reports thereon to the War Department.[12]

This directly contradicts Soviet General Derevenko's admission to General Gay that American POWs were being held at Wiener Neustadt, Austria, in late May, and it contradicts General Deane's letter the day before – 'information which indicates that 15,597 United States liberated prisoners of war are now under control of Marshal Tolbukhin' – which the Soviets later admitted. It also contradicts the memorandum from Lieutenant Clark which stated, just forty-eight hours earlier, that 20,000 US POWs were still being held by the Red Army – along with 20,000 British and others.

It is also difficult to reconcile with Eisenhower's own concern over the fate of Western Europeans in Soviet hands, the day before, and with Barker's report of the Halle Conference.

However, the Eisenhower cable does square perfectly with the official line put out by the War Department in Washington on 31 May 1945. On the very day Eisenhower sent his cable saying that 'only small numbers of US prisoners of war remain in Russian hands' *The New York Times* printed a special announcement from the War Department saying that 'substantially all' of the American soldiers taken prisoner in Europe were accounted for. This not only wrote off any remaining prisoners, it also wrote off those listed 'missing in action' who had not yet been accounted for. The War Department announcement, from

119

Undersecretary of War Robert P. Patterson, continued: 'This means that it is not expected that many of those who are still being carried as missing-in-action will appear later as having been prisoners of war.'

This statement – and Eisenhower's cable – essentially put an end to the wrangling with the Soviets over POWs that had been going on for the previous three months. No evidence was cited to counter Lieutenant Clark's memorandum. Once the Halle Conference had failed, it became almost inevitable that some 20,000 Americans would simply be abandoned in Russian hands. And if America – the strongest of the Western Allies – was not going to confront the Soviets over their missing POWs no one else stood a chance. The British were exhausted after six long years of war. They could not fight the Soviets alone. At least 20,000 British POWs had to be written off, along with large numbers of French, Dutch and Belgians.

Again on that same day the American Red Cross issued a press release saying that 99 per cent of all POWs had already been returned. This press release had been sent to the State Department for approval on 21 May, even before the end of the Halle Conference.

This incredible story of abandonment is even told, in a bowdlerised version, in the official history of the repatriations, 'RAMPs: The Recovery and Repatriation of Liberated Prisoners of War', written in 1947. Even this watered-down version remains 'restricted' though forty-six years later. On the subject of Western Europeans in the Soviet zone in 1945, RAMPs says:

> In mid-May 1945 it was estimated that there were 340,000 prisoners of war of the United States, British, French, Belgian and Dutch nationality under Soviet control. At the same time it was estimated that there were more than 700,000 displaced persons of French, Belgian and Netherlands nationality under Soviet control, making a total of 1,040,000 persons to be moved from the Soviet area to the area under the control of Supreme Headquarters (SHAEF). The actual repatriations accomplished later on showed that the estimate of east–west movement (from the Soviet zone) was an overestimate as only about 450,000 persons of all categories and nationalities were recovered from the Soviet forces.

In other words the shortfall, even according to RAMPs, was some 590,000 people.

Records in *The Military and UNRRA [United Nations Relief and Rehabilitation Administration] of European Refugees* indicate that the figures for these missing men (nearly all from the Soviet zone) are: Belgium – 40,000; France – 350,000; and Netherlands – 150,000.

In return for the 450,000 people that the Western nations received from the Soviets, the Allies returned – forcibly and otherwise – 2,034,000 Soviet POWs and other citizens by 1 September 1945, over 200,000 more than SHAEF had originally estimated. (In a review of the official history of the repatriations made in 1952, the US Assistant Chief of Staff, an army Intelligence officer, recommended that all this information be suppressed.)

Other records in the US National Archives give the estimated numbers of other people – Eastern Europeans and enemy POWs – who were also swallowed by the Gulag. They indicate that two million Poles were deported to the labour camps. The Soviets also took 4 million Germans, 230,000 Italians and a large number of Austrians, Rumanians, Czechoslovakians, Bulgarians and others into slave labour. Stalin even offered to take German POWs captured by the Western Allies. He would gladly find space for them in his forced labour camps.

The Soviet Union lost 13.6 million men and over 21 million citizens overall in the war. And most of the prewar occupants of forced labour camps – Ukrainians and other victims of Stalin's purges of the 1930s – were long dead from overwork and starvation. So in 1945 the Soviets were desperate for labour to rebuild their devastated country. However, Stalin's generous offer to take the German POWs was declined.

The decision of the American War Department to effectively write off 20,000 of its own men, could not have been taken lightly. Truman had been vice president for only eighty-two days when Roosevelt died. There was little time for on-the-job training. Although the war in Europe was only weeks away from conclusion, there was still the war in the Pacific to fight. The invasion of Japan alone was expected to cost a million casualties and much of Southeast Asia and Indonesia was still in Japanese hands.

On 16 July 1945 the atomic bomb was tested successfully, but on 31 May no one knew whether it would work. The Soviet Union had not, yet, declared war on Japan. Plainly, the overriding political consideration was to stop all this carping about prisoners of war and get Russia into the war against Japan. When faced with a million casualties, 20,000 men is a small price to pay.

Churchill's priorities were different, though. He was committed to the great anti-Bolshevik war against Stalin. But war-weary Britain could not take that on without its American allies.

## CHAPTER 22

# The British Bulldog

ALTHOUGH EISENHOWER COULD write off his own men, he could not be quite so cavalier with the British. On 1 June 1945 he wired the War Office: 'Anxious to ascertain the number of British PW still to be located in Germany and Austria [and] in Russian rear.'

The men on the ground were harder to handle. Eisenhower issued orders to disband the Special Allied Airborne Reconnaisance Force (SAARF) teams who had been used to help in extracting POWs beyond the reach of the Allied ground forces. Operational officers, under British Brigadier Nichols, begged him to cancel the stand-down from active duty which had suddenly been ordered.[1]

Meanwhile the forced repatriations continued, to keep Stalin sweet. A cable to Secretary of State Stettinius from Ambassador Caffery in Paris records on 1 June 1945: 'SHAEF Forward informed 12th Army Group that normal repatriation procedure should be applied to 7,000 White Russian POWs held by Seventh Corps.'

The British would still hang tough though. On 1 June the British Ambassador in Moscow was instructed to ask for the publication in *Pravda* of the statement made by Richard Law in the House of Commons responding to General Golikov's accusations, and to protest that British repatriation teams had not been allowed into Poland or Soviet-occupied areas of Czechoslovakia and Austria.[2]

Alexander was certainly no further forward in getting back British POWs – whatever their number – in return for the men, women and children he was handing over to the Soviets. On 1 June he reported: 'No British Commonwealth PW transferred to us by Marshal Tolbukhin though small parties have come through Russian lines. No known estimate of British Commonwealth PW still in Marshal Tolbukhin's zone.'[3]

Later that same day though, Alexander heard of 'some thousands of liberated Allied PW including British and Americans in adjacent areas of Czechoslovakia majority of whom Russians may be expected to hand over to you at Graz in exchange for Soviet citizens'.[4]

Despite McNarney's 'understanding' that no American or British ex-POWs were being sent to Odessa after 30 May, the Americans were still concerned about Allied ex-POWs being taken east. The US State Department's chief political adviser to Alexander at SACMED, Alexander Kirk, cabled Secretary of State Stettinius: 'Department should see MX 24501 of May 31 from Deane at Moscow to AGWAR concerning Russian plans to abandon port of Odessa as evacuation point of Allied nationals who will be evacuated in future through Graz, Austria to British Eighth Army.'[5]

Admiral Archer at the British Military Mission in Moscow had been pursuing the case of Company Sergeant Major Manzie, who had been seen in a Russian hospital at Schubin for two and a half months, suffering from frostbitten feet. Archer first wrote to Golubev about Manzie on 17 March. Golubev wrote back on 27 March, saying that all the sick and wounded were being airlifted to Odessa. On 19 April Archer wrote to Golubev pointing out that Manzie had still not turned up. Then, on 2 June, Golubev replied that Manzie was not registered at the hospital at Schubin and there was no record of him passing through earlier. In that same letter, Golubev said that three other British soldiers reported to be at Schulitz were not there either.

Admiral Archer also heard from General Basilov on 2 June, saying that he was making enquiries about the whereabouts of Lance Corporal Chambers, as requested. He also mentioned that seventy-one Englishmen had been handed across the lines in Austria on 1 June. Otherwise, he asserted the Soviets knew nothing of British POWs behind their lines.

'At present we have no information about the presence of Englishmen, awaiting repatriation, on the territory of Austria controlled by the Red Army,'[6] Basilov wrote.

There were certainly some Americans there. Ignoring the change of POW policy in Washington and at SHAEF, General Deane continued to pursue the matter in Moscow. On 2 June 1945 he had a meeting with General Slavin and General Golikov and confronted them with General Marshall's 30 May cable, claiming there were still 15,597 'liberated' US POWs in Marshal Tolbukhin's 3rd Front Area – Austria. Deane asked how these men and other US prisoners still in Poland and Rumania would be repatriated.

The Soviet generals avoided making an 'official statement', but Golikov added he was 'sure the shortest and best route would be used for evacuating these men'. So Golikov admitted that the men in

Austria, written off by McNarney's cable, *did* exist. And Deane was discussing with the Soviets the repatriation of men who, according to Washington and to Eisenhower, had all been returned.

After the meeting General Deane sent a top-secret cable to General Marshall (and copied to Eisenhower at SHAEF and McNarney, senior American general at Alexander's headquarters): 'Concerning those liberated prisoners of war in Marshal TOLBUKHIN's area, estimated in excess of 15,000, GOLIKOV assured me that they would be evacuated westward in accordance with the HALLE agreement. He confirmed my previous belief that ODESSA was to be abandoned as a transit camp . . .'

Once Deane had his admission that the Soviets were holding over 15,000 US POWs (and presumably almost 8,500 British – or 6,500 if Macmillan was right and 2,000 had been handed over) and that they would be repatriated westwards, he sprang on the Soviet generals the fact that he possessed intelligence which said that Americans were still being shipped eastwards, ostensibly towards Odessa. General Golikov simply responded by again charging the Allies with abusing liberated USSR POWs.

Churchill took up the matter of the missing prisoners from Austria directly with the Soviets. On 17 June 1945 Stalin cabled back: 'With regard to Austria, I have to repeat what I have already told you about the summons of Soviet Commanders [Tolbukhin et al.] to Moscow and the date of their return to Vienna.'

Without the backing of Truman there was little Churchill could do in the face of this obtuse reply.

The British were also having to contend with still more Soviet bluster. On 31 May 1945 the British Embassy in Moscow had received a letter from Vyshinski at the People's Commissariat for Foreign Affairs, in reply to a letter of complaint from Mr Roberts, dated 12 May. Vyshinski stated that British ex-POWs had been despatched with 'maximum speed' to Odessa and he was surprised at the British complaints. The only problem had occurred with British POWs who did not notify themselves to the Soviet authorities. Nor could Vyshinski understand British complaints about the access of repatriation officers to assembly camps under the Yalta Agreement. After all, the British had been allowed into the camp at Odessa, and 'Apart from Odessa, no other camps exist and consequently references to the various collecting camps are without any foundation.'[7]

It was not possible to furnish the British with lists of liberated POWs before they reached Odessa. Vyshinski also said that Mr Roberts's assertion that there was no Soviet organisation dealing with repatriation questions in Austria 'does not correspond with the facts'. Vyshinski rejected all the British accusations and said that questions raised in connection with overland repatriations had already been solved. The Soviet authorities were fulfilling all their obligations under the Yalta Agreement, he maintained.[8]

In a cable to the Foreign Office and the War Cabinet, dated 3 June, Clark Kerr pointed out that Vyshinski's claim about the British being allowed to exercise control of the camp at Odessa was quite untrue. He contested the statement that 'no other collecting points existed'. Despite the Soviet claim that they could provide lists only from Odessa, some other lists had been provided. But Clark Kerr could see no point in continuing protests as Roberts's original letter had been intended to pave the way for better arrangements for the overland exchanges, which had now been agreed. Clark Kerr was concerned, though, that the Soviets would be given rights of inspection or facilities denied to Britain and its allies – 'experience hitherto suggests that strict reciprocity should be observed'.[9]

The Foreign Office replied on 15 June 1945: 'We should not leave unchallenged any Soviet assertion, whether made in public or otherwise, which we believe to be false.' And Clark Kerr was urged to reply to Vyshinski in 'firm tones'.[10]

On 4 June the Associated Press reported how difficult it was to get into the Soviet zone of Austria. 'Unsmiling Russian soldiers, with tommy guns ready, guard every bridge, every highway, and every byway. It takes a special pass from Marshal Tolbukhin to get by them and such passes are hard, if not impossible, to obtain.'

Despite what Deane had been told in Moscow, the Americans were playing down the POW question in Austria, at least as far as the media were concerned. AP reported:

The only Americans known to be in the Russian zone of Austria are some officers and men at Melk, midway between the American lines on the Enns river and Vienna.

Heads are counted for convoys enter there almost every day, and every driver must be accounted for when they return. Relations have been cordial generally among Americans and Russians stationed along the demarcation line. But this cordiality changed more or less to formality after a tour last week by a Russian general. The next day the Russians established and placed barricades on all unbarricaded bridges over which traffic was not authorized.

The general's visit and the subsequent action came after some Americans had visited Vienna. The Russian captain who let the

Americans thru was understood to have been demoted to a private. The lieutenant colonel who told the captain to let the Americans pass was reported docked three months' pay.[11]

Things may have been frosty on the front lines, but on 4 June Alexander finally reported: 'Negotiations . . . beginning today between representative Commanders 8th Army and representative Marshal Tolbukhin in Graz to arrange transfer point at Graz or other suitable location in neighbourhood. Will inform you of result when known.'

On that same day Alexander intervened personally and cancelled the orders for the forced repatriation of the remaining Cossacks, since no British POWs had been received in exchange. Yet in his memoirs Macmillan asserts that the return of the Cossacks, White Russians and a large number of Yugoslavs – Croats who fought for the Nazis – handed to Tito's communist forces 'was a great grief to me . . . [but] at least we obtained in exchange some 2,000 prisoners and wounded who were in the area and had been in German hands'.[12] For up to 38,000 Cossacks, this was a poor rate of exchange.

According to Nikolai Tolstoy it was recently admitted by the Chief of Staff in Austria, Brigadier Toby Low, that there was in reality never anything more than a pious hope that placating the Soviets by delivering up the Cossacks might possibly pay dividends in this respect. In 1985 Low made a public statement that, after handing over the Cossacks, British prisoners of war in Austria were returned 'much sooner than we had reason to expect'. But when he was pressed on this point by author Nikolai Tolstoy, Low conceded that the alleged link between the two operations amounted to no more than wishful thinking: 'I think we both [Soviet and British] felt obligated to the Yalta Agreement, and if we didn't play our part they were unlikely to play theirs,' Low told Tolstoy.[13]

The deal had been botched. Even at the time many of the officers in that theatre of war had reservations about the repatriation of the Cossacks. But most were swayed by Macmillan's authority. He was a minister of state, a direct emissary of Churchill, and at the time the orders were given Macmillan had recently returned from London and was, presumably, carrying the full authority of the Prime Minister for his actions. US government documents show that none of the 15,597 US POWs were returned, and we only have Macmillan's word for it that 2,000 of the 8,462 British POWs may have been released. The rest disappeared in the East.

## CHAPTER 23

# Murder in Murmansk

✝

ON 5 JUNE 1945 the War Office reported to the Foreign Office's prisoners-of-war department: 'We have received information from various sources that there were in the middle of May large numbers of our ex-prisoners of war in Czechoslovakia, including some 1,900 in or near Prague.' The great majority were British, according to BBC correspondent D.M. Graham who visited Prague on 15 May.

On 19 May a large evacuation of these men by train and by truck had been arranged but a new Soviet general took over and stopped the evacuation. He wanted to know on whose authority the trains, trucks and transports were being used, and returned the ex-POWs to Prague.

Meanwhile more had been pouring into Prague, the city was filling up. Two camps contained 2,500 between them and more men were billeted in civilian accommodation. However, those men in or near Prague were certainly not there on 1 June 1945, according to Monsieur Dunant of the International Red Cross Committee, although he had met a few hundred British and American prisoners south of Dresden. By 5 June the War Office still had not been able to discover what had happened to them and asked the Foreign Office to make enquiries with the Czech government.

Those who had escaped from Prague earlier had some interesting tales to tell about the attitude of the Soviets. While they reported that the Soviets were not actually unfriendly, they simply ignored the liberated POWs, many of whom were spread out across Czechoslovakia in outlying work camps. But as the Soviets got a tighter grip on the country, their attitude became more surly. The fact that no evacuation seemed to be taking place put the wind up the British ex-prisoners, many becoming convinced that they were in the front line of an inevitable war between the Soviet Union and Britain.[1] The British government had taken the same attitude. When disarming the German army, General Montgomery had been told to store their weapons near to the formations, so that they could be re-armed quickly in the case of a Russian attack.

While the efficacy of a general protest about a large number of men missing from Czechoslovakia had to be weighed, the Foreign Office continued its policy of pressing on individual cases. On 5 June the British protested to the Soviets about the treatment of Private Tasker. They had last enquired about him on 28 March after he was seen on 5 January in a prison camp liberated by the Soviets. On 25 February they reported that he had been sent to Odessa, but he had not turned up there. In fact he and another British ex-POW called Barratt had been arrested in Budapest, accused of being anti-communist Hungarians and held with German prisoners of war. On 31 May Tasker was transferred to a French camp at Bronowitz near Moscow. From there he managed to get a letter to the British Embassy.

The embassy complained that the Soviets must have identified Tasker before he was sent to Bronowitz, and now demanded he be shipped to Odessa or handed over to them in Moscow.[2]

On 4 December 1945 the Soviet Ambassador in London sent a note to the Foreign Office, explaining that Trooper Tasker had been held for a long period at Krasnogorak because the Soviet authorities had to make a detailed investigation into 'the circumstances of his entry into the Soviet army area'. They pointed out that he had no papers proving his nationality and citizenship.

In his reply on 16 January 1946 the new Foreign Secretary, Ernest Bevin, pointed out that the easiest way for the Soviets to have checked Tasker's bona fides was to contact the British authorities.

'Quite apart from the fact that this was the duty of the Soviet government under the Yalta Agreement,' Bevin wrote, 'the very desirability of ensuring . . . that Tasker was not an enemy agent masquerading as a British subject might have suggested the advantage of allowing a British officer to interview him.'

Not only was the Soviet explanation not satisfactory, Bevin enquired whether there were any other individuals who claimed to be British subjects but who were suspected of being German spies.

'If this is the case, the relevant British authorities would be glad to confirm or deny their British nationality,' he said.[3]

The case of Barratt, who was arrested with Tasker, was also pursued well into 1946.

The response to such enquiries was a snow job. 'The Soviet Embassy in London is constantly sending a flood of protests about the treatment of individual liberated Soviet citizens, most of which are extremely flimsy and seem to be designed to merely irritate,' the Foreign Office complained. They themselves had 'plenty of material . . . for making well-founded protests'.[4]

On 7 June 1945 Allied officials expressed puzzlement at the hailstorm of Soviet accusations, and on 11 June Britain finally directly denied charges made by Golikov, and hinted that the accusations expressed Soviet frustration at the Western Allies' failure to repatriate Poles and citizens of the Baltic Republics of Estonia, Latvia and Lithuania, now part of the USSR. However, the British had begun to put pressure on the Norwegians to comply with Stalin's demands for repatriation of Polish and Soviet citizens from the Baltic Republics who had fled to Norway.

The question of British prisoners of war in Soviet hands was still on the agenda in Parliament. On 5 June 1945 Sir James Grigg told the House of Commons:

> Since I gave an answer to a number of hon. members on 29 May a further 8,500 British Commonwealth prisoners have reached this country, making 164,500 in all, since the beginning of this year. No appreciable groups of prisoners now remain awaiting repatriation in the areas occupied by the British and American armies. Assurances have now been given by the Soviet authorities that British prisoners in Austria and other southern areas in their occupation will be transferred westwards under arrangements similar to those made with SHAEF.

Again, Grigg is reporting Soviet assurances that British prisoners in Austria would be transferred westwards – prisoners who, according to the McNarney cable, did not exist.

The fate of US POWs was still a topic for discreet discussion in Moscow. The subject came up at a reception given by Stalin for Truman's emissary Harry Hopkins on 6 June 1945. Chief US political adviser Robert Murphy says in his memoirs that Hopkins was 'bubbling with enthusiasm about his meetings with Stalin' and that he had 'changed our perspective at SHAEF'. Hopkins had said: 'We can do business with Stalin! He will cooperate!' However, whatever was said or agreed between Hopkins and Stalin about prisoners of war during this critical period of 30 May to 6 June 1945 has remained classified.

At a 6 June meeting between General Deane and Soviet General Golubev, the 15,597 American prisoners in Austria were discussed again. Deane also asked the whereabouts of other Western European citizens, saying that 'Holland and Belgium believed that they had more war prisoners to be evacuated'.

Golubev answered curiously that: 'Belgium and *Norway* should not worry about repatriation of their citizens, but that it would be well for them to concern themselves with speeding up repatriation of Soviet citizens from their countries . . .'

Deane's minutes of the meeting continue: '. . . Golubev said he was surprised to hear the claim that there might be 5,500 US prisoners still in Marshal Tolbukhin's area, and that these were supposedly being evacuated through Odessa. General Golubev said this was not so.'[5]

Golubev's mention of Norway – rather than Holland – in his reply is interesting. Around this time, Norway allowed the forced repatriation to the Soviets of over 80,000 people from its soil, including Poles and citizens of the Baltic Republics which had been overrun by the Russians. Many were shot by NKVD firing squads as soon as they landed at the Murmansk docks.

The British Naval Attaché in Stockholm expressed concern about people committing suicide rather than be returned to the Soviet Union from Norway. The American Embassy there reported: 'He had heard that the Soviet firing squads in Murmansk had been very busy dealing with repatriated citizens by way of that port.'[6]

Harriman reported from Moscow that, though he could not verify men were being executed in Murmansk, certainly the bulk of repatriates were placed in forced-labour battalions and sent to construction projects in the Urals, Central Asia or the far North under police supervision.

'The attitude of the Soviet authorities toward surrender and anti-state activity is, of course, well known to Soviet citizens not yet repatriated and they can have few illusions concerning the treatment awaiting them on their return,' he wrote.[7]

What few people then realised was that even the soldiers who had fought their way to Berlin suffered a similar fate. Stalin believed that the Soviet Union was on the brink of an industrial revolution and Central Siberia and Kazakhstan were going to be the new Ruhr. After three days' drinking, looting and raping in the ruins of Berlin, most were shipped east to the new industrial towns being built there. Few ever saw their homes and families again.[8] Stalin's plans for this industrial miracle were so grandiose that, in the early 1950s, according to the estimates of one camp record-keeper, there were 28 million people in the Gulag. The plan was bound to fail though. People do not work at their best when they are starved, beaten, brutalised and imprisoned.

However, Stalin's thirst for control over human beings knew no bounds. On 6 June 1945 the Soviets protested that Polish officers who had been POWs in Finland were being smuggled into Sweden.

Meanwhile, Soviet-occupied Europe was full of British ex-POWs who were gradually being rounded up, like those seen by author Alexander Thomsen in Berlin on 7 June 1945. 'I visited Dr Lehner's neighbours in Wannsee and there found four British soldiers,'[9] he wrote in *In the Name of Humanity*, describing the time shortly before he himself was seized by the Soviets and shipped to the Gulag.

The British government considered making a public protest. A draft press statement, dated 8 June 1945, read:

His Majesty's Government have abundant evidence of the presence in territories under Soviet control of many Allied stragglers . . . There is also the clearest evidence that the speedy overland repatriation of British subjects was deliberately obstructed or forbidden by Soviet officers in some cases after it had begun . . . Soviet authorities refused all permission for British aircraft to land behind Soviet lines to help in their reciprocal evacuation – even after all hostilities had ceased.[10]

## CHAPTER 24

# Fiddling the Figures

On 5 June 1945 Colonel W.P. Schweitzer, chief of the RAMPs Division at SHAEF, let it slip that 25,000 of the US servicemen who had been returned from German POW camps had originally been listed not as prisoners of war but as missing in action (MIA). This figure was announced by Allied Command from its headquarters in Paris and was reported in the *New York Herald Tribune* on 6 June.

The US War Department had listed some 77,500 US servicemen as 'prisoners taken' in the European theatre. These were confirmed prisoners, reported by the Germans, via the Red Cross. But by 5 June, nearly a week after the War Department had announced that 'substantially all' prisoners had been returned and no more MIAs were expected, only some 90,000 men had come back. If all the 77,500 listed US POWs had been returned, plus 25,000 MIAs, the Americans should have had a grand total of 102,500 liberated men, not 90,000.[1] So by the War Department's own figures, there was a shortfall of 12,500 known POWs – not to mention any other MIAs who might have been captured rather than killed by the Germans, and later taken by the Soviets.

This shortfall cannot be accounted for by men released later. In the second half of 1945 only 1,000 US POWs were repatriated, and just a handful of stragglers are reported after that.

Similar wonders have been worked on the British figures. According to the official returns, there were 199,592 registered POWs on 24 March 1945. But only 168,746 British POWs returned in all, giving a shortfall of 30,846.

Recently a document headed: 'Figures showing prisoners of war unrepatriated as at 0600 hrs on 8 June 1945' was discovered in Canadian archives. It shows that the British government still expected 31,809 British prisoners of war to come home after that date.[2] However, according to Brigadier Venables' report headed 'Repatriation of British, US and Other United Nations Prisoners of War as of 7 June 1945' and distributed on 11 June 1945, a total of 167,819 British POWs – 159,129 via SHAEF, 4,409 from AFHQ and 4,281 via Odessa – had already been returned by the 7th. In all, just 168,746 were returned.[3] So after 7 June only 927 British prisoners were returned, of the 31,809 expected – a shortfall of 30,882. This figure is suspiciously close to the 30,846 you get if you simply subtract the 168,746 returned from the 199,592 expected.

The British government maintains that all the POWs were returned and the 199,592 is an estimate, not a true figure. That is not true. The returns are broken down in detail by camp and by area. The 199,592 was not plucked from the air but built up by the Germans, month by month, over six years of war. After the German camp records were captured, no statement was issued saying the reported figures were wrong, nor have the German records been used to belie the figure 199,592 British POWs held since. What's more, the 8 June figure for unrepatriated POWs is also broken down. The British not returned home are made up of: Army – 7,156; Royal Navy and Royal Marines – 1,757; RAF – 11,218; Canadians – 3,292; Australians – 2,360; New Zealanders – 2,573; South Africans – 1,243; Indians – 1,627 and Colonials – 857, though the document remarks that another 660 unclassified Dominion or Colonial prisoners had been returned home.[4]

Brigadier Venables, British POW chief at SHAEF, skilfully minimised the shortfall in his 7 June report, which read: 'The total number of British and Dominion Prisoners of War repatriated is less than the total expected which is 175,000.' He was simply quoting the smaller 'British and Dominion' POW figure of 175,000, rather than the 'British and Commonwealth' figure of 199,500.

He went on: 'It is believed that there are more British and US PWs to be recovered and the War Office/War Department are endeavouring to ascertain the number and if possible the location of such personnel.'

Venables gave his own reasons why 'the total number of British repatriated may be less than anticipated'. In his report of 7 June 1945 he said this would be

> due to one or more of the following reasons: a) numbers in hospitals in Army Areas and on the continent; b) stragglers in Russian and SHAEF areas; c) those unwilling to declare themselves for one reason or another; d) unreported deaths, particularly those occurring on forced marches during the winter when the Germans attempted to prevent Allied personnel being recovered.

Venables also noted that 'the same assumptions applied equally to US and other nationals'. But the remarkable thing is that the Americans got back more prisoners of war than they expected. Only 76,854 were listed as captured, and 91,252 US POWs were actually returned.[5] This is because of 'the large number of missing in action personnel recovered as prisoners but never officially reported as prisoners, due to lack of time between their capture and recovery', Venables explained.

But if the same assumptions applied to the British – that more men were captured in the closing weeks of the war and not reported – they should have got back more than 199,592, not 30,000 less.

On 9 June 1945 the War Office in London finally answered Eisenhower's 1 June telegram asking how many British prisoners remained in Austria and Germany and 'in Russian rear'. The total given is 8,551, including about 1,400 Australians, Canadians, New Zealanders and South Africans.

Extraordinarily, evidence has been recently uncovered of a German camp for British and Commonwealth POWs in Austria that seems to be missing from the maps and documents so far released. It contained 101 Canadians, 454 Australians, 701 South Africans, 174 New Zealanders, 171 merchant seamen of all nations, 900 RAF and 6,050 British army personnel. That little lot adds up to exactly 8,551.

This figure is also remarkably close to the figure of 8,462 mentioned for British POWs in Austria alone. It is certainly a lot smaller than the 20,000 British POWs under Soviet control mentioned in the Clark Memorandum of 30 May, or the 31,000 unrepatriated prisoners listed on 8 June.

However, the telegram to Eisenhower indicates the possibility of more British ex-POWs elsewhere behind Soviet lines. It says: 'Interrogation of (ex PW) repatriates indicates some hundreds probably living in PLZF, POLAND, etc, but no figures.'

But even if there were only 8,551 behind Soviet lines on 9 June, no more than 927 ever returned.

While the War Office was being mealy-mouthed about the figures, Winston Churchill was urging President Truman to stand up to the Soviets, who were urging the Allies to withdraw to specified lines. On 9 June 1945 Churchill cabled Truman about the critical situation in Austria, where thousands of British and American prisoners remained captives of Tolbukhin's Third Ukrainian Division:

> Our missions have been ordered by Marshal Tolbukhin to leave by the 10th or 11th June. They have not been allowed to see anything outside the strict city limits . . . On the other hand the

Russians demand the withdrawal of the American and British forces in Germany . . . Would it not be better to refuse to withdraw on the main European front until a settlement has been reached on Austria?

Despite this plea the troops would be withdrawn anyway.

Averell Harriman was still complaining of the difficulties of keeping track of prisoners of war in the Soviet Union. In a top-secret cable on 11 June 1945 he reminded the Secretary of State that the Russians had never signed the Geneva Convention and that during the war 'they refused all attempts of enemy governments to come to an agreement regarding the treatment of POWs'. Harriman added that Russian repatriates were met by Soviet guards and marched to unknown destinations and that 'trainloads of repatriates have been going through Moscow enroute east. No contact may be had with the prisoners while the train remains in the Moscow railyards.'

Harriman went on to say that those repatriates accused of anti-state activity were probably being shot, while most were destined for forced-labour camps.

Harried by repeated complaints about the treatment of Soviet citizens in Allied hands, the British government responded in the press on 11 June 1945. The *Daily Telegraph* pointed out that very large numbers of the Soviet citizens liberated by the British and American armies had been serving in the Todt or other German military organisations. Many were wearing German uniforms. But realising that the vast majority had been forced to fight for the Germans, the British government decided to give them the same treatment as liberated POWs of any other Allied power.

Despite the almost complete lack of parallel help in Soviet-held territory, the *Telegraph* insisted that the fullest facilities had been afforded to Soviet repatriations teams.

The *Telegraph* went on to print a British statement which answered the Soviet complaints, point by point. Soviet citizens had only been held in the same camps as German prisoners in Egypt because General Sudakov, a Soviet official, had classified them as prisoners of war. Even then they were kept separate. They had not been subjected to anti-Soviet propaganda. And in response to complaints that some of them had been in contact with Poles, they were moved on to a new camp until they were embarked for Odessa.

The Soviets had complained that the repatriation of their men was slow, but that was because they had not provided any ships. British shipping had to be diverted from other duties.

The Soviets had complained that 1,712 Soviet citizens had been held in three camps in the United Kingdom and their presence concealed. But the British government had already explained that these camps were under American control, so informing the Soviets was not a matter for the British government. Besides, the Americans *had* told the Soviets, the previous autumn. General Vasiliev, head of the Soviet Mission in London, had visited the camps and, from January 1945, weekly reports were given to General Dragun, the Soviet liaison at SHAEF.

The Soviet complaint that 340 Soviet citizens in the UK had been withheld from them referred to a group of people who claimed that they were not Soviet citizens at all, on grounds that the British authorities accepted as valid. The majority were Poles from east of the Curzon line, the armistice line after the 1919–20 war of intervention which largely formed the pre-World War II Polish border. Arrangements had been made with the Soviet authorities for the joint examination of their cases.

Soviet prisoners in Norway had remained in captivity, under German guard after Germany's capitulation, the British government conceded. But there were no Allied forces in Norway when Germany surrendered. Keeping the Soviets in camps was the only way they could be fed. For a few days, the German guards had to be used to run the camps until other arrangements could be made.

Although the problem of repatriating the huge numbers of Soviet prisoners of war and displaced persons was vast, there were 130 Soviet repatriation officers to deal with it. Meanwhile, British POWs in Soviet hands were suffering unnecessary hardships.

On 12 June Truman cabled Churchill that, despite Churchill's objections, he had decided to withdraw Allied forces from the Soviet zone of Germany regardless of the POW situation in Austria. This greatly weakened the Allied bargaining position on the missing prisoners, as Churchill had pointed out. Perhaps Truman believed that strict adherence to the tripartite agreements would shame the Soviets into reciprocation.

Once the decision had been made, Churchill had no choice but to go along. On 14 June he cabled Truman: 'Obviously we are obliged to conform to your decision, and the necessary instruction will be issued . . .'

But Churchill had not entirely given up and urged a united front in the face of Stalin's demands: 'As to Austria I do not think we can make the commanders on the spot responsible for settling the outstanding questions . . . I consider the settlement of the Austrian problem is of equal urgency to the German matter . . .'

The treatment of prisoners of war was also raised in Parliament. Lord Dunglass, Undersecretary for Foreign Affairs, said that all the complaints made by Moscow over the treatment of their prisoners in British hands had been investigated but 'have proved to be quite unfounded'.[6]

In the House of Commons on 12 June Captain Gammans MP asked the Secretary of State for War if all British Commonwealth prisoners of war liberated by the Soviet armies had yet been returned to the UK and, if not, how many were unaccounted for.

Sir James Grigg replied:

Since the beginning of this year close on 168,000 British Commonwealth prisoners have reached this country or their country of origin overseas. This is nearly 3,500 more than the figure I gave on 5 June in reply to my hon. and gallant friend the Member for Wycombe (Sir A. Knox). There are still some prisoners in parts of central and southern Europe occupied by the Soviet Forces but figures are not available. Arrangements are being made for their transfer westwards to areas in British and American occupation.

Captain Gammans then asked: 'Have representations been made to the Soviet Government to supply lists of the names of these prisoners-of-war, in view of the fact that the war has been over for more than a month?'

Sir James replied: 'There certainly have been representations. I do not think it is a very hopeful line of [enquiry] to ask them to supply lists. The representations have been in the main, if not entirely, pressure to send the prisoners back to our lines.'

Sir Joseph Nall asked: 'How many are there still unaccounted for in the official records?'

Grigg said: 'I do not think my hon. Friend can have read the answer that I gave last week. I referred to that and suggested that it is impossible to give the exact figures.'[7]

Lord Croft had repeated Grigg's statement in the House of Lords in answer to a question from Lord Rennel.

The parliamentary answers to questions about missing prisoners of war were beginning to become rather vague. The government could barely conceal its unease and embarrassment. While it was undeniable that British POWs were still being held in the Soviet zone, without American support there was little the British could do about it. They still vaguely hoped that Stalin would do the decent thing and hand the men back. Slowly it dawned on them that kindly old Uncle Joe was not the ally that they had convinced themselves he was. He was an enemy who would use any weapon he could lay his hands on to destroy the already weakened British Empire. Quietly, the whole issue of POWs in Soviet hands began to slip off the political agenda.

The Soviet government did not take kindly to Sir James Grigg's statements in the House of Commons. A Reuters' report on them had been published in *Pravda* and *Trud* on 14 June under the headline 'Grigg's Unfriendly *Demarché* in Commons'.[8]

Sir Archibald Clark Kerr cabled London from Moscow, saying that under the circumstances he did not think it worth while asking the Soviets about new cases of liberated British prisoners of war in Hungary and Rumania until the Foreign Office supplied some more recent information. Protests had been made before to no avail. He could, of course, lodge a general complaint.[9]

## CHAPTER 25

# A Great Discrepancy

†

IN AN ATTEMPT to analyse Soviet actions towards Allied POWs, the US army thoroughly debriefed their POW contact officers. One of them, Lieutenant Colonel James D. Wilmeth, revealed in a secret report that he had failed in his mission of locating US prisoners in Poland because of Soviet non-compliance and obstructions.[1]

Another secret report came from Lieutenant Colonel William F. Fenell, who had been in charge of repatriations at Odessa when some 2,000 American prisoners in Poland disappeared.[2] He was extensively debriefed at SHAEF on 17 June 1945 by General Harper and an Intelligence officer.

Fenell said that at Odessa he and a number of other American officers had been 'called in by Russian Intelligence and grilled very minutely' on American army organisation and their personal and political beliefs. Fenell was questioned on his feeling about the Soviet Union. His personal attitude was that 'war against Russia would be a world catastrophe' and to prevent it 'strong American forces were needed in Europe and firm diplomacy to stand up for American rights'. This is not exactly the sort of treatment repatriation officers expected from their allies. One can imagine the howls of protest that would have followed any political interrogation of a Soviet repatriation officer in the West.

Colonel Fenell had worked with a Soviet major who told him that regardless of Fenell's rank or orders he would 'do as the Russians ordered because he was in the Soviet Union and was in their power'.

Fenell said that he had witnessed Soviet repatriates being shot out of hand when they debarked at Odessa and that, from what he had seen of the Soviet handling of German prisoners, he doubted 'very much that any significant number of them will ever return to their native land, since they will not be able to survive the treatment given them'.

On 18 June 1945 a secret OSS report gave further details of this 'informal interview with Lt. Col. William F. Fenell . . . who recently returned from Russia where he was stationed at . . . Odessa, since early this year, mainly as a contact man with the Russians on problems connected with repatriation of American prisoners of war freed by the Russians'. It said: 'Toward the end of his stay he apparently became persona non grata with the Russians for he was suddenly ordered to leave by the American command and take the first boat out of Odessa, regardless of where it was going.'

Under the subtitle of 'Treatment of American PWs' the OSS report of Fenell's debriefing read:

> American PWs freed by the Red Army were in the main treated very shabbily and came to hate the Russians. Many of them were robbed of watches, rings, and other personal possessions which they had managed to retain even after extended periods of captivity under the Germans. Their food at Odessa was very poor, consisting mainly of soup with cucumber in it and sour black bread. The Russians generally tended to throw obstacles in the way of repatriation, frequently calling off shipments at the last minute and insisting always upon clearance from Moscow for every prisoner released. American PWs at Odessa were guarded by Russian soldiers carrying loaded rifles with fixed bayonets, and Russian security was more stringent there than German security had been in the various Stalags and Oflags. A number of American officers who went to Poland at various times to coordinate the hunt for liberated PWs were ordered out very quickly at Russian insistence.[3]

Much the same treatment had been meted out to British ex-POWs.

Although Eisenhower had dropped the matter of missing US POWs he continued to press generally about prisoners of war and displaced persons. On 19 June 1945 he cabled to the US Military Mission in Moscow:

> A further approach to the Soviets regarding numbers of Western Europeans in Soviet-occupied area of Eastern Europe is urgently necessary. About 1,200,000 French have been repatriated. Less than 100,000 remain in SHAEF-occupied areas. French insist total POW and displaced persons is 2,300,000. Even allowing for several hundred thousand unaccounted trekkers, discrepancy is still very great. About 170,000 Dutch have been repatriated, with

less than 25,000 in the SHAEF area. Total Dutch estimate of deportees is 340,000.

So according to Eisenhower's figures up to 1,100,000 French and 145,000 Dutch POWs and DPs were still being held by the Soviets. Eisenhower pointed out that these figures were 'causing the Dutch and French governments considerable anxiety'.

In response to Eisenhower's cable, the US Military Mission in Moscow wrote to General Golubev on 20 June 1945, almost three weeks later:

> We have been requested by General Eisenhower to make an urgent appeal to you for an estimate of the number of displaced Western Europeans who are now in Soviet-occupied areas of Eastern Europe.
>
> Thus far, about 1,200,000 French have been repatriated. Less than 100,000 French remain in German areas occupied by British-American forces. This makes a total of 1,300,000 French accounted for, exclusive of those who still remain in Soviet-controlled territory. French authorities insist that the total number of prisoners of war and displaced persons amount to 2,300,000. Even allowing for several hundred thousand unaccounted individuals, there still remains a great discrepancy.
>
> About 170,000 Dutch have been repatriated. Less than 25,000 Dutch still remain in Germany under control of British-American forces. However, the Dutch authorities estimate that there were originally 340,000 Dutch nationals deported, thus leaving a great discrepancy.
>
> The Belgian authorities also reported a discrepancy, but it is comparatively smaller than those of the French and Dutch.

On 25 June 1945 the US Military Mission in Moscow sent Eisenhower a cable with the Soviet reply. It was not encouraging:

> . . . we represented [your] queries . . . to GOLUBEV and have received the following reply . . .
>
> '1. I do not have the exact data on the moving around of persons from Western Europe and therefore cannot say much about them.
>
> '2. I know that there have been freed by the Red Army: French: About 250,000 of which 202,456 persons have already been sent home and about 50,000 who are getting ready to be sent home. Belgians, 27,980 persons freed of which 25,920 have been sent home, the remainder in the process of being turned over.'

The discrepancy between the Soviet and SHAEF numbers for both the French and the Dutch is unsettling. But worse is the Soviet claim that they 'cannot say much about' the hundreds of thousands of Western European soldiers and citizens who had apparently disappeared in Soviet-occupied territory.

On 30 June 1945 the Soviets and the French signed an agreement in Moscow for the return of 500,000 to 600,000 French prisoners and deportees. Until that time only two members of the French repatriation mission had been allowed in Russian territory.[4] Despite this agreement, not all French prisoners of war were returned. In 1993 French authors and TV companies were still investigating their fate.

Nearly a month after he had claimed that 'only small numbers of US prisoners of war still remain in Russian hands', Eisenhower sent a 'secret, priority' cable to General Deane in Moscow. Dated 25 June 1945 it read: 'Possibility that several hundred American prisoners of war liberated from Stalag Luft I, Barth, are now confined by the Russian Army in the Rostock area [of East Germany] pending identi-fication as Americans is reported by an American who recently returned from such confinement.'

The American was Staff Sergeant Anthony Sherg. He had been one of 1,000 air force officers and NCOs who left Stalag Luft 1, at Barth, immediately before the Red Army took over the camp, when they heard a rumour that air transport had been laid on from Wismar. The group of ten in which Sergeant Sherg travelled was arrested by Soviet soldiers and held in jails in Bad Doberan, then Rostock. Ten other Americans were seen under similar circumstances in Rostock.

'Russian authorities demanded identification papers which no prisoner possessed, and refused to consider dog tags proof of the Americans' status,' Eisenhower wrote.

After twenty-five days in jail, Sherg escaped and made his way to the British lines. Eisenhower reported:

> From his own observations and conversations with other former prisoners he believes several hundred Americans may be held in like circumstances in the Wismar–Bad Doberan–Rostock area . . .
> Immediate representation should be made by you to Russians with a view to recovery of any British/United States PW who may at present be held under similar circumstances by the Russians.[5]

Deane put questions to the Soviet authorities but it was not until two and a half weeks later that he got any sort of answer. On 12 July he cabled Eisenhower: 'Golubev today informed me that he is still con-ducting an investigation concerning the possibility of American prisoners of war being in the Wismar–Bad Doberan–Rostock area . . . He has promised to let me know the results of the investigation and I will inform you.'[6]

General Deane eventually was to write in his memoirs that the POW crisis caused his darkest days in Russia. He also wrote: 'If in my sketchy account of the prisoner-of-war episode I have given the impression that I plumbed the depths of discouragement and despair, I can only say that that impression is correct.'[7]

While the Soviets were frustrating Allied contact officers at every turn, the British and US forces were living up to the Yalta Agreement. Soviet liaison officers were infused into the Allied command structure and went about their business of assisting Allied forces to repatriate, forcibly or otherwise, Soviet and Eastern European soldiers and citizens who were in British- and American-controlled territory. A cable dated 29 June 1945 from Eisenhower's Deputy Commander, British Air Marshal Tedder, informed London:

> . . . we now have 153 Soviet Liaison Officers working under the direction of Major General Dragun who is charged with the responsibility of assisting us in the problem of repatriation . . . Each Army Group has an organization to handle repatriation matters, and in these organizations we have woven Soviet Liaison Officers who are doing valuable work.

But the Soviets were simply not reciprocating.

'Before the Halle Conference we had made numerous attempts to visit PW camps in the Russian zone and always met a firm refusal,' Tedder wrote. Even the tour of camps in the Soviet zone promised at the Halle Conference never materialised. Tedder reported:

> After the Halle Conference General Golubev asked to visit camps where Russians were being kept. We agreed and asked him for permission to visit camps in the Russian zone. He agreed to allow one of our Officers to visit five camps. One of my representatives started on the trips accompanied by a Russian Major who stated he had the necessary orders. After visiting the first and nearest camp the Russian officer produced orders signed by General Golubev restricting our Officer's visit to the one camp. This is the only instance of Soviet authorities permitting US or British Officers to visit camps in their area, which is in sharp contrast to the liberal policy pursued by us.[8]

In the Mediterranean theatre, Alexander reported similar experiences. On 24 July 1945, he cabled London:

1. I should like to point out that I have given the Russian authorities every help, facility and assistance to go where they like in Italy and to see anything which affects or interests them.

2. With regard to these camps they must realise that if we wished to hide anything from them we would not give them the freedom they now enjoy . . .

3. The treatment given to British representatives in Russian occupied territory is very different.[9]

Despite the fact that Allied repatriation officers were denied access to the camps in the Soviet zone, Eastern Europe was closed and allegations concerning the fate of tens of thousands of Allied prisoners of war were flying to and fro, the 1947 RAMPs report says blithely:

The information available indicates that no special problems were encountered in recovery and evacuation of ex-prisoners during the month of June [1945] and that all United States ex-prisoners were recovered or accounted for during June, as these operations with respect to our own personnel were considered complete at the end of June.

# CHAPTER 26

# Poland and Potsdam

✝

ON 1 JULY 1945 *The Times* of London reported complaints made by Australian ex-POWs about their treatment by the Soviets: 'Hatred, suspicion and ill-treatment were the portion of Australians who escaped from German prison camps into Russia, according to Gunner Vivian Cox, formerly of the 3rd Tank Regiment.'

Cox had recently returned to Sydney via Odessa after being a prisoner for four years. He had escaped from Poland and spent two months in Russia, during which, he said, he was confined in filthy quarters under armed guard.

> In two months in Russia I received no food but boiled barley and black bread. The Russians refused to let any of us send messages home, and cables we tried to send to the British Consul were torn up in front of us. Everywhere we met hatred and suspicion. Polish home rule was just a joke and a Russian corporal had more real power than a Polish general.[1]

Despite the unresolved POW problem in Austria and indications that the new Polish authorities were nothing more than Russian puppets, on 1 July 1945 the Allied armies withdrew from occupied areas of the Soviet zone and, on 5 July, full diplomatic recognition was given to the Polish communist regime. Orders were issued that no more Germans were to be allowed through Allied lines. The American and British armies refused to accept the surrender of large numbers of German soldiers, who had put up stiff resistance while retreating from the Red Army, and had been wandering about the countryside ever since. They were turned back to the Soviet lines, captured by the Soviets and shipped into forced-labour camps which eventually held over four million Germans and other Axis prisoners, many of whom disappeared for ever.

Slowly the Iron Curtain was falling across Europe. Vast numbers of people would find themselves trapped on the wrong side of it.

On 12 July 1945 the War Office cabled the British Military Mission in Moscow with information about British ex-POWs at Hindenburg, Beuthen, Sosnowiec and Gleiwitz. The Military Mission was to ask the Soviet authorities about these men and arrange for them to be returned to Britain as soon as possible.

The answer the following day indicates a subtle shift in British policy over the former prisoners of war, after months of banging its head against a brick wall.

'You will have gathered from my previous telegrams that the Russians have been as unhelpful as possible over the recovery of ex-PW,' Archer cabled back. The Military Mission would continue to put general enquiries about missing British POWs to the Soviet authorities, 'but without more definite information, such as names, there is little hope of a useful answer'. And Archer recommended that the War Office would stand a better chance if they dealt with the Polish authorities in Warsaw.[2]

On 13 July 1945 Foreign Secretary Anthony Eden approved withholding a Russian family which the Soviets were demanding be forcibly repatriated in accordance with the Yalta Agreement.

The Prime Minister's office spelt out the policy quite clearly:

> Under [the] agreement signed at Yalta we are bound to return to the Soviet Union all undoubted Soviet citizens (ie persons coming from territories within the 1939 boundaries of the Soviet Union). The question of the use of force for this is another matter, but it would be very dangerous to suggest to the Soviet government that we claimed the right to keep undoubted citizens if they do not wish to be repatriated.[3]

The husband and wife had been captured during the liberation of France. Although the husband claimed to be Polish, both were undoubtedly Russian, but their daughter had been born during their captivity in England and was, therefore, technically British. The parents had made friends with some English families, who pledged their support, and the Foreign Office were afraid of a public outcry if the family were sent to their deaths at the hands of Stalin's henchmen. The matter was referred upwards to Lord Dunglass – who later, as Sir Alex Douglas-Home, became prime minister – then to Eden.

Eden eventually agreed to let the family stay in Britain. He wrote to the Foreign Office officials handling the case: 'All right, keep the family. But delay our answer as long as we can so that we can get as many people out as we can. I have some fear of reprisals.'[4]

The fact that Eden feared reprisals indicates that there were still British POWs in Soviet hands in mid-July. The War Office was almost certain that some 200 British former prisoners of war were in hiding in Poland, but the Foreign Office pointed out that their emergence after a period of hiding 'may not be without risk'.[5]

The newly installed British chargé d'affaires in Warsaw, Robert Hankey, was already having problems with liberated British POWs there. Three had written to him and he cabled the Foreign Office asking for general instructions on what to do with British soldiers in Poland.

'As it is evident that Russian authorities have in many cases ignored the Yalta Agreement about freed British subjects, I hesitate to hand them over to the Russians for conveyance to the Elbe or Berlin unless so instructed,' Hankey wrote. Instead, he had issued the soldiers documents stating that they were under the protection of the embassy. Hankey pointed out that the French Ambassador was also ignoring their repatriation agreement with the Soviets and was smuggling French citizens out of Poland via Katowice and Prague, but he did not want to send British POWs by that route until a British consul was established in Katowice.[6]

Three weeks later Hankey was still having trouble. On 8 August 1945 he cabled the Foreign Office: 'Ex-prisoners of war outside Warsaw are not being brought into Warsaw for the moment because conditions here make organisation of an adequate collecting centre impossible.' He was also concerned about whether the 300 zloty a day he was handing out to British prisoners would have to be paid back.[7]

Robert Hankey went on to become head of the Foreign Office Northern Department in 1946. During a debate in the House of Lords on 17 March 1976 the then Lord Hankey claimed that the government would have been subjected to an irresistible storm of criticism if it had not forcibly repatriated unwilling Soviets – because it would have imperilled the return of British prisoners liberated by the Red Army.[8]

The Americans were doing no better. Out of thousands of liberated US POWs known to have been in Poland, only 231 had been registered by the Polish between 1 February 1945 and 28 May 1945, according to the US Embassy in Warsaw in a message dated 18 July 1946. In London, General Bor-Komorowski of the Polish Resettlement Corps spoke darkly of 'American flyers who are guests of the Russians'.

Some clue as to the fate of these people may have been given at the Potsdam Conference, where the Big Three wartime victors met on the outskirts of Berlin on 15 July 1945.

In his memoirs, Churchill says that, during a disagreement over Poland's border and population shifts, Stalin complained of being short of labour for food, metal and coal production because of the war casualties. When Churchill also complained of coal shortages Stalin said: 'Then use German prisoners in the mines, that it what I am doing.' A little later Stalin added: 'Our position is even more difficult than yours, we lost over five million men in the war, and are desperately short of labour.'

Details of the discussion about prisoners of war and forced repatriation at Potsdam remain highly classified to this day. Indeed, there may not even be a record of them. In his account of the Potsdam Conference senior American diplomat Robert Murphy remarked: 'The American Government made no official transcript of the proceedings because over zealous security officers ruled against admitting stenographers to plenary sessions.'[9] But it is known that POWs and forced repatriations were discussed at Potsdam. Harold Macmillan mentioned the fact to the then US Ambassador to Italy, Alexander Kirk. Field Marshal Alexander was also informed.

It was at the Potsdam Conference that Truman told Stalin of the Western Allies' 'new weapon' – the atomic bomb which had been tested for the first time on 16 July, the day after the conference started. On 26 July 1945 the Big Three sent an ultimatum to the Japanese demanding their immediate surrender, otherwise Japan 'would lay herself open to complete and utter destruction'.

In closing his account of Potsdam, Churchill says: 'I take no responsibility beyond what is here set forth for any of the conclusions reached at Potsdam . . . There were many other matters on which it was right to confront the Soviet Government, and also the Poles . . . I had in view, namely, a "showdown" at the end of the Conference.'

But Churchill was not there at the end of the Conference. Defeated in the July 1945 election, he was replaced at the conference table by Clement Attlee.

The change of government had no effect on POW policy. Attlee and his Foreign Secretary, Ernest Bevin, had been members of the War Cabinet – Attlee as Deputy Prime Minister, Bevin as Minister of Labour and National Service. Indeed, every British prime minister until Harold Wilson in 1964 had first-hand knowledge of the POW problem.

On 26 July the Military Mission in Moscow informed General Golubev that telegrams had been received in the United Kingdom from

Privates Turner and Ashmore, at a hospital in Kharkov, whose presence had never been notified by the Soviets. And on 1 August Mr Roberts at the British Embassy again complained of the treatment meted out to British POWs, including assaults on those returned from Odessa. The Soviets, he complained, were still maintaining that Odessa was the only collecting point for ex-POWs and the only place Allied officers were allowed to visit. He wrote:

> The Odessa route is now closed so far as liberated British POWs are concerned, and except for the notification and prompt repatriation of any further British personnel who may still remain in Soviet hospitals or camps (to which my government attach great importance) there would appear to be no longer any action which the Soviet authorities could usefully take in the matter.

# CHAPTER 27

# Intelligence Operations

✝

SINCE THE BEGINNING of April 1945 a little-known aerial photography operation named Casey Jones, conceived by OSS General William Donovan, served as secret cover for attempts to pinpoint American and British POW locations for future rescue or negotiated release.

Sixteen squadrons of American and British bombers (some of them unmarked) photographed some two million square miles of Soviet-occupied Europe at the very time thousands of Allied POWs were being secretly withheld in Soviet camps.

It is known that a series of secret air battles took place between the Soviets and the Allies from April through to August 1945, with the loss of many aircraft. In July 1945 two British Anson bombers engaged in aerial reconnaissance photography were shot down by the Soviets near Klagenfurt in eastern Austria where the 300 British POWs who had escaped into Alexander's lines had reported that other British and US POWs were being shipped eastwards.

In August 1945 the Soviets filed more than 300 airspace violations complaints against the Americans and British. The Soviets, of course, knew precisely what was going on in operation Casey Jones. US Air Force Lieutenant Colonel Juergan Kuczynski, who was stationed in Strategic Bombing Command near Frankfurt and was involved with the aerial photography, was later discovered to be a Soviet agent.

Similar operations took place in the Far East. On 29 August 1945 a US B-29 bomber was shot down over Korea on a POW rescue mission.

However, aerial reconnaissance operations like Casey Jones or the operations of secret agents could not be relied on to pinpoint locations of prisoners if the Soviets continued to conceal them and move them to the depths of Siberia.

On 6 August 1945 with the obliteration of Hiroshima, the Soviets – and the Western Allies – saw the power of the atomic bomb. Stalin declared war on Japan on 8 August 1945, the day the second atomic

Top: When Boris Yeltsin visited George Bush in Washington in June 1992, the Russian president said that American POWs from World War II, Korea and Vietnam had ended up in Soviet labour camps – and that some of them might still be alive. No one ever asked him how many British POWs had been taken, or whether there were any survivors.

Bottom: At the height of Stalin's power, there were more than 28 million people in the Soviet Gulag. Often the camps were in remote parts of Siberia, like this one in Marble Canyon of the Kodar mountain range in northern Chita region. Escape was impossible and 30,000 British POWs could easily have been swallowed up.

Top: The shape of the post-war world was decided at this table at Yalta, in the Crimea, in February 1945. Churchill, Roosevelt and Stalin also came to an understanding about the return of prisoners of war, liberated from German prison camps. The failure of this agreement left tens of thousands of Allied POWs in Soviet hands.

Bottom: While the 'Big Three' – Churchill, Roosevelt and Stalin – decided the big issues in the Livadia Palace, Yalta, their foreign ministers – Eden, Stettinius and Molotov – thrashed out the details at the Vorontsov Palace. Their bungling of the wording of the Yalta agreement would lead to an exchange of stiff protests between them later.

Top: Although Churchill and Stalin were all smiles in front of the cameras, Stalin knew that Churchill had tried to strangle the Bolshevik state at birth in 1919. Stalin also knew, through Kim Philby and other Soviet agents, that Churchill was planning to attack the Soviet Union again, once Hitler was dead.

Bottom: Churchill, Roosevelt and Stalin with the foreign ministers Eden, Stettinius and Molotov behind them in the grounds of the Livadia Palace, Yalta, on 11 February 1945. The agreement the wartime allies had just signed laid the foundations for the Cold War, which would soon have its own prisoners of war and other casualties, just like any other war. The other three in the picture are, from left to right, Lord Leathers, Sir Alexander Cadogan and Averell Harriman.

Top: Infantrymen of the US First Army meet Soviet soldiers from the Ukrainian First Army on the damaged bridge at Torgau. The River Elbe quickly became the dividing line between the Soviet and Allied zones.

Bottom: For a Soviet citizen, not to have fought to the last drop of blood for the motherland was the ultimate disgrace. Soviet prisoners of war found themselves marched straight out of German prison camps into Soviet labour camps. Large numbers of Allied POWs went with them.

The defeated German armies were paraded through Moscow on their way to Soviet labour camps. Of four million taken, one and a half million returned. Many men of other nationalities were caught up in this human tide. With twenty-one million Soviet citizens dead, they were desperately short of labour.

By the time the victorious allies reconvened in the Berlin suburb of Potsdam in July 1945, Roosevelt had died and been replaced by his vice-president of eighty-two days, Harry Truman. And before Churchill could stage his promised showdown with Stalin at the end of the conference, he had been voted out of office and replaced by the Labour leader Clement Attlee. Of the Big Three, only Stalin remained in power.

Top: Two of the major players in the 1945 POW crisis: Air Marshal Tedder points out an Allied fly-pass to Marshal Zhukov at the Potsdam Conference.

Bottom: General Eisenhower thought the POW crisis might be resolved by Marshal Zhukov who, Eisenhower believed, would depose Stalin. They met at Potsdam with General Montgomery.

Top: Field Marshal Alexander turned up at Potsdam too. He tried to alert his superiors to the fact that the Soviets were not returning Allied prisoners of war from the camps in Austria. He also stopped the handover of the Cossacks when the Soviets failed to hand back British POWs in exchange.

Bottom: The Potsdam Conference had its round table too. At Yalta, Roosevelt felt that the Western Allies were negotiating from a position of weakness because of the concessions Churchill had already made to Stalin at their meeting at Moscow. Here, at Potsdam, Stalin was completely in control.

Top: Even though the Western Allies told him that they had successfully tested an atomic bomb, at Potsdam Stalin refused to back down over Poland and rejected a call for free elections in Rumania, Bulgaria and Hungary. He did join in the ultimatum sent to Japan, but did not declare war until the dropping of the atomic bomb on Hiroshima on 6 August 1945 assured an easy victory.

Bottom: Several British ex-POWs saw the inside of the famous Lubianka prison in Moscow. Military policeman James Allan, who escaped from Stalag 20A at Thorn in Poland, witnessed the first German air-raid on Moscow from a KGB cell there, before being sent to a labour camp.

Top: The Russian camp at Tambov saw a lot of Allied prisoners during the war and after it. Here, camp commandant Yevdokimov addresses French prisoners released to fight with de Gaulle. Allied citizens held there later were not so lucky.

Bottom: The Frenchmen had been captured in German uniforms. Here they march from Tambov in Russian uniforms before being sent to Tehran.

Top: These three German prisoners of war were released in 1953, after the Soviets had said that they held no more German prisoners of war. All returning German POWs were interrogated by the Allied authorities.

Bottom: Many returning German POWs said that they had seen British prisoners in captivity in Russia. They reported that there were special camps for foreigners and that British POWs were working in tank factories and radar installations.

Top: Unlike World War II, the Geneva Conventions were not applied in the Korean War and no official lists of prisoners of war were exchanged. However, Chinese newsagencies returned pictures of British POWs.

Bottom: Although these pictures were returned without identification, it was a relatively simple matter to find out who these men were from the family and friends of the missing.

Top: Guarded by Chinese soldiers with rifles at the ready, these British prisoners of war were posed for the cameras in a North Korean prison camp. Among them, recognisable from their cap badges, are men of the Gloucester Regiment.

Bottom: The last two years of the Korean War were fought solely over the POW issue. The United Nations debriefed returning POWs, some of whom had seen other UN POWs who did not come back.

French serviceman Paul Catrain was captured in 1940. After being discovered by a journalist in the Ukraine, Catrain returned to France in 1993. He had made his presence known to the French embassy in Moscow in 1980, to no avail.

Top, right: Grave markers are a rare thing in the Gulag. Most inmates were buried in mass graves. This rudimentary cross was found in an abandoned graveyard outside one of the huge mining camps at Vorkuta in Arctic Siberia.

Top, left: This large cross marks a mass grave near the Yur-Shor mine in the former Soviet republic of Komi. Millions died anonymously in the Gulag. Some of them were British. Russian records may yet show exactly who they were.

Bottom: The camps at Vorkuta have now been demolished, but former inmates still live in the area. People who survived the horrendous conditions in Vorkuta said that they saw British there.

On the bleak landscape of Vorkuta, there is now a monument to the victims of Stalinism – including British POWs – who died in the mines there.

bomb was dropped on Nagasaki, ensuring the end of the war. By then US policy-makers saw that, although the US had long urged the Soviets to join in the war against Japan, they were no longer needed. Nevertheless before Japan surrendered on 2 September, the Red Army proceeded to swallow up huge tracts of Manchuria, half the Korean peninsula and the northern islands of Japan. Soon the Soviets were demanding a place in the postwar occupation of Japan.

As the Red Army drove deep into Manchuria, Korea and China, they uncovered some Japanese POW camps where British and American prisoners were being held. During the closing days of the war with Japan, US military Intelligence 'Mercy Teams' were sent into China and Manchuria to arrange for the wellbeing of the Allied POWs. Generally, Japanese troop commanders co-operated with the Mercy Teams, but Soviets and Chinese communists denied Mercy Teams access to camps in areas under their control. American OSS teams who were searching for Allied POWs in Manchuria in August and September 1945 met with hostile and sometimes violent reactions from the Soviets and communist Chinese. In one incident OSS agent John Birch was killed.

Moscow sent a delegation to Hanoi to forcibly repatriate any French Foreign Legionnaire POWs held by the Japanese who were citizens of the Soviet Union or of any of the Eastern bloc nations. These men were duly surrendered to the Soviets by the British occupation forces.

An estimated 800,000 Japanese prisoners of war out of Japan's million-man army on the mainland were marched into Siberian forced-labour camps. In his memoirs, *Speaking Frankly*, Truman's Secretary of State James F. Byrnes conservatively estimates that half a million of them were still there in 1947 and probably remained there for ever. Of these men 316,339 were known by name or had been heard from while in captivity, according to one recently uncovered report from General MacArthur's headquarters dated 12 December 1950.

Some few thousands who did come out of the camps in the 1950s were debriefed on their experiences in the Gulag. Eight boxes of Japanese ex-POW debriefings once existed. Seven are now in America's National Archives. American researchers say the other one contains hundreds of references to large numbers of American POWs in the forced-labour camps. It remains secretly held by the CIA, according to both a senior archivist and a former top CIA officer they have interviewed.

There are also said to be similar boxes of the debriefs of the small number of German POWs who came out of the Soviet Union during the Adenauer era. These so-called Wringer Reports are still classified top secret.

At the time General Patton was one of the few who criticised Soviet conduct – and was publicly castigated for it. In his diary entry for 8 August 1945, he wrote: 'Lt. General Gowlina of the Polish Army came to see me . . . He told me some of their methods . . . more than two million Poles have been taken to Russia for slave labor.'

That same day, Patton added a cryptic note: 'Strange to say, I had a letter from General Sibert [G-2 12th Army] on the question of the Russians, so that apparently for the first time in his career, he is on to a good scent.'

General Sibert was Eisenhower's chief of Intelligence for the Communications Zone and was deeply involved in POW matters and Soviet repatriations. It was General Sibert who had 'discovered' – and, in August 1945, was pushing for the use of – Hitler's Intelligence chief, General Reinhard Gehlen. Gehlen's network of high-level Intelligence agents was still in place in Russia and Eastern Europe. He and forty of his top aides surrendered to the Americans. It was not difficult for Sibert to convince the War Department of the value of Gehlen, his agents and his extensive files – he had fifty-two crates of them hidden near his chalet in Bavaria.

The only top-ranking SS man to be captured during the war, Gehlen was flown to Washington, wearing the uniform of an American general. Sibert became Gehlen's army Intelligence controller in some of the first American covert actions of the Cold War. Gehlen's organisation became a unit of the CIA, after its founding in 1947, and later formed the core of Federal Germany's Intelligence service, the Bundesnachrichtendienst, with Gehlen as its director. The Bundesnachrichtendienst, naturally, handled the Wringer Reports.

On 10 August 1945 SACMED political adviser and US Ambassador to Italy Alexander Kirk sent a cable to the new Secretary of State James F. Byrnes:

We have learned from our British colleague [Harold Macmillan] that in accordance with Churchill's promise to Stalin at Potsdam, General Basilov will arrive at AFHQ in next few days to arrange visit to British POW camp near Cisenatico. Russians claim that some ten thousand occupants of this camp are Soviet citizens whereas British claim they are Poles from east of Curzon Line. Field Marshal Alexander was not enthusiastic about receiving this mission but decided to do so when he was informed that Churchill had given his promise at Potsdam.

General Basilov was a deputy POW repatriations commissar. He demanded the forcible repatriation of 'approximately 30,000 Soviet citizens' in the Polish Corps in Italy, who had fought heroically on the Allied side – a demand Alexander continued to refuse. More contentious was the Ukrainian SS division, who had fought for the Germans and were being held by the British in Italy. At a meeting with Alexander on 18 August, Basilov demanded their return under the Yalta Agreement.

While the Cossacks had been high-profile horsemen with little place in modern warfare, the Ukrainian 'Galizien' division was a highly disciplined, well-trained unit of 10,000 dedicated anti-communists. They were not returned. The British declared, falsely, that they were Polish from east of the Curzon line. After the forced repatriations had finished, the Ukrainians were moved from Italy to Britain for eventual resettlement in the Empire.

The British Embassy's reluctance to continue its futile protests to the Soviet government had been noted. On 10 August 1945 the Foreign Office cabled Moscow:

> In view of withdrawal of Red Army from Poland . . . I agree there is now no need to approach Soviet Government and that we can deal exclusively with Polish authorities whom His Majesty's Chargé d'Affaires in Warsaw will no doubt keep up to mark.
> 2. I agree that the case of the three men mentioned in Warsaw telegram No. 7 [Stamp, Dimmock and Nesbitt] calls for protest when full details are available but prefer to take the matter up with Soviet Ambassador in London . . . since Soviet authorities deliver all their protests through this channel. At the same time I shall request that all other British ex-prisoners be released and sent to Warsaw for repatriation together with any men who may be still in Soviet hospitals.

But plainly His Majesty's chargé d'affaires in Warsaw was not keeping the authorities there up to the mark.

> You may be interested to know that 21 Army Group have sent us copies of Field Security Reports on two British PsW who have been in Russian hands in Poland [the Political Division of the Control Commission for Germany wrote to the POW Department in London on 11 August]. These reports indicate that there are still a number of British and Allied PsW in Poland who have not been repatriated. The following places are mentioned as centres where they are held up: Bromberg, Graudans, Deuenberg. Both

prisoners complained of ill-treatment by the Russians. One stated that he had been put with German PWs in Warsaw and kept without food and with only meagre clothing because, so the Russians told him, he had not fought well enough. The other stated that the Russians had not treated him as an Allied national and that they had taken away from him all his possessions except his clothes.

Now that there was a clear division of duties between the embassy in Moscow and the chargé d'affaires in Warsaw, Whitehall began preparing the case of the 'three men' mentioned in the 10 August telegram to Moscow, to present to the Soviet Embassy in London. On 14 August 1945 A.J. Gardener at the POW Department of the Foreign Office wrote to Major R.G.L. Moore at PW5, the Directorate of Prisoners of War, about Privates Stamp and Dimmock who had escaped from a German POW camp in January 1945. 'From then until July [they] worked for the Soviet authorities contrary to the provisions of the Yalta Agreement,' Gardener wrote. 'In addition, they report that they were robbed of their watches, boots and greatcoats.'[1]

On 16 August 1945 Mr Hankey in Warsaw turned in a full report to the Secretary of State:

Private Raymond Stamp 4452668, 2nd Battalion Durham Light Infantry and Private Harry Dimmock 4975907, 8th Batt. Sherwood Foresters were sent on February 18th from Stalag XX B at Wilenburn to No.13 Working Camp at Langenau, from which they escaped on the 21st January 1945 on the approach of the Red Army, fearing that they might be marched westwards into Germany. They hid for two or three days in a house at Heinrichschau [a handwritten footnote says this should be Heinrikan 80 km NE of Deutsch-Eylau in East Prussia], where they were joined by Private James Pegg (1874992 of 55th Field Company, Royal Engineers) and a deported Ukrainian girl with whom he had escaped from German forced labour.

The house was visited by Red Army troops on their arrival in the village and Stamp, after being relieved of his wristwatch and great coat, was brought before a Russian NCO interpreter who told him that he would be given papers for repatriation via Odessa. They waited from 9am to 4pm for the appearance of an officer competent to issue the papers until the interpreter, who was sympathetic, grew tired of waiting and sent Stamp back to the house from which he had been taken. Dimmock had remained there unnoticed. No further steps were taken by the Russian detachment, which moved on west.

Pegg and the Ukrainian girl (whom he later married in Warsaw) had some time previously escaped from a column of slave workers being marched to the west, but had been caught by the Gestapo. Pegg pretended that he was a Russian and they were sent to a concentration camp for Russian civilians at Dershau, whence they were taken to Hexengrund, near Gdynia, which was uncovered by the Russians on 4 April. Pegg contrived to see the Russian commandant at Gdynia and explained who he was. He then boarded a lorry going in the direction of Bydgoszcz in the hope of finding a British officer, whom the commandant believed to be there. However, the lorry went instead to Heinrichschau and Pegg found himself and the girl set to work as cowherds together with Stamp and Dimmock on a farm under the control of a Soviet Mission sent to requisition livestock, and to organize the despatch of butter and beet-sugar to the Soviet Union.

After his arrival Pegg, who had learned to speak Russian, was able to some extent to prevent the continued maltreatment of Stamp and Dimmock by the Russian guards under whom they were made to work. Their hours were from 4am to 9pm every day. Their food was insufficient and frequently rotten. In more than four months they were unable to obtain even the smallest amount of milk, butter or sugar with which to sustain themselves. On one occasion Stamp and Dimmock were sent to the guard-house for 15 hours without food by a drunken guard who picked a quarrel with them. They were unable to see an officer and were sent straight back to work on being released. As a result of malnutrition they suffered badly from bleeding gums, but they were denied any medical attention and compelled to continue work. On two other occasions Dimmock was sent to the guard-house for refusing to work when he felt too ill to do so.

The Ukrainian girl was regarded by the Russians as a collaborator with the Germans, by whom she had been deported, and was accordingly made to share in the indignities of the other persons doing forced labour on the farm. The three soldiers protected her from assault by the Russian guards. Dimmock himself witnessed the rounding up and raping of twelve-year-old girls by the guards. On the night of 12 July 1945, the three soldiers and the girl escaped to Deutsch-Eylau, where Pegg explained their situation to the Russian commandant. He gave them a warrant to go by train to Torun, whence they came to Warsaw on the 14 July with the assistance of the Polish Red Cross.[2]

On 8 January 1946 Foreign Secretary Ernest Bevin protested to the Soviets over the treatment of Stamp, Dimmock and Pegg. He also expressed some pique at the way the Soviets had been responding to his queries. 'His Majesty's Government note with some surprise that the Soviet Government should seek to disqualify their representations on grounds which apply equally to the far more numerous complaints received from the Soviet Government in respect of Soviet citizens liberated by British armed forces,' he wrote. At the same time, the Foreign Office was lodging complaints about two other ex-POWs, Hales and Newdick.

On 15 January 1946 the Soviet Embassy in London said that it was impossible to check out the complaints lodged by the British and New Zealand governments – Newdick was a New Zealander. He had not passed through Cracow, the Soviets said, and the Foreign Office's note did not give the names of the individuals involved in his maltreatment. Consequently, the Soviet government could not accept the British and New Zealand governments' protest.[3]

Pressed again, the Soviets replied on 1 February that British ex-prisoners of war Stamp, Dimmock, Pegg, Hales and Newdick had avoided returning home by the organised route. Having converted themselves into fugitives, they had tried to hide from the Soviet military authorities who, consequently, 'could not take care of them, and can bear no responsibility for the condition in which these individuals found themselves'.

Miss Maclean at the Foreign Office noted that these men would no doubt have been delighted to have returned by an organised route if they had been given the opportunity.

On 20 August 1945 the War Office reported that George Hayhurst of the Royal Engineers and two other British prisoners of war were at Zimnevody Lager, Bromberg. There was another man, Thomas Kavin of the Seaforth Highlanders, at Sypniewo, sixty kilometres northeast of Bromberg. And the French repatriation officer in Prague reported fifteen British subjects, probably ex-prisoners of war, at Ruckers, a village between Nachod and Glatz.[4]

While these protests and counter-protests were circulating behind the scenes, Major Turton MP had tabled a parliamentary question asking the Secretary of State for War how many British officers and men who had been prisoners of the Germans had not yet been repatriated and how many of these were in territory now controlled by the USSR and awaiting repatriation.

Major Moore at the War Office suggested a reply along the following lines:

> The number of British Commonwealth (excluding India) officers and men who were prisoners of war in Germany and who have not been recovered or accounted for by Allied Forces is 690. All prisoners of war notified by the Soviet Authorities having been released by them have been repatriated with the exception of one officer and nine other ranks who were in hospital at Kharkov.

Moore asked Gardener at the Foreign Office to have this reply cleared by the Northern Department. It seems to have passed their scrutiny, as it was given almost word for word in the House of Commons by James Lawson on 21 August 1945, adding only that the figure of 690 was as of 11 August 1945.[5]

The reply is a masterpiece of underhanded wording. It refers, not to prisoners of the Germans, but only to 'men who were prisoners of war in Germany'. Many of the missing POWs had been held in Poland, Czechoslovakia and Austria. Germany, too, had changed its borders radically since 7 May. East Prussia had been divided between Russia and Poland. The new Polish administration had also taken over Pomerania and Silesia, moving the eastern border of wartime Germany hundreds of miles to the west. The exchange between Moore and Gardener shows just how disingenuous this answer was. Under the heading 'Further information for the Secretary of State', the civil servants added: 'It is known that there are still a number of ex-prisoners of war who are living in Poland and Czechoslovakia with local families.'

## CHAPTER 28

# A Show of Force

†

AND STILL THE complaints and counter-complaints continued. On 22 August 1945 the Commissariat of Foreign Affairs told Sir Archibald Clark Kerr that the Soviet government saw no grounds for their complaints about the treatment of British ex-POWs. It also pointed out that there had never been camps for British ex-POWs at Lvov or Volkovysk and that 'British repatriation officers who visited Lublin in the first half of March had the possibility of convincing themselves that no camp for British prisoners of war existed in Lublin'. These were breathtaking lies.

While the British made out that they had complied strictly with the provisions of the Yalta Agreement, the Soviets had established at the Potsdam Conference that 10,000 Soviet citizens, about whom the British authorities had not considered it necessary to inform them, were being held at Camp 5 near Cisenatico in Italy. Another 30,000 were being held secretly in Germany. Soviet repatriation officers were not allowed into those camps. Soviet citizens were being attacked there and propaganda hostile to the Soviet Union was being spread. The Soviets demanded immediate admission to the camps and information on other camps where Soviet citizens were being held.[1] Clearly this gave the Soviet authorities yet more reasons to continue holding Allied men.

As complaints via the Soviet Embassy in London and the British Embassy in Moscow were making no headway, the British government tried routing its protests through the Military Mission in Moscow again. On 25 August 1945 the War Office asked them to enquire about Sergeant Clarke of the Royal Artillery who had been reported by civilians to be in Soviet headquarters at Neurode and was 'possibly unwilling to leave'. The Military Mission was also asked to investigate the case of '19 exPW some with wives reported to have been sent by Russians to Liegnitz during the last 10 days'.[2] And they should find out what was happening to Private Lythgoe of the South Staffordshire Regiment who was 'shortly leaving hospital at Bad Aldheide' and Lance Corporal J.S. Russell of the Duke of Wellington Regiment who was 'staying with Lythgoe at same place'.[3]

The Military Mission was not prepared to play ball, though. Tired of banging their heads on brick walls too, on 28 August 1945 they cabled back to the War Office:

> Should be glad to know whether you agree my policy previously stated that this Mission shall not (repeat not) take up with Soviet General Staff cases where ex-PWs are in Polish territory.
>
> If you agree this policy, you will no doubt not wish Mission to take up cases at Neurode and Liegnitz which are in ex-German now Polish territory. Bad Aldheide is not shewn on available atlases but sounds in same category.
>
> Must point out that, as you probably know, results of requests to Soviet repatriation department have been almost uniformly fruitless and while we are anxious to do everything possible to recover ex-PW, feel that best results will be obtained by limiting requests to those occasions where demands for information and locations of ex-PW are most clearly justifiable.[4]

One can sympathise with the British Military Mission. They knew, realistically, they could expect no satisfactory answers from the Soviets. But to refuse to take up these cases effectively abandoned British POWs in Soviet hands, without so much as a word of protest.

In mid-August 1945 Eisenhower went to Moscow believing that Marshal Zhukov, his opposite number in the Soviet army, would soon be Stalin's successor and 'after that the United States would have no major difficulties in dealing with the Soviet Union', he said. Both Harriman and General John Deane told him he was wrong. It appears that, at about this time, Eisenhower and a few of the highest US officials were assured by the Soviets that, if 'mistakes' had been made in shipping Allied prisoners to Eastern labour camps with German POWs, they would be released through the Siberian port of Vladivostok or Dairen (Lu-ta) near Port Arthur in Manchuria, where some of the Allied prisoners from the war in the Pacific, held by the Japanese in Manchuria, were being liberated.

Indeed, there is some indication that a small number of Allied prisoners from the European theatre, shipped to Siberian labour camps with Western European civilians and Germans, may have been released secretly during the Soviet repatriation of Allied ex-POWs of the Japanese in Manchuria. But all US ex-POWs were screened by the

Intelligence service MI5-X who made each ex-prisoner sign a pledge not to disclose any information on methods or routes of escape, or any other facts concerning their experiences as prisoners. Each prisoner was warned in the pledge to be particularly careful not to speak to anyone from the press. The pledge also forbade them giving any account of their prisoner-of-war experiences in books, newspapers, periodicals, broadcasts or lectures. Disciplinary action was threatened for the disclosure of any information. American researchers have spoken to US POWs who escaped from the Soviets and are still living. They say that these threats, and genuine concern for possible future American escapees, ensured their continued silence. With British ex-POWs, interrogation by MI5 and orders to remain silent were standard practice. Plainly, if ex-POWs could not speak out, their concerns for comrades who had not returned could not be aired.

Eisenhower had misjudged Zhukov's position. He had not taken into account the Marxist-Leninist dread of military takeover – known to communists as Bonapartism. Stalin saw Zhukov as a rival and after Zhukov's return in triumph to Moscow in 1946 he was banished to a series of obscure regional commands. By the time Eisenhower realised this, it was too late. Both the American and British people had already been told by the War Department and War Office that all their prisoners were home, so domestic public opinion could not be used as leverage with the Soviets. Nor could the matter even be discussed openly.

By the beginning of September 1945 the Allied governments were forced into doing a tally. At Yalta, in February and March 1945, British Foreign Secretary Anthony Eden had estimated that the Soviets had already overrun 50,983 British POWs who were then in Soviet hands. But by 1 September 1945, after the prisoner exchanges, General Golikov stated officially that just 23,744 British POWs had been freed by the Russians. That alone indicates at least 27,239 British prisoners remained in Soviet captivity.

Despite other documents showing that the number of missing British prisoners of war in Soviet hands had clocked up to over 30,000 by the end of the war, the British authorities spent much of September 1945 grappling with the case of five dead Indians. Fighting in the British army, the five men had been captured in North Africa. They had been shipped to POW camps in Italy, then moved to Germany where they were liberated by the Soviets. Two died in a Soviet hospital. The other three died soon after the British authorities located them. The British complained that they had been kept in filthy conditions and fed meagre and inappropriate food – and their presence had not been notified to the British. Notes between the War Office, the Foreign Office, the Indian High Commission and the Soviet Embassy flew all month.

Appalled by the violence Allied troops had to use in the forced repatriation of Soviet citizens and others claimed by the new governments in the Eastern bloc, Eisenhower requested a review of the policy. Backed by Robert Murphy, US political adviser in Germany, he urgently cabled Washington on 4 September 1945. The answer came back, under the name of Secretary of State Byrnes, but it was actually from H. Freeman Matthews. Matthews was State Department Director of European Affairs and a colleague of Alger Hiss. Both he and Hiss had advised Roosevelt at Yalta.

Matthews instructed that American policy should involve close co-operation with the Soviet Union in this matter. Particularly important was his caution on POWs: 'Department has been anxious in handling these cases to avoid giving Soviet authorities any pretext for delaying return of American PWs of Japanese now in Soviet occupied zone, particularly in Manchuria.'

During the autumn of 1945 the United States began to make large payments to the Soviet Union, mostly in the form of massive shipments of military aid and vehicles ostensibly used in the Soviets' eight-day war with Japan. It is possible that this massive postwar aid was intended to encourage the Soviet Union to release the remaining Americans and British.

In Manchuria itself, unprecedented events were occurring. The US forces made several demonstrations of military power to the Soviet forces. One day in the first week of September, before the last American prisoners of war had sailed, US carrier aircraft made a show of force over the harbour of Dairen which excited the Soviets a great deal. On 13 September 1945, after the prisoners of war had sailed and the large numbers of men from the European theatre Eisenhower had hoped for had not turned up, another major show of force was made at Dairen by cruisers and destroyers of the US 7th Fleet.

Apparently the order for this show of force came from such a high level that senior officers at the scene were not informed of the reasons for it. American researchers have uncovered a secret report by US army Lieutenant Colonel Donovan, who was in charge of a POW repatriation team on the scene. He reported:

> This worried Admiral Settle considerably and he sent a strong protest to his headquarters . . . Although some Russian officers came to see him after the cruisers and destroyers had departed

161

. . . I do not know if they were lodging a protest against the second naval demonstration or not. The Admiral was at a loss for a reasonable explanation. His information from Fleet headquarters stated that the show of force would be repeated off Port Arthur . . . The Admiral had told me that a 'show of force' is technically rather a belligerent action.

This US show of force over the POWs was one of the first actions of the Cold War.

Exhausted after a long war, the British were not up to making a show of force. Months after the first men had gone missing there, the Foreign Office were still in a dilemma about what to do about British ex-POWs in Poland. One view was that they could make their approach through the Military Attaché in Warsaw. This was all very well in a few isolated cases, but most of the missing men had been in Red Army hands. On the other hand, they could ask about men they knew to be in Soviet hands. But as the men had gone missing from Poland, the Soviets would simply say that the Red Army had pulled out of Poland so the Foreign Office had better ask the Polish authorities.[5]

The British government were not faring much better with their demands for details of British and Commonwealth ex-prisoners of war being held in Germany. They were protesting that others were being held without notification in Hungary and Rumania.[6] And on 10 September 1945 Colonel F.J. Errol wrote to the Foreign Office asking about POWs who were still in Czechoslovakia.[7]

They had recently got one back from Russia. On 26 September 1945 a cable from American chargé d'affaires in Moscow George Kennan, drafted by Edward Page, an interpreter and personal aide to Harriman, was sent to Secretary of State James Byrnes. It reported the recent release by the Soviets of a British POW who had been held incommunicado at Krasnogorsk, where high-ranking German officers including Marshal Paulus and General Sevdlitz were also held. The reason for the Americans' interest was that, earlier, in a Moscow prison, the British POW reported seeing an American, Stanley Young. Young had not been returned.

Young was still in Soviet hands when, in September 1945, several weeks after Japan's surrender, the Council of Foreign Ministers met in London. The meeting was attended by Commissar for Foreign Affairs Molotov, Secretary of State Byrnes and Foreign Secretary Ernest Bevin who discussed, among other things, prisoners of war and the continuing forced repatriations. Byrnes said in this autobiography, *Speaking Frankly*, that, while in London

Mr Molotov came to see me, on instructions from Moscow . . . [Molotov] wanted to complain of the way in which the surrender terms [with Japan] were being carried out. He complained particularly about the way the Japanese Army was being demobilized. It was dangerous, he said, merely to disarm the Japanese and send them home: they should be held as prisoners of war.

The Americans should do what the Red Army had done with the Japanese they had taken in Manchuria, Molotov said – 'make them work'.

Charges that prisoners of war were being withheld flew back and forth. In Byrnes' account of the meeting: 'The Council had discussed a complaint from the Soviet Union that France was failing to repatriate Soviet citizens. France in turn complained that the Soviet Union continued to refuse to repatriate nationals of France.'[8]

But the Soviets held all the cards. White House aide Charles E. Bohlen said: 'If Molotov had walked out of the meeting, the Council of Foreign Ministers would have been delayed. The result might have been widespread public criticism in England and the United States of the ill-treatment of the Soviets.'[9]

In *Spycatcher*, Peter Wright says he read all the secret Soviet NKVD Intelligence transmissions intercepted during the London Council of Foreign Ministers in September 1945, and that this traffic was taken up with numerous messages from Moscow 'detailing arrangements for the return of Allied prisoners to the Soviet authorities, groups like the Cossacks and others who had fought against the Soviet Union'.

'Many of the messages,' says Wright, 'were just long lists of names and instructions that they should be apprehended as soon as possible.'

Despite his instructions from Washington, on 4 October 1945 General Eisenhower tried to stop the forced repatriations. The thousands of missing Allied prisoners from the European theatre that he believed had been shipped, by mistake, to Siberia with the Germans had failed to show up in the repatriations from Manchuria. The return of the Allied POWs held by the Japanese and liberated by the Russians had ended. The repatriation points at Mukden (Shenyang) and Dairen were now closed. At that time, 26,400 Soviet citizens were still in American hands. There was no point in sending them back to certain death, if the Soviets were not going to reciprocate. But the State Department overruled Eisenhower and ordered the completion of the repatriation program.[10]

The Allies' options were closing fast. Their embassies and military missions could get no joy from the Soviets. Molotov had blustered his way through the London conference with the Allies quaking at the political consequences of a Soviet walkout. A show of force had done no good. The only thing that the Allies could do was continue the forced repatriations and hope against hope that the Soviets would reciprocate.

## CHAPTER 29

# Permanently Lost

†

On 30 October 1945 Secretary of State for War James Lawson told the House of Commons that the Soviet government had not yet given permission for British search teams to enter Soviet-occupied Germany to look for missing British and Dominion prisoners of war. Asked whether the Soviet government had given any reason for this 'extraordinary refusal', Lawson said that it was a matter for the Foreign Office. He refused to answer any additional questions. However, with hindsight, it seems almost certain that the Soviets delayed the entry of Allied officers into their zone until they had moved all the POWs into the Soviet Union itself.

Clearly further returns were still expected. When consolidated casualty figures were issued in London on 29 November, *The New York Times* reported: 'A further statement of casualties will be issued when the fate of all reported missing persons is determined and when all the prisoners of war are repatriated.'[1]

(For many years after the war, thousands of returning Western European and Japanese survivors of the Gulag gave troublesome live-sighting reports of many American and British POWs in the forced-labour camps. Most of these were immediately separated from other records and filed under jurisdiction of the Intelligence agencies, effectively burying them. Fortunately, some were misfiled and resurfaced later – like the report by the Pole who had seen British, American, French and other Western European POWs in the camp at Tambov. It was first filed at the OSS on 20 December 1945.)

Inside the military, the missing men still had to be dealt with. Bureaucratically, they were still alive on active service. Somehow they had to be written off. The British with their traditions of secrecy and their long experience of foreign wars found this easy. American efforts were more laboured. On 31 October 1945 a US army report stated that a total of 97,879 POWs (known by name and excluding those listed missing in action) were taken in the European and Mediterranean theatres. It says that 90,532 had been returned by that date – leaving a shortfall of 7,347. According to this report, a total of 6,595 US army personnel in the European theatre were still being carried as live POWs, 'not yet returned to military control'. This directly contradicts the US War Department's 31 May 1945 statement that 'substantially all' the American POWs had been returned. A handwritten note on the original 31 October report reads: 'Capt. Pench – I phoned Col. Ballard & suggested he do some more work on this – P.'

Lieutenant Colonel L.L. Ballard was the Chief of the Strength Accounting Office in the War Department's Chief of Staff Office. And he did, indeed, do more work on these figures. On 25 February 1946 he sent the National Headquarters of the American Red Cross in Washington a 'chart showing Missing in Action (including captured) US Army personnel for the period 7 December 1941, through 31 December 1945'.

In this covering letter Colonel Ballard outlined his difficulties:

It will be noted that the items 'Prisoners of War (Current Status)' and 'Missing in Action (Current Status)' are still large. The reason of course is that as of 31 December 1945 these categories reflected latest definite reports available for statistical compilation, and the situation to date has not materially changed. You will appreciate that for statistical purposes these casualties cannot be moved to other categories until detailed disposition records have been processed. In many cases, final disposition must await a legal determination of death under PL 490 which may take up to next September, even though investigation to date leaves little logical doubt that a given man is permanently lost . . . The foregoing data was classified 'Restricted', but has been approved for release to you.

The chart shows that as of 31 December 1945 for the German theatres, the US listed:

| Captured | | Other Missing in Action | |
|---|---|---|---|
| | | *MIA* | |
| Returned to Mili. Control | P.O.W. (Curr. Stat) | Declared Dead | (Current Status) |
| 90,937 | 5,414 | 11,753 | 2,997 |

According to this 5,414 Americans were still listed as 'P.O.W. (Current Status)'. So since 31 October 1945 Ballard had managed to shrink the figure for 'Prisoners Not Returned to Military Control' – essentially the same category as 'P.O.W. (Current Status)' – of 6,595 men to 5,414. But in the two intervening months only 435 US prisoners – stragglers – had been returned. This still leaves a decrease of 746 men from P.O.W. (Current Status) between 31 October 1945 and 31 December 1945.

The War Department had issued Presumed Findings of Death on these 746 individuals during that period. There was no harm in this. Even if the man was not dead, he was, in Colonel Ballard's words, 'permanently lost'. It seems that, by the end of October, the War Department had been able to make legal Presumed Findings of Death in at least 5,900 cases, as the figure for 'Prisoners Not Returned to Military Control' – when you add the 25,000 US MIAs returned to the 77,500 registered US prisoners and subtract the 90,000 US prisoners who returned – was some 12,500, not 6,595.

The 11,753 Declared Dead under the category 'Other Missing in Action' represented Presumed Findings of Death (PFDs) as authorised by US law. However, these PFDs were drawn both from the MIA (Current Status) list and the POW (Current Status) list, decreasing the numbers in those categories and increasing the number Declared Dead.

Perhaps this is why Colonel Ballard felt obliged to explain to the Director of the Relief to Prisoners of War of the Red Cross that for 'statistical purposes' the numbers in the POW (Current Status) and the MIA (Current Status) were 'still large'. Ballard also pointed out to the Red Cross that these casualties cannot be moved to other categories 'until each man can be found legally, to be dead'. And this could only happen after an 'investigation to date leaves little logical doubt that a given man is permanently lost'.

But the most striking aspect of these documents is the revelation that the Chief of the Strength Accounting Office's main function was to resolve each outstanding case by determining – as soon as enough time elapsed to make it legally possible – that each man is 'permanently lost', and therefore, officially, dead.

It is also interesting to note that the POW (Current Status) and the MIA figures add up to just over 20,000 – the figure first mentioned in the Clark memorandum of 30 May 1945, the day before the War Department said they were 'substantially' all home. Juggling figures between categories – turning known POWs into MIAs, before making a Presumed Finding of Death – also became the practice after the Korean War and, particularly, the Vietnam War.

Instead of making an honest effort to resolve the fate of each man on its merits, the US War Department seemed determined to write each man off bureaucratically as quickly as possible. Instead of finding out what had actually happened to their POWs, many of whom seemed to have ended up in the Soviet Gulag, the American War Department merely awaited 'a legal determination of death under PL490 which may take up to next September'.

The bureaucratic precedents for this action were created in World War I, when the missing from the American Expeditionary Force were written off. It is hard to imagine that the British War Office acted any differently as they managed to trim the 31,809 British prisoners of war expected to come home on 8 June 1945 down to just 2,780 unaccounted for by February 1946, when just 927 had returned in that time. But the British, of course, did these things behind closed doors. And the newly re-established democratic governments of Western Europe likewise wrote off hundreds of thousands of their own citizens. Once the Americans had abandoned their own POWs, what chance did any other weaker nation have? And who wanted to risk a war with the Soviet Union anyway?

The secret existence of hundreds of thousands of Western citizens in the Gulag may have become the original glue that stuck the NATO alliance together. The prisoners themselves, though, were doomed to a life of perpetual slavery by the fears of their own political and military leaders.

The United States must bear the heaviest burden of guilt. As the sole possessor of the atomic bomb and the most overwhelming military force in history, it was the only power in a position to call Stalin's bluff. When the US government decided not to, Churchill, then Attlee, had to go along.

Once this policy had been established the security services (which at that time in Britain included Burgess, Maclean, Philby and Blunt) had to be given access to the records to 'weed' them before they went into the archives. Numerous documents and records from 1945 and 1946 relating to prisoners of war and forced repatriations are retained on the grounds that they cannot be found or that they are still classified top secret and cannot be released for reasons of 'national security'. Many are in the hands of the CIA, but other documents critical of this issue went to the FBI. Some went to director J. Edgar Hoover by name. At the time, Hoover was attempting to halt army Intelligence involvement in the investigation of the missing POWs in a dispute over jurisdiction. In Britain, the relevant files are closed for seventy-five years or simply 'retained by the department', which should indicate that they are in everyday use. In practice, it simply closes them for ever.

There are also records of many burials in US national cemeteries of American soldiers who were in combat units and whose year of death is listed as 1946. These men 'died in combat' when no action was taking place. Could they perhaps simply have been written off? At that time there was a central identification system for remains brought back from Europe similar to today's discredited Central Identification Laboratory in Hawaii that has been fraudulently misidentifying remains – or sometimes rocks and animal bones – as those missing from the Vietnam War. It is not inconceivable that these fraudulent identifications started long before the war in Indochina. The coffins of the men who 'died' in 1946 could similarly be full of rocks and pig bones.

The Central Identification Laboratory in Hawaii is still in operation. In 1987 some attempt was made to force it to clean up its act. Up until that time, it had lacked a dental X-ray machine, camera equipment and even hot water. $200,000 was spent on new equipment. Its offices were expanded, a library of technical publications was established, and the whole compound was surrounded by a high-security fence. Nevertheless, there are still frequent complaints about the dubious methods the laboratory uses in making its identifications (for more details see *The Bamboo Cage* by Nigel Cawthorne, 1991).

And later in 1948, in one documented case, the US government paid some $55,000 (the equivalent of $500,000 today) to the Soviets, for disinterring and shipping home seventeen sets of American remains. The Americans have shown a similar inclination to pay for remains of soldiers missing from the Vietnam War, but refuse point blank to offer money for live prisoners. That, they say, would be paying ransom for hostages.

Reports of Allied prisoners being held by the Soviets continued into 1946. The catalogue of the National Archives in Washington lists a memorandum from the State Department Special Project Division, dated 6 February 1946, regarding a conversation between Colonel Kavanaugh from the War Department, a Captain George and a Mr Baily, regarding the 'Doolittle fliers'. The Doolittle fliers were crew members of the daring surprise Doolittle Raid on Tokyo, a one-way bombing mission in April 1942 by sixteen B-24 bombers from the aircraft carrier USS *Hornet* who ditched on mainland China. They had been interned by the Soviets. (Although a memo containing the details of this conversation is listed in the catalogue of the Washington National Archives, the memo itself is missing.)

In an attempt to buy back Allied POWs, the forced repatriations continued into 1946. Although on a far smaller scale than the mass movements of the summer of 1945, they were just as horrifying. Of the 271 Soviet inmates of the Nazi concentration camp of Dachau in West Germany, 135 were forcibly repatriated in a violent incident that left 11 of them dead of suicide, and 21 severely injured in suicide attempts. A British soldier involved in the forced repatriations from Bergen-Belsen also reported suicides and said that women would kill their own children rather than have them handed over to the Soviets.

Despite the secrecy that surrounded these operations, news was beginning to reach the public. On 20 February 1946 Pope Pius XII denounced the forced repatriations in an allocution. The operations continued nonetheless. Of some 3,000 Soviets concentrated at Platt-ling, 1,590 were forcibly returned on 24 February 1946 in another violent operation. Five men killed themselves rather than face the NKVD, and many others attempted suicide.

However, perhaps as a result of the Pope's allocution, the forcible repatriation of the prisoners held at Plattling seems to have marked a high-water mark in Allied policy on this matter. As late as 10 December 1945 the War Department had been refusing official permission to Reinhard Gehlen's controller, General Sibert, to initiate covert activity against the Soviets. However, official approval was forthcoming in March 1946, although it is certain that some Intelligence activity in the Soviet zone had been under way unofficially for some time.

The results of these Intelligence operations in the Soviet zone are, so far, not officially available. But former American Intelligence agents, who have spoken out, claim to have been members of a team which brought out small groups of British and American prisoners who had been held by the Soviets. These men were being secretly returned from rendezvous points inside Soviet-held territory in 1946, the former agents say. At the time though, cover stories were used to disguise the real nature of these missions.

# CHAPTER 30

# Spies and Slaves

✝

IN JANUARY 1946 enquiries were still being made about Reginald Harold Barratt, a British POW who had escaped from a prison camp in Germany and made his way to Budapest. On 24 December 1944 he had been arrested by the Soviets at Szarvas, accused of being an anti-communist Hungarian and held with German prisoners of war. A former Dutch POW, Lieutenant E.J.C. van Hootegen, had seen him being taken. 'Barratt had Intelligence service papers on him but these were destroyed by the Russians,' Van Hootegen said when the Dutch Ambassador allowed the British Military Mission to interview him on 29 March 1945. The information was sent to the War Office in London, encoded on a one-time pad.[1]

The British Military Mission in Hungary asked the Soviet members of the Allied Control Commission about Barratt. On 23 June the Russians replied that Barratt had not been detained by their forces and they did not know where he was. An approach to the Soviet Embassy in London also proved fruitless.

Barratt's wife had last heard from her husband in a letter from him from a POW camp on 3 June 1944. She heard nothing more until March 1945 when she received a letter from Lieutenant van der Pol of the Dutch air force. He had been living in Budapest with Barratt. As van der Pol could speak fluent German, he decided to escape westwards. He managed to reach southern Italy and was flown to England in an American plane. Van der Pol said he had heard that Barratt had been sheltered in northern Hungary by a Hungarian count, but that the Soviets had come and taken Barratt away.

Mrs Barratt wrote to the Air Ministry with van der Pol's story. They made enquiries and, on 8 June 1945, cabled Mrs Barratt: 'Information received from Moscow that your husband 937633 W/O R.H. Barratt is now safe in Russian hands.' The Soviets would not say why they were holding Barratt and she could get no further news.

171

Then Mrs Barratt got a letter from Baron Nikolaus von Maasburg, who was then in Italy. He said that he had been in jail in Hungary with Barratt, who was also using the name Godden. Rifleman Godden was a fellow British POW who had escaped from Stalag 8B. Swapping identities between escaped POWs was a common practice, used to keep the Germans confused. Mrs Barratt wrote to a friend in Hungary to try to contact her husband. She also visited the Soviet Embassy in London where she was received very coldly.

Von Maasburg said that he had been held with Barratt at the 'Russian Field Law Court' at Ivanka near Bratislava. When von Maasburg left, Barratt was being held at Czecklis Castle near Treseburg, at the war tribunal of the Second Ukrainian Army.

According to von Maasburg, Barratt had been working with a colonel from British Intelligence in Budapest, organising the resistance against the Germans and helping the Soviet advance. Escaping from the Gestapo, he had been picked up by the advancing Soviets. They treated him well at first, as an escaped Allied POW. But shortly afterwards he was put in prison on the suspicion – or excuse – of being a Nazi. The Soviets had told him several times, in von Maasburg's presence, that enquiries were being made through the British Embassy in Moscow and that, as soon as a reply came from London, he would be released. Before he left Czecklis Castle, von Maasburg promised that if he ever escaped he would write to Barratt's wife. He also promised to contact the British authorities and tell them of Barratt's plight. Von Maasburg also carried a message from Barratt about another of their cellmates, Major Dombrowski, a former Polish Intelligence officer. Barratt said he was being groomed as a Soviet agent to be infiltrated through Turkey.

In May 1946 Captain Knorr, a Polish officer, also contacted Mrs Barratt. He had been incarcerated with Barratt, before von Maasburg's capture. He too reported that Barratt had been held with Dombrowski.

After he had left Barratt in Czecklis Castle, von Maasburg had been moved to a filthy cell in Theresienstrasse in Vienna, which he shared with one of Hitler's cousins, a man called Schmidt. Schmidt died of typhus and tuberculosis and, on 16 June 1945, von Maasburg managed to escape and made his way to the American zone.

Barratt was standing up well to his ordeal, von Maasburg said. He was greatly respected by the Russians and looking forward to being back with his wife and daughter. He advised Mrs Barratt to make enquiries through the British Embassy in Russia as he had probably been taken to Moscow.

'If he hasn't come back yet,' von Maasburg wrote Mrs Barratt on 3 March 1946, 'they have other purposes with him, and it will be very urgent, to get him out as soon as possible.' Von Maasburg had confided what those other purposes might be to the British authorities in Vienna in January 1946.

'Barratt believed the Russians were holding him for eventual employment as a Soviet agent in England and were checking his bona fides through Moscow and London,' he said.

Mrs Barratt took up the matter with her MP and the British Embassy in Moscow continued to ask that Barratt be handed over without delay to the British authorities, along with Pilot Officer Albert and Lieutenant John Clements, two Hungarians, who had been working behind the lines for the British (and who had presumably taken English names when they joined the RAF).

The Soviets said they had no knowledge of these three people, but referred throughout to Albert and Clements by their Hungarian names, Harajzti and Vajda.[2]

In February 1946 a young Hungarian was on a smuggling trip into Czechoslovakia. At the border town of Novo Mesto he saw an east-bound train coming into the station. As it slowed to a halt, Soviet troops leapt off and formed a ring around the train. Seeing the soldiers, the young Hungarian and his fellow smugglers hid. They were just a few yards from the train.

Inside the boxcars, the young smuggler could see soldiers. They were prisoners – the boxcars were locked and the small windows criss-crossed with barbed wire. At first he thought the soldiers inside were German or Hungarian prisoners of war, but a companion recognised that they were speaking English. The railway line led east – into the Soviet Union.[3]

Information concerning Allied prisoners still being held by the Soviets also came in through military channels. On 15 June 1946 a report from the Headquarters of the United States forces in Austria entitled 'USSR – American Army Personnel in Confinement' was sent to the Director of Intelligence, the General Staff of the US army. Under 'Summary of Information' it stated:

The following information was obtained from a former forced laborer who claimed to have been confined in an unregistered lager with Subject personnel. Informant claimed to have been released through an error committed by the commandant of the Moscow hospital where she was transferred because of infantile paralysis.

Approximately 60 km from Moscow, in the direction of Kaline, there is an unregistered labor camp. The confinees, 150 men and 50 women, work in coal mines in the vicinity of the camp. Among those confined are three American Air Force soldiers who were captured by the German Wehrmacht, Czechoslovakia, during April 1945. These men are:

Charlie, 21 years, 170 cm, blond, blue eyes, has paralyzed right shoulder.

Joe . . . 165 cm, dark blond, dark eyes, has stomach wound and is confined in lager infirmary.

Albert, 27 years, 170 cm, black eyes, has stiff left hip and burn scar on left side of face, is from Texas.

The lager confinees will never be repatriated and are not permitted to write letters.

Another camp where Allied ex-POWs were held was in Novosibirsk in central Siberia. A letter to the leader of France's National Constituent Assembly, dated 17 August 1946, from the Deputy of the Bas-Rhin department of Alsace said:

I have brought to the attention of the Minister for ex-Prisoners of War the testimony of Mr Joseph Bogenschutz, 55 Grand Rue, at Mulhouse (Haut Rhin), who was repatriated on last July 7 from Russia, from Camp 199-6 at Inskaya, which is 70 kilometers from Novisibirsk [sic], and who states that about 20 Alsatians and Lorrains were still in the Camp at the time of his departure.

Bogenschutz states that he wrote at least three cards a month through the Red Cross (Red Crescent) since September 1944 and that none of these cards ever arrived. He states that the Camp Commander is a German and that instead of repatriating Alsatians, he selects Germans for repatriation.

Bogenschutz, in addition thereto, alleges that there still remain American, British, Belgian, Polish, Romanian, Luxemburg, etc. nationals in the Camp.

French Deputy Henri Meck reported this matter to the American Embassy on 17 August 1946.

Other US documents indicate that, in 1946 and 1947, US Fifth Army Intelligence and the FBI were investigating the interrogation of American POWs in postwar Soviet-controlled Poland by at least two American-born Soviet Intelligence officers, one of whom was known by name. (The name is now blacked out on released copies of the documents.)

CHAPTER 31

# The Tank Factory

✝

DESPITE THE INFORMATION trickling in that Allied prisoners of war were in the Soviet Union, by mid-1946 most of the prisoners in Soviet hands had been given up as 'permanently lost'. A State Department document from the Special Projects Division, dated September 1946, indicates something of the methods used in reaching the conclusion that the Soviet-held POWs were deceased. Edward McLaughlin, assistant chief of the division, wrote:

> The War Department has informed this Department that its overseas commanders were recently queried as to the probability of personnel now carried in a missing status being located alive, and that the answers from all commanders reveal that no information had been brought to light by intensive investigations which would indicate the possibility that any will be found alive.

However, the American public were not about to give up so easily. On 25 October 1946 a number of Chicagoans wrote to Secretary of State James F. Byrnes. They claimed to be relatives of American citizens 'now held illegally as slaves on farms in Yugoslavia and in mines in Russia'. They asked the Secretary of State to ban the Yugoslav delegate from the United Nations General Assembly until these men were freed.[1]

By 1947 the figures had been tidied up in the RAMPs study. With the American figures this was simple. Although the final revised total for US prisoners from the European theatre through all channels is given in 1947 by RAMPs as 91,252, including the 2,858 shipped from Odessa – at least 10,000 shy of the numbers that should have returned – the large number of MIAs meant that they actually got back more POWs than were expected. But the British figures were not so easily squared away. So they were simply shrugged off. The report states: 'The number of British prisoners of war recovered by the Allied Expeditionary Force was reported as 168,746. (Including 4,310 from Odessa.) The number fell short of the 176,000 expected in advance.'

This shortfall of 7,000 missing prisoners was attributed, in part, to 'unreported deaths in forced marches', as Brigadier Venables had done before. The figure 176,000 approximates to the 175,000 figure Venables used, which is actually the figure of British and Dominion prisoners held in German camps. Only hidden deep in the arithmetic of the RAMPs report – in the combined total of British and American prisoners held – is the 199,500 which throughout the last months of the war was the official figure of British and Commonwealth prisoners of war held. Perhaps the large numbers of Indian, African and other colonial POWs did not matter.

The RAMPs report was classified, so even the official excuses were hidden from the public gaze. In Britain such secrecy is a matter of course. But it was not good enough for American families who were awaiting the return of loved ones. In the American National Archives there are stacks of petitions with tens of thousands of signatures, handed in at the White House in 1947, urging Truman to demand that US search teams be allowed into Soviet-controlled territory to locate the missing American prisoners and remains. Some contain notes from families who believed their loved ones were under Soviet control. These apparently went unread. A brief memorandum attached to the petitions by a Pentagon colonel says: 'File. No action necessary.'

During 1947 forced repatriations continued. In May 1947, a year after Churchill's 'Iron Curtain' speech at Fulton, Missouri, which effectively began the Cold War, Operations Keelhaul and Eastwind forcibly repatriated 255 Soviet citizens. There are indications that a relatively small number of British and American POWs were secretly repatriated by the Soviets in return for these men. Others may have been smuggled out later. A limited operation of this type could have been used to still criticism within the Intelligence services of a policy of outright, total abandonment.

American researchers say that returned prisoners were, in the cases they have discovered, threatened with death if they ever revealed the circumstances of their imprisonment. This threat was made ostensibly to protect the lives of remaining POWs, and sources and methods of intelligence-gathering. However many men were repatriated this way, it can only have been a drop in the ocean compared with the number who disappeared into the Gulag for ever.

Although the entire forced-repatriation policy was still being conducted in the utmost secrecy, news again slipped out. In the House of

Commons on 21 May 1947 Richard Stokes MP asked Foreign Office Minister Christopher Mayhew if there had been attempted suicides among the Russian prisoners returned under Eastwind. Mayhew replied that there had not – but this was not the case.

Another interesting reference to the forced repatriations came up in the US Senate. In 1953, when more Allied prisoners were in the process of disappearing at the end of the Korean War, the Senate Foreign Relations Committee was holding hearings to confirm the nomination of Charles E. Bohlen as United States Ambassador to the Soviet Union. The senators were less interested in Bohlen's credentials than in any light he could shed on the meeting of the Big Three at Yalta, where Bohlen had been Roosevelt's interpreter and an adviser on Eastern Europe. The 'Sell-out Theory', which alleged that the Democratic party was full of 'fellow travellers' who had 'sold out' to communism, was particularly fashionable at the time and the Republican senators wanted to accuse Franklin Roosevelt's Democratic administration of negotiating a bad if not treasonable agreement. In his defence of Yalta, Bohlen made some revealing comments on the bloody continuation of the forced repatriations in 1945–7. Senator Homer Ferguson asked him: 'Even after we knew that these people were committing suicide rather than go back, we forced them to go back . . . How do you account for the fact we did not sense what was going on and refuse to carry out an agreement that not only enslaved these people but took their lives?'

Bohlen replied: 'There were 60,000 American prisoners in Poland and Germany under the control of or about to be under the control of the Red Army, and the purpose was to get those prisoners back.'[2]

If Bohlen's figure is correct, the number of US servicemen who disappeared is greater than the documents available indicate – only 28, 662 Americans in total were returned by the Soviets, according to their own official repatriation statements of record.

Of the two million people whom the Soviets claimed were their citizens in British and American hands in 1945, all but 40,000 were ultimately repatriated. In all, around 1,000 committed suicide or were killed by Allied forces when they refused orders to return. The Ukrainian SS Division and a large number of individuals were kept by the Western Allies for Intelligence purposes. The existence of these individuals was supposed to be concealed from Stalin, but he learnt about it soon enough from moles in British Intelligence.

As a quid pro quo, Stalin held Americans and British. Some may have been used for Intelligence work, but most were exploited for their technical expertise. On 4 August 1947 the US forces Counter Intelligence Corps (CIC) in Goettingen filed a report. It told the story of Hans Joachim Hofman, a German prisoner of war recently returned from the Soviet Union. He had information about Allied prisoners being held in Siberia.

After Hofman had been released by the Prisoner of War Processing Centre at Dachau on 17 July 1947 he went to the American Red Cross Club in Ulm. He gave a CIC agent there three pictures of American soldiers. Hofman claimed to have talked with one of the men depicted, in Siberia. His name was Viktor Boehm, and he told Hofman that he had emigrated to the US in 1928 and had served in the US army during World War II. He had been taken prisoner by the Germans. He was held in Oelmuetz, Silesia, and on or around 5 May 1945, his guards changed. From then on he was a prisoner of the Soviets.

Boehm was transported to Siberia and on 17 July 1945 he arrived at Novosibirsk Camp 311 near Krasnoe where, Hofman said, he was set to work in a tank factory. Hofman worked there too and they got to know each other. Boehm could speak German and handed over the pictures of himself and the other two Americans.

But Boehm was not the only American working in the factory, Hofman said. There were some 200 of them – along with another 900 Allied prisoners of war, mostly British and French.

This story could have been dismissed as the bizarre ravings of a returned POW. But the CIC agent backs his report with an appendix. It is the testimony of Ernst Schmidt who had returned to Munich after escaping from a Soviet internment camp. In the camp, he said, there were Germans, Austrians, Italians, Americans, English, Belgians, French and Dutch nationals. There were 35,000 men there in all, although most were Germans and Austrians.

Inmates had to work fifteen hours daily from 0500 hours to 2000–2100 hours. If they did not work hard enough, prisoners were punished with strokes of the lash. If they collapsed under this punishment they were killed. The guards were GPU personnel with bloodhounds, the GPU being one of the former Soviet Union's many state security agencies.

The conditions were poor. The daily rations were half a litre of soup, potatoes, two lumps of sugar, rotten beets and some undefinable vegetable – probably grass. There was no bread and the rations were dished out twice a day. There were no medical facilities, no camp doctor and no medicines. And there were no Swiss relief packages or CARE packages. Any charity packages were confiscated by the guards and traded with the local populace for liquor and cigarettes.

Any decent clothing was taken from the prisoners, divided among the guards and traded off. Valuables were packaged up and sent to Moscow.

Schmidt knew the names of some of the Allied POWs he had been in the camps with. One was First Lieutenant Fred McMorran. He was around thirty years old and came from Florida. Before he arrived in the camp in January or February, he had been with the American occupation forces in Vienna. Another was the Englishman Tom Ryan, who was twenty-two or twenty-three years old, from Cambridge. He had arrived in the camp on 15 February 1947.

Schmidt felt sorry for the Allied nationals who were treated as POWs and received far harder treatment than the Austrians or Germans. They were separated from the others while working and more was demanded of them, though their rations were the same as the others'. These Allied POWs, Schmidt said, had often been captured in Vienna and Berlin, where they were occupation troops. There were also members of the Foreign Legion. Americans and Englishmen were usually transferred from the camp after eight days to a more permanent destination. Their documents were sent to Leningrad. In the camp there was a large spy network. Anyone who confided in these spies was liquidated. This was done in front of the assembled members of the camp.

Another German recently returned from Soviet captivity in June 1947 wrote from Regen in West Germany that an American and a British citizen were held by the Soviets. They had been detained in Germany since the outbreak of the war and were treated as prisoners of war by the Soviets, even though they had never been in the Wehrmacht.

A third report came from a German named Naumann who had been picked up by a GPU officer in Dresden. He was taken to the GPU's three-storey headquarters on Zittauerstrasse in a small cream Opel. There, on the first floor, he was stripped and searched. All his identification was taken away from him.

He was interrogated by a man in uniform with one large and two small stars on his shoulders, and accused of being an American spy. When he denied it, he was threatened with beating and even death.

He was interrogated from 9.30a.m. until 4p.m., when he was locked in the jail at the back of Zittauerstrasse.

The next night he was interrogated again, but this time for only three quarters of an hour. Then he was returned to his cell. In a nearby cell he saw seven prisoners all dressed in American uniforms, though they spoke German. In his cell there were ten other prisoners. One was a Russian soldier who was accused of attempting to shoot his superior officer during a heated dispute over the interrogation of an American soldier.

Naumann was held in that jail until 22 January 1946. Then he and twenty-seven other men were transferred to the Muenchnerplatz jail in Dresden. They were marched to the prison, guarded by Soviet soldiers and police dogs. The jail was completely manned by Soviets and he was held with Paul Lutbold and a lawyer named Riedl, both political internees. During his seven-month stay at Muenchnerplatz, twelve people died of starvation.

While there, he saw five Americans and two Englishmen, he said. He talked to the Englishmen and one of the Americans. The American was from Detroit and his name was Noble. His son was in the same prison.

He did not know how long the Englishmen had been held. One of them was called John Speigel and both of them came from Baghdad. They may have been stationed there.

Walter O. Hoelter, the CIC special agent who debriefed Naumann, says he realised that this report might sound fantastic in many places, and the information in it might not be true, but the subject had been interrogated in great detail on three occasions. Each time the facts he had given coincided.

Naumann claimed that he had been interrogated by the Soviets again on 12, 13 and 14 July 1946 in the city prison. Violence was used in an attempt to make him confess to being a spy. He was interrogated again on 17 August 1946, then released on 21 August, though none of his identification documents were returned to him.

He went home. On 13 September he left Dresden and escaped to Bamberg in the West. For his pains he had been arrested and charged with illegal border crossing. He was handed over to the Military Government for appropriate action.[3]

CHAPTER 32

# The Readjustment

†

WINSTON CHURCHILL HAD won the war against Hitler magnificently. His immense personality stiffened British resistance to fight on alone against the might of the seemingly invincible Germans. He forged an alliance with Stalin, worked with Roosevelt to get America into the war, and helped to plan the final victory. His thirty-six-year war against Bolshevism had not gone so well, though. Without Truman's support, he had been unable to administer the coup de grâce.

On 5 March 1946, Churchill made a speech at Fulton, Missouri, where he thundered: 'From Stettin in the Baltic to Trieste in the Adriatic, an iron curtain has descended across the Continent.' This iron curtain was a military and ideological barrier between the Western capitalist democracies and the communist bloc, led by the Soviet Union which, Churchill warned, desired an 'indefinite expansion of its power and doctrine'. By then, the Cold War between these competing ideologies already had over 30,000 British casualties – the missing POWs.[1]

Lady Soames, Churchill's daughter who often travelled with him during the war, says that her father was 'deeply anxious (especially after Yalta) that Stalin's government would not abide by the various agreements'. But she stressed Britain's impotence as 'the minor partner in the Big Three'.[2]

In America, despite the US army's G-2 Intelligence unit and Reinhard Gehlen's SSU (Strategic Service Unit), the US government felt they required more indigenous human Intelligence from inside the Soviet Union. Kennan was recalled to Washington and, in 1948, as chief of the State Department's Policy and Planning Staff, he produced a plan for what was to become a covert action agency: The Office of Policy Coordination. This would later become a major component of the CIA.

The man who was put in charge of The Office of Policy Coordination at the State Department was Frank Wisner, an ex-OSS agent who had served in Rumania and Yugoslavia where a number of known US POWs had disappeared. Wisner recruited Richard Bissell, Desmond Fitzgerald, Cord Meyer Jr and others, who later became senior CIA officials. Their job was to develop a network inside Soviet-occupied territory. However, to do that they were obliged to liaise with the British Intelligence services, where they were betrayed by Philby, Burgess, Maclean and Blunt. Many of their recruits turned out to be double agents working for the KGB. Wisner eventually committed suicide in 1965.

Kennan returned to Moscow, briefly, in 1952, this time as Ambassador. He was declared persona non grata on 3 October 1952 after comparing the Soviet government to Hitler's Nazi regime.

On 23 December 1948 the American Embassy in Bucharest reported some consternation in Rumania. In February 1948 the Rumanian government had reached an agreement with the Soviet government for the return of the 177,000 Rumanian POWs held in the Soviet Union. However, by December 1948 the repatriations had come to a standstill and less than 40,000 men had been returned. Popular concern about the remaining prisoners has been fanned by a decree which appeared in the 23 November 1948 *Monitorul Oficial*, declaring all persons 'reported missing during the war, beyond the frontiers of Rumania, during the period of June 22 1941 to May 9 1945' legally dead.

Large numbers of Rumanian families had never received official notice that their captured relatives were prisoners of war of the Soviets, but they had heard indirectly that they were alive, through men who had been returned. It was widely believed that Rumania's communist government was preparing to say that these prisoners no longer, officially, existed and they would be making no further effort to secure their liberation.[3]

Feelings were running high in all the defeated nations. Under the Geneva Convention, prisoners of war were supposed to be repatriated speedily at the end of hostilities. While America had largely complied, both Britain and France were still holding prisoners of war in 1948. The last enemy POWs were repatriated from the British Isles on 12 July 1948. Others, though, from the North African campaign – as many as 46,000 as of 6 April – were held by the British in the Middle East. By 1 December 1948 the International Committee of the Red Cross (ICRC) reported they had all been released.

The French had reduced the numbers they were holding to 96,000 on 1 July 1948. France was still holding 3,000 POWs in the French zone of Germany, but the French government assured the International

Committee of the Red Cross that they would all be released by 15 December 1948.

The 60,000 prisoners of war in Yugoslavia were due to be repatriated by 18 January 1949, the Yugoslav authorities told the ICRC. About 40,000 prisoners of war remained in Poland. Although the Polish authorities had given no official plan for their repatriation, the ICRC had heard by 1 December 1948 that two convoys of discharged POWs had recently left Poland for Germany.[4] These may have been prompted by the 'vigorous government protest' the British lodged with the government in Warsaw in November.[5]

Although, looking back, it can be seen that the Geneva Convention had reached the pinnacle of its success during World War II, in 1949 it was seen as a failure. And on 21 April 1949 a new Geneva Convention was inaugurated by the International Red Cross in Switzerland.[6]

In April 1949 the Allied authorities found that the Soviets had suddenly started returning an average of 1,400 German POWs a day to the British zone. They were immediately debriefed by the military authorities at Goettingen. Out of every 1,000, 150 were held for longer interrogation and of that number 40 to 50 were taken to Bad Driburg for a third and much more thorough questioning. At Goettingen there was a staff of around fifty conducting this examination work. They came from British Intelligence, the army, navy and air force. In Bad Driburg there were another thirty-five to forty examiners.

At that time it was thought that another 400,000 German prisoners were being held in the Soviet Union, but it was difficult to get an accurate figure because the Soviets were constantly moving POWs from one camp to another.[7]

As those who had survived came back, they were a ready source of Intelligence. On 2 October 1950 a 'reliable German source' reported from Baden-Baden that there were still about thirty Allied prisoners being held in Prison Camp number six, about five kilometres northeast of Odessa. Among them were one or two Americans, 'probably arrested for spying in 1945'. One of these men was Harry Lepselter of 1284 St John's Place, Brooklyn 13, New York.[8] When this report came to light recently, American reporters checked and found that a Lepselter family had indeed lived at that address in the 1940s.[9]

Another German returnee said that in May 1950 he had been a prisoner at Halle. In the next cell were two Americans who communicated with him using a tap code. Their names were H. Claus Moore of Newark, Delaware and Captain Andrew Maisano. They had been visiting girls in Magdeburg when they were arrested.[10]

Another American report shows three American servicemen in their late twenties and early thirties had been kidnapped while sightseeing in Berlin. They were shipped to Dresden the next day and had been seen in an MVD (Ministry of Internal Affairs) prison there.

On 22 March 1950 two German prisoners of war returned from the Soviet Union said they had been employed on the construction of a new institute at Marfino, Moskva Oblast, during the first half of 1949. One of them had experience in radio engineering. From the antennae and the ultra-shortwave apparatus, he concluded that the installation was for high-frequency research. Another returned German POW confirmed this.

Between them they gave detailed information about the electrical supplies, the scientific apparatus and the equipment in the machine shops. The machine shops were manned by Soviet civilians, but the scientific personnel who were segregated in a main building were guarded by MVD men.

There were between sixty and seventy scientists and technicians employed in research work. All the scientific personnel were MVD prisoners serving long terms. Most of them were Soviets, although the returnees positively identified one German. Others, they heard, were English, French, Italian and Baltic nationals. A German engineer told one of the POWs that the imprisoned technicians had been promised a reduction of their sentence when they obtained satisfactory results in their work.

Auxiliary sections of the institute employed about 150 German POWs from the nearby Camp 7815 and about 20 Soviet civilians, most of whom were employed in the new construction. In September 1949 the German POWs from Camp 7815 were completely evacuated and Soviet civilian internees were housed there instead.[11]

Many returning German POWs talked of the Allied prisoners they had seen in the Gulag. Some of their debriefs – heavily censored – have been released.

On 15 December 1954, for example, Mrs Johanna Korner reported that in a Soviet prison in Berlin-Lichtenberg she had seen an American soldier. He was from Milwaukee, about thirty-one years old, and spoke little German. He was transferred to Siberia, she said.

A report about Captain Robert Dewes (or Davis) of the US army was also made. But the details of the date of the sighting, whereabouts of Captain Dewes, date of the report, the informant, the sentence, the action taken and, for that matter, anything else about the sighting of Captain Dewes were all blacked out when the report was declassified.

Philip Graves, an American officer, was seen on 8 January 1951, working in the Soviet officers' mess in Budapest. The informant said Graves had been captured by the Germans, then later taken by the Soviets into the USSR, before being moved to Hungary. He had passed a note to a Hungarian woman to be delivered to the American legation. It asked that his wife – Mrs Alice Graves of 7123 Toland, Dallas, Texas – be notified of his welfare.

On 4 June 1955 an Austrian returnee said he had seen four US airmen in a labour camp in the Karaganda region some 2,250 kilometres southeast of Moscow in 1948. One of them was named William, another John. The informant had photographed the four airmen, but the pictures were confiscated by the Soviet guards because the men were in uniform. They still seemed in good condition, in 1948.

Another Austrian returnee reported to the American Embassy in Vienna on 1 September 1955 that he had seen an American sailor in Vorkuta between 1949 and 1952. His name was William Vasilievsky Bizet and he had been born in Russia, around 1911, of Russian parents. His father's name was Vasilievsky. Before World War II Bizet and his mother had emigrated to America and settled in California. There his mother married a Professor Bizet of the University of California, who adopted the boy and gave him his family name. Bizet attended elementary and high school in America, but the informant did not know whether he had been to college. Before the war Bizet had worked as a bank clerk in San Francisco. He was married with a child.

He had been on patrol duty with the US navy in 1945 when he was captured by the Soviets. The informant thought he had been an officer, probably a lieutenant. He was sentenced to eight years' forced labour.

When the informant met Bizet in Pit 40, Vorkuta, a mining camp in Arctic Siberia, Bizet was sanitation chief. He received the same treatment as the other prisoners. But he was a very good comrade, his fellow inmate reported, and was naturally friendly.

He was approximately 1.68 metres tall with a round head, round face and dark blond hair. He spoke fluent Russian. After a dispute with a Soviet official in 1952, Bizet was transferred, probably to another camp at Vorkuta. Bizet had said that the Soviets never recognised his American citizenship since he was born in Russia. Because of that, the informant believed that Bizet was probably exiled to another part of the USSR upon the completion of his sentence in 1955.

An unnamed American had been seen by a Japanese returnee in a camp at Narinsk, in lower Yenisei, Siberia, in July 1947. The American, who came from the Mississippi river area, had been moved on in

August 1947. The Japanese informant thought the American had been a US Intelligence agent in Harbin, Manchuria, up to 1945 and had been arrested and sentenced as a spy. Another report said that he was about forty years old in 1946, bald, with a moustache.

In September 1946 an air force lieutenant called 'Kah' (perhaps a man known simply as 'K', or 'Kay') had been seen in the Muenchnerplatz prison in Dresden, German returnee Heinz Peter Kaldonek reported when he returned to Bonn in 1954. He was with the 23rd Air Force Regiment, from Detroit. He had been shot down by the Soviets on 17 or 19 August 1945 – after the end of the war – over Grossenhain, near Dresden, and held on suspicion of espionage. Kaldonek said he was transferred to the prison at Muenchnerplatz from the General GPU Stalle, Zittauerstrasse 32, Ville Pietsch, Dresden. The informant had last seen Kah when the American was moved to a higher floor of the prison on 1 September 1946, but the informant had promised to tell the American authorities if he ever reached the West.

German returnee Isle Koenke reported on 29 June 1954 that on 10 February 1953 he had met Major Harry Hopkins in the courtyard of a prison at Rasaifka, 200 kilometres east of Moscow. They were in transit eastward. Hopkins was between thirty-five and forty years old, about 1.65 metres tall, medium build with close-cropped blond hair, blue eyes and an oval face. He spoke good German with a marked American accent, Koenke said. Hopkins claimed to have been an officer at Tempelhof airfield in Berlin in 1945, after Germany's capitulation. He was arrested in Berlin by the Soviets, but did not say which sector or why. In 1946, he had been sentenced by a Soviet military court to ten years' forced labour for espionage.

Koenke said he had been sent to work as a doctor in a women's forced-labour camp. It was not unusual for unqualified people to be used as doctors in the Gulag. Women doctors were used almost universally in male camps, as part of the humiliation and demoralising of the inmates.

Hopkins told Koenke that he had escaped and made his way to Moscow where he had contacted the US Embassy. They assisted him to open a practice in Moscow under an assumed name. But eventually he had been found out and, at the end of 1952, was sentenced to another twenty-five years' forced labour.

A day or two after their meeting, Hopkins was taken off the train at Gorki and Koenke did not see him again.

These stories were only the very tip of the iceberg.

## CHAPTER 33

# Those who Returned

✝

A HANDFUL OF Allied prisoners were returned openly. One was Frank Kelly, a private in the Royal Army Medical Corps. He was captured at Arnhem and taken to Stalag 4B, which was liberated by the Soviets. Kelly was a young man in no particular hurry to go home. He met some German girls and enjoyed the free-and-easy atmosphere of postwar Leipzig. Soon he was picked up by the Soviets as a spy.

They released him and told him to make his way to the British headquarters in Berlin. Before he could leave he was picked up again. He found himself in a cell with Germans, Poles, Danes and other flotsam Hoovered up by the Soviets. A Pole – a stool pigeon Kelly thought – told him to 'confess' so that he could get privileged work.

After five months in Leipzig jail Kelly was sentenced to fifteen years. There was no trial. He was doubly miffed because one of the Germans in his cell only got eight years. Kelly's sentence was later reduced to ten years, again without a hearing. He served eight.

Kelly was taken east to the Lubianka, then to Vladimir jail 320 kilometres north of Moscow. He later wrote: 'God, it's not funny to be just a bit of worthless unwanted humanity, kicked around, nameless, unknown, believed dead probably.' Deprived of proper food, warmth and clothing, and packed in a tiny cell with Frenchmen, Germans, Lithuanians and Japanese, he was afraid of dying, forgotten.

'If I died no one would ever know about me,' he used to think. 'It would be a kind of forgotten life. They would think I died years before somewhere in Germany. It used to make me feel mad, caged, lost, wanting to shout out: "I'm alive, I'm alive – I've been alive all the time." And sometimes I wouldn't give a damn. Sometimes I wanted to die.'[1]

He hoped that his mother, back in England, believed he was dead. He could not bear the thought of her fretting.

Like the other prisoners, Kelly was allowed to write two letters a year – to Stalin and to Molotov, asking for clemency. He received official replies registering the plea, but that was all. In desperation he wrote to the Official Prosecutor, begging to be shot. The official reply simply said: 'No.' He wrote to the British Embassy, but doubted that his letter got through. He was not allowed to address any letter to England, though.

Kelly fell into despair. His cellmates tried to cheer him up. They were more stoical about their situation.

'I don't remember anyone asking me what I had done to get into prison,' he recalled. 'I don't think anyone ever asked that kind of thing. People in prison were just unlucky.'

An Austrian suggested that he try for a transfer to a prison camp. There had been a lot of trouble in the camps, he explained, but it was good there – 'You worked and you got paid.' Then they heard that 200 men had been shot in one of the camps.

Kelly's spirits revived when he met an American, Sergeant Robert Cummings, who had been captured in Czechoslovakia. It was good to speak English again.

'That was the first time in all those years that I really knew what was happening to anyone else,' Kelly said.

But his whole attitude to his imprisonment changed when a German doctor was thrown into his cell. The doctor was an epileptic who had frequent fits, and Kelly began a campaign to get him proper medical attention.

Kelly began to make trouble. He spent over 200 days on hunger strike, often for as long as 17 days at a stretch. He made several suicide attempts. One gained the perverse admiration of Alexandr Solzhenitsyn. In *The Gulag Archipelago*, he wrote:

> The Englishman Kelly, in Vladimir Special Purpose Prison, very skilfully cut his veins with the door wide open and the jailer right there on the threshold. [A footnote adds: He did it with a piece of enamel from the washbasin. Kelly hid it in his shoe and his shoe stood by the bed. Kelly dropped his blanket over the shoe to cover it, got out a piece of enamel, and cut his wrist vein beneath the blanket.][2]

Despite periods of solitary confinement, Kelly's campaign began to work. The prison authorities relented and allowed medical treatment for the epileptic German. This gave Kelly renewed strength. He refused all food except for bread and water until he was released. Despite the casual brutality of the Soviet prison system, they refused to let Kelly starve himself to death. When he was weak, they would take him to a hospital cell and give him glucose injections.

Finally, Kelly became more trouble than he was worth. He and the epileptic German were released. On 16 November 1953 Kelly was handed over to the British authorities in Berlin. He was promptly arrested.

The British authorities had had good warning of his return. On 12 November 1953 *The Times* reported from Moscow:

> Russia has agreed to release a British soldier who was arrested after the war and sentenced to 10 years' imprisonment for espionage, the British Embassy announced today. The soldier, Private F.J.W. Kelly, Royal Army Medical Corps, will be deported from Russia.
>
> The British Minister, Mr Paul Grey, was told of the Russian decision when he was summoned to the Soviet Foreign Ministry yesterday. Private Kelly, who is in a Russian prison, will be handed over to British military authorities in Berlin 'at a time to be notified'. Mr Grey was told that the case had been reviewed by the Soviet legal authorities, who had decided to substitute deportation from the Soviet Union for completion of the sentence.

It was no surprise to the British authorities that the Soviets were holding Kelly. They had enquired about him six years before. *The Times* story went on:

> The British Embassy in Moscow in 1947 asked the Soviet Foreign Ministry whether reports that Private Kelly was detained in the Soviet zone of Germany were correct. They replied on February 28, 1948, that Private Kelly had been sentenced to 10 years' imprisonment under Article 56, section 6, of the Soviet criminal code. The Embassy continued to approach the Foreign Ministry on the question and last June asked the Foreign Ministry to use its good offices to secure a remission of the sentence.[3]

*The Times* also reported Kelly's release in Berlin on 16 November:

> Private Kelly of the RAMC, a British soldier who is believed to have been held a prisoner in Russia since the beginning of 1945, was handed over by the Soviet authorities to British military police at Karlshorst today. The British authorities had been asked by telephone to collect the soldier. Private Kelly was wearing a grey civilian suit and overcoat and a Russian fur hat, and looked pale and thin but otherwise in good spirits. He will remain in the British Military Hospital at Spandau until he is sent on to western Germany tomorrow.[4]

Two days later, on 18 November, *The Times* reported that Kelly had arrived in West Germany by car. He was detained on a holding charge of being absent without leave and held under close arrest in Hanover.[5]

On 22 November 1953 *The Times* reported from Bonn that Kelly was being released 'without prejudice to further proceedings' – in other words, the charge against him still stood. Although he was technically free, Kelly remained in the British military hospital in Hanover, suffering from the effects of malnutrition over a long period in Soviet prisons and was 'receiving every care and attention'. *The Times* noted that he would not be required to attend the court of enquiry into the circumstances of his absence until he was medically fit.[6]

On 4 December 1953 General Sir Richard Gale, Commander-in-Chief of the Northern Army Group, decided that no disciplinary action would be taken against Private Kelly. A staff officer visited Kelly in hospital to tell him of the decision. Confined to his bed, Kelly was on a special diet to abrogate the effects of the malnutrition he still suffered. However, he was allowed a glass of champagne to celebrate.[7]

On 10 December he was briefly allowed to meet the press. Two weeks later he was flown to RAF Benson in Oxfordshire, and taken to the RAF hospital at Wroughton, Wiltshire.[8]

It may seem odd that a man who has just spent eight years in a Soviet jail should be charged with being absent without leave. But after nine years' captivity – including his time in a German POW camp – the threat of an indefinite stretch in a British jail is a good way to shut someone up.

The only prisoner of war to return late from the Vietnam War was treated the same way. Marine Private Robert Garwood managed to get out of Vietnam in 1979, six years after the American withdrawal from Southeast Asia. He was charged with four capital offences, including desertion, collaboration and striking a fellow prisoner. Only years later did he speak out about the other Americans he had seen who had been left behind in captivity. Even then his testimony was largely ignored. The court martial had smeared him as a traitor.[9]

Kelly was not the only Englishman in the Soviet prison system at the time. Len Wincott was certainly there. Leicester-born Wincott had been one of the Invergordon Mutineers. In 1931 he had led a strike on board the Atlantic Fleet, after the seamen's pay was cut. In 1932 he joined the Communist Party and in 1934 moved to the Soviet Union. When he became disillusioned with communism and decided to return to Britain, he was arrested and sentenced to ten years in the camps and life banishment. Another Briton in the Gulag met him in a camp at

190

Arshan in the late 1940s and he was still alive in the Soviet Union in the mid-1970s.

The Englishman who had seen Wincott at Arshan was Eric Pleasants, a merchant seaman from Norwich. During World War II, Pleasants had the misfortune to be on Jersey when the Germans invaded. He was captured and, after several abortive escape attempts, ended up in a concentration camp. To survive, he volunteered to join the SS.

Pleasants was not a very good SS man, according to his own account. On his only mission – he was sent into Denmark – he got drunk before he reached the border.

With the end of the war, Pleasants was in trouble. He knew he would not be looked on favourably by the British authorities. They might even hang him as a traitor. So he remained in the Soviet zone and joined a circus as a strong man. The Soviets love circuses and he did very well. But it was only a matter of time before the truth came out.

In 1946 Pleasants was arrested. He confessed to having been in the SS. But this was not enough for the Soviet interrogators. They forced him to confess to spying for Britain too. He was sentenced to twenty-five years for being in the SS, twenty-five for sabotage and twenty-five for espionage, to run concurrently, plus five years' internal exile in the USSR.

In the camps Pleasants often heard of Englishmen up in Inta in the Arctic. The camp there was known as the 'city of the lost' and held 45,000 condemned souls. As well as Wincott, Pleasants met a young Englishman named Piddington in Lubianka jail. He had served four years in the labour camps and was about to be released.

In the camps he met a young man from Blackpool who had joined the Communist Party at seventeen and decided to go and see Russia. In Moscow he was arrested for 'speaking out of turn'.

There were also a number of young Estonians who had been born and brought up in England, and were consequently British nationals. Pleasants also met a Spaniard, Raoul Faube. Orphaned during the Spanish Civil War, he had been taken to Russia. When he asked to go back to Spain, he was told that it was impossible as he was a Soviet citizen – and he was sentenced to twenty years in the labour camps for being politically unsound.

There was always a great deal of interest in England in the camps. One man Pleasants met wanted to know if England had come under Soviet occupation.

After seven years Pleasants' sentence was commuted and he was handed over to the British authorities in Berlin. They decided that he had been punished enough in the Soviet Union and he was released.[10]

191

There were Americans in the camps too. At that time the State Department said there were more than 5,000.[11] One of them, John Noble, was released after smuggling out a postcard to relatives in Germany in 1955. Since then he has dedicated his life to trying to bring out the other Allied prisoners he saw during his captivity.

Although born in America, John Noble was of German stock and he was working in his father's camera factory in Dresden when America entered the war. He was interned, though he was still allowed to work as long as he did not leave the city and reported regularly to the police.

When the war ended things became more difficult. The Noble family festooned their house with American flags and it became a centre for American POWs and displaced persons who were trying to get across into the Allied zone. Although they were left alone at first, the Soviets soon found an excuse to arrest Noble and his father. They were held at Muenchnerplatz prison in Dresden. Later Noble was moved to Muhlberg, the former German POW camp which the Soviets were now using. There Noble met a fellow prisoner, a young woman. She was British.

Noble was moved on through other prisons, including Buchenwald, where some inmates complained that they were treated worse by the Soviets than they had been by the Germans. At a jail in Weimar he heard through the prison's tap-code grapevine that other Americans, British and French were being held there. Noble discovered later that two of the Americans were William Verdine and Homer Cox.

At Weimar Noble received notification that he had been tried in Moscow and sentenced to fifteen years' slave labour. Noble asked: 'Why? For what reason? On what charges?' He was told: 'If there are any questions, ask them where you are sent.' And he was pushed from the room.

At Orsha in Byelorussia he saw a partially obscured name written on a prison wall – Roberts, Robertson or Robinson, Maj. USA – dated mid-August 1950, just a few weeks before Noble got there. (In the summer of 1945 Italian chemist, writer and concentration camp survivor Primo Levi reported seeing black men in American uniforms in a camp in Byelorussia.)[12]

Noble was then moved on to Vorkuta in northern Russia where he went to work shifting slate in a coal mine in freezing conditions. Vorkuta is a huge coal mining settlement in the Arctic circle. A vast system of camps spread out from the pit heads. Conditions there were appalling. The equipment was old and there were not even minimum safety standards. The slave labourers lived in wooden huts ruled over by common criminals who, compared to the political prisoners, were treated well. Food was meagre – thin soup and black bread, barely enough to sustain a man through long hours of back-breaking work. And if you failed to meet your production target, your rations were cut.

Many prisoners deliberately maimed themselves to avoid going down the mines. But this was considered sabotage and their sentences would be increased.

In the camps there Noble met some Canadians and heard rumours about Americans. These included Private William Marchuk, Private William Verdine and two Americans he was to meet later, Homer Cox and Leland Towers.

In the camps he met Spanish communists who had been organising the shipment of material to the loyalists during the Spanish Civil War. When Franco won, they stayed on in the Soviet Union. But a year later they were arrested for 'espionage'. Noble noted that the ex-communists in the camps were particularly disillusioned with what they considered the Kremlin's perversion of Marxism.

He also met Poles, Latvians and Estonians, slaves from Iraq, Iran, Italy, Mongolia, China, Czechoslovakia and, later, two North Koreans who had been accused of disloyalty to their regime. And there were Russian and Ukrainian Jews, victims of Stalin's pogroms of 1949–53. There were Greeks who had been taken by the communists during the Spanish Civil War and Hungarians and Germans – both communists and Nazis.

In Noble's camp there was a Frenchman called René who had been attached to the French government unit in West Berlin. His wife was in the women's compound. There was an Englishman called Chapman in Camp 10. He was a British soldier, captured by the Germans in Holland, liberated from a Nazi POW camp in 1945 by the Soviets, then promptly re-arrested and sent to Vorkuta. When Noble met him in mid-1954 his mind had been almost completely destroyed. And there was a good-looking blonde Englishwoman called Robinson in the women's camp.

Noble also met Americans. Russian-born William Vlasilefy had become a naturalised American citizen and spent much of his early life in the western states. He said his family still lived in Seattle. He had joined the US army in the early 1930s and on his discharge moved to China where he went into business. In 1949, when the Chinese communists took over, they arrested him in Peking and sent him to the Soviet Union as a slave labourer.

In the camp hospital Noble met Roy Linder, who had been born in Vancouver, British Columbia, but had become an American citizen. He became a stunt flier, performing at the Michigan State Fair. Later he flew as an observer in the Spanish Civil War and, during World War II, became an army pilot in China. After the war he rose to become a colonel in the USAF, and one of the commanding officers at Templehof airport in West Berlin. In 1949 he had been kidnapped in West Berlin and dragged into the Soviet zone. After a year in the Lubianka he was sent to Vorkuta as a slave labourer.

Noble did not trust Linder and suspected he had done a deal with his captors. Linder was given a pardon and released. Later he sent a note to Noble saying he was living in the nearby village of Vorkuta and working in the powerhouse as a free worker. He had a girlfriend in Rostov in southern Russia and hoped to go and meet her. Noble has no idea whether he was ever allowed to leave the Vorkuta area, or what became of him. But it was usual for former slaves, after completing their sentences, to stay in the area of their camps in life-long exile.

Noble heard of other Americans in the camps. One was an engineer who had been seized while working for the Soviets in Vladivostok. The last Noble heard of him he was in Lubianka jail.

A Yugoslav prisoner Noble met later, claimed to have met eight Americans who had recently been shot down over the Baltic. The American air force acknowledge that several B-29s and B-50s had been lost. One of the American flyers told the Yugoslav that he was afraid they would never get back to the US. The Soviets had reported them dead, saying there were no survivors from the crash. According to the USAF, these B-29s and B-50s were on routine flights over the Baltic. However, they were almost certainly being used to probe Soviet radar. Flights would have continued up until the late 1950s when the high-altitude U-2 was introduced. The missions would have been clandestine, and they would probably have had a false manifest as a cover story. The USAF admitted that the planes had been downed at the time, pretending that the Soviets had taken aggressive action against them when they accidentally strayed off course near Soviet airspace. More recently, however, their true purpose has been admitted to.

As prisoners funnelled through Vorkuta from camps in Tadzhik and Irkutsk in Soviet Asia, Omsk in Siberia and Magadan in the Far East, Noble heard that many Americans, including veterans of the Korean War, both GIs and officers, and South Korean soldiers, were working as slave labourers. From what he heard, they were POWs captured by the communist Chinese and North Koreans, and shipped to the Soviet Union for safekeeping. At that time, Noble estimated that between 25 and 28 million people, including POWs, were in the slave-labour system.

According to a German Gulag inmate called Godfrey Lias, 50–60 million people – a quarter of the population of European Russia – had been forcibly moved to the industrial towns built by the German and Japanese POWs in Siberia and Kazakhstan. While at a camp in Dzezkazgan, in Kazakhstan, he met an American called Johnny T. Alexander Dolgun, an American official at the US Embassy in Moscow who was snatched by the Soviets and imprisoned in the Gulag. Alexander had also heard that there was an American officer captured in Korea at Dzezkazgan.[13]

An Austrian prisoner known as 'Erwin Germanovitch' told Lias that Germans and Austrians were treated much better than the English. In a book he wrote about his experiences, Lias also mentions the existence of 'camps of silence'. These were secret camps in remote places where the inmates were not allowed to write or receive letters, never even saw any local people and had no idea where they were.[14]

In 1953, with the death of Stalin, things began to loosen up in the camps. On Beria's birthday, 14 April, there was an amnesty for all those serving a sentence of five years or less. The new relaxed regime led to a strike at Vorkuta. The authorities crushed it by shooting down 200 men in cold blood.

Noble did not benefit directly from the new regime. Even though it was acknowledged that he was an American, he was still denied a Red Cross postcard, a right he demanded under international law, even though, as he was not technically a POW, he was not legally entitled to the cards. But a friend let Noble use his mail privileges and he managed to get a coded postcard to a relative in Germany. This was passed on to Noble's father who had already been released and returned to the US with his family.

With proof positive that John Noble was alive in a camp at Vorkuta, Eisenhower, who was then President, took up the case. He had already successfully pushed for the return of Homer Cox. Noble was taken with two other Americans – Privates Marchuk and Verdine – to a repatriation camp at Potma. Marchuk had been arrested when he got drunk in a bar in Berlin and wandered into the Soviet zone. Verdine had been kidnapped while on sentry duty on the frontier demarcation line.

The repatriation camp was full of Yugoslavs, Austrians, Germans, Greeks, Spaniards and Hungarians being fattened up ready for their release. Plainly, the Soviets did not like the criticism they had received for returning the half-starved Kelly.

Noble's touchdown at Idlewild – now Kennedy Airport – on 17 January 1955 was upstaged by an article in the communist newspaper *Taegliche Rundschau*. It alleged that Noble was one of a number of British and American agents in Germany during the war who colluded with the Nazis during their final hours. Noble, apparently, had done a

195

deal between the Wall Street bankers, Bomber Harris and the Nazi high command to destroy the Soviet zone, while preserving capitalist investments. Ironically, unscathed by the bombing of Dresden, the Noble family's camera factory was taken over by the Soviets.[15]

When John Noble got home the State Department showed him files of 500 to 700 American soldiers who had been kept by the Soviets and asked him if he'd seen any of them. He hadn't. Then, in 1987, he met then-Secretary of State George Schultz and brought up the subject of 5,000 US servicemen listed in 1954 as still being held by the Soviets.

'He told me he knew there were Americans still in the USSR,' said Noble. 'He said: "We send them notes, but they just throw them back at us." '[16]

## CHAPTER 34

# Special Camps for Foreigners

✝

WILLIAM VERDINE ALSO reported that he had heard numerous rumours of prisoners of war from Korea being in the Gulag.[1] William Marchuk had heard that the eight US flyers shot down over the Baltic in 1950 were dead – others had seen their bodies removed from the plane. But Noble, as already noted, had heard they were alive.

Marchuk reported that he had received information from Otto Herman Kirschner, a German POW, who had met nine American pilots in a camp at Kirov prior to January 1955. One was a major, another a captain, but they were not in uniform.

Japanese prisoners of war were being returned through China at this time. Back in Japan, some of the returnees reported that there were Soviet interrogation centres for American POWs, mainly airmen, along the Yalu River. Local Chinese told the repatriates that a group of seven 'US spies' were later taken to the USSR.

One Japanese returnee had seen an American airman in a military hospital in Siberia in October 1953, who said he had participated in the World War II bombing of Japan. Interrogated three times after his return to Tokyo in 1953, the informant said that the American had been shot down in 1951. He was a lieutenant and knew practically no Russian.

Another Japanese POW said that Soviet guards, fellow prisoners and labourers told him that there were 12 or 13 Americans, crew members of a military plane downed by the Soviets, at Khabarovsk prison in April–May 1953.

Germans were still coming home, with fresh reports. An American captain, around fifty years old, tall, slender, with greyish-blond hair, had been seen in Vorkuta in 1950. He was said to have been seized by the Soviets while travelling inside the USSR accompanying lend-lease shipments during World War II. He was sentenced to fifteen years' forced labour and was transferred to Vorkuta from a prisoner-of-war camp in Stalingrad.

An Austrian returnee reported to the American Embassy in Vienna in 1955 that he had seen Second Lieutenant Otto Gechli in January 1952 at a railway station by a camp at Tscheljabinsk. He was on his way from Magnitogorsk to Moscow for questioning. Gechli had been an artillery officer but was seconded to the American Military Attaché's staff in Rumania. He said that his parents were born in Switzerland and had emigrated to America where they lived in Queens, New York. He was kidnapped in Bucharest in 1947 and taken to Baden where he was badly treated during questioning and had lost most of his teeth. Then he was moved to Sopron, Hungary, where he contracted tuberculosis. He had been to Magnitogorsk, reportedly in a special camp exclusively for Western Allied officers.

A second Austrian returnee informed the American Embassy in Vienna in 1953 that he had met Otto Gechli at Verkhni-Uralsk. He said that Gechli was thirty-two years old and spoke English, French, Rumanian, Hungarian and German. He was taken to Moscow frequently, where the Soviet authorities tried to persuade him to work for them. He would not co-operate and they sentenced him to death for espionage. The sentence was later commuted to twenty-five years. Gechli was still at Verkhni-Uralsk when the informant left in June 1953.

A German returnee had also seen Gechli at Verkhni-Uralsk. The German said that Gechli had been sentenced to twenty-five years for espionage in 1948, in Moscow. The interrogator asked the US Department of the Army about Gechli. They said they had no information on him. Other memos the interrogator sent enquiring about Gechli were not replied to.

On 21 June 1955 the *New York Herald Tribune* said that an Austrian returnee had reported seeing an American POW in a Soviet prison. The man had been arrested by the Soviets after escaping to the USSR from a Japanese prison camp in World War II.

Another officer in the US army, a Captain Jimmy Fabian, had also been seen in the Gulag after 1948, at Verkhni-Uralsk, and at a Soviet camp on the Mongolian border. A Jimmy 'Sabian' had also been reported. Allegedly, Fabian had been kidnapped in Czechoslovakia in 1948. Several Austrians reported further details of Jimmy Fabian's captivity. He was said to be between thirty-two and thirty-five when he was seen in October 1953 at a camp near Omsk. He had previously been at a camp near Taishet. In December 1954 he was transferred to a 'special camp for foreigners' in Tschurbai-Hui, forty kilometres south-west of Karaganda, Kazakhstan. He was last seen in this camp by Austrian POW Karl Pauer on 26 May 1955. Pauer said that Fabian had been arrested on the Austrian side of the Czech frontier in 1948 or 1949. His job there was to locate American property in Austria, Czechoslovakia and Hungary. He spoke excellent German and Hungarian. He was unmarried. Fabian wanted food parcels and could be contacted through Post Box 5110/80, Moscow.

Another Austrian POW, Richard Ludwig, reported that Fabian was born in Chicago about 1925 and was an officer in the US army. The informant was with Fabian at Tschurbai-Hui from 2 October 1954 until 25 May 1955, when the informant was repatriated. He said that Fabian was allowed to write, but the answer cards he sent out never came back. He had never received any food parcels.

Yet another Austrian POW said that Fabian was born about 1917, was 1.8 metres tall, weighed approximately 80 kilogrammes, had brown eyes, black hair, and a large red birthmark covering the right side of his face. He spoke Russian, English and German and was working in a section for 'Displaced Persons' in Tschurbai-Hui. This Austrian also reported that Fabian had been born in Chicago where his parents still lived. Fabian had served as a lieutenant in the 'Rainbow Division' of the US army. He was arrested by the Soviets with another officer in May 1948 at Gmünd in the Soviet zone of Austria. At Soviet headquarters the two officers were separated. Fabian was sentenced to twenty-five years for espionage and sent to the Gulag. He had been in camps at Omsk and Gengir. When the Austrian last saw Fabian in June 1955, he was in good condition, and asked the Austrian to let the US authorities know his whereabouts.

A fourth Austrian recently returned from Vorkuta had also seen Jimmy Fabian – this time at the Soviet Kommandatura, Vienna IV, Ploesslgasse, in December 1946. He had also seen Fabian at Sopron, Hungary, in September 1947. Fabian was an 'oberleutnant' (first lieutenant) and was born in 1919. He was 1.9 metres tall, slim with a light red birthmark about 7 by 7 centimetres on his left cheek. He was educated at 'Oxford or Cambridge' and was living at Sievering in Vienna when captured.

Although details vary the stories these four Austrians tell mesh together so convincingly that it is impossible to believe that Jimmy Fabian did not exist. Throughout the late 1940s and 1950s reports of British and American prisoners still being held poured out of the Soviet Union. But the Cold War secrecy regulations in force meant that they did not enjoy wide distribution within government and military circles.

199

Certainly, neither the public nor the families of the individuals named were ever informed.

French prisoners who returned from Tambov and other camps in the mid-1950s also reported seeing British prisoners of war. Armand Malumian, a dual French-American national, returned from Vorkuta in 1955. He reported seeing two Englishmen there – Harry Keating and Peter Cartwright. The Ministry of Defence say they have no record of these men.[2]

Another Frenchman who spent seven years in Vorkuta said he had seen Eric Pleasants and an Englishman called Lester.[3] An Austrian returnee also told the British authorities that he had seen a Major 'Money' or 'Mony' Lester or Lesters in the camps. Born in 1902, Lester told the Austrian he was captured in early 1949 while travelling from Graz to Vienna, and sentenced to twenty-five years on 14 October 1949. Again the Ministry of Defence say they have no record of such a man.[4]

In *A Hidden World*, published in 1963, Eastern European Raphael Rupert, related the story of his nine-year captivity in the Gulag:

> I only met one Englishman during the whole of my time in Russia, Alec Peters. He had been attached to the British Military Mission in Rumania and was about to sail from the port of Constanza when he was arrested. The Russians had politely asked him to come ashore 'just for two minutes' to deal with final customs formalities. These 'two minutes' had so far lasted eight years. His family had sailed without him. He was quiet, dignified and courageous.[5]

The Ministry of Defence said that various refugees and repatriated Austrian prisoners of war reported a Peter, Petersen or 'Major' Petersen. The MoD says – even though they don't seem to be too sure of his name – that he was of Rumanian origin, although he claimed to have renounced his Rumanian nationality and become a British subject. This claim, the MoD says, was not substantiated. He was not a member of the British Military Mission either, but he did act as a legal adviser to the British Consulate in Bucharest between 1945 and 1948 when he was arrested by the communist authorities.

'As he was not a British subject, the British government had no formal standing in this case to make demands of the Russian or Rumanian authorities,' said Mr John Harding at the Army Historical Branch in a letter to the author in 1992. 'However, his case was raised by Britain and Peters was apparently released in Rumania in the mid-1950s.' History does not record whether he ever saw his family again.

In October 1953 seven Norwegians were released by the Soviets after eight years' imprisonment and told journalists in Berlin on 25 October that the Soviets were still holding scores of other Western prisoners, including an American major. Alexandr Solzhenitsyn also remarked on an American major in the Gulag, but his mind had gone and he would talk to no one. One of the Norwegians, Otto Larsen, a forty-one-year-old partisan who had been arrested when he refused to work for the Soviets after the war, said he met the American in June that year in a prison near Sarask, 480 kilometres south of Moscow.

'I did not remember the major's name,' he told the United Press wire service, 'but he told me the Russians arrested him in Germany. He appeared to be between thirty-five and forty years old.'

The Norwegians said the Soviets also held Spaniards, Austrians, Germans, Turks, Frenchmen, Italians and Finns.[6]

Long after World War II was over an American woman, Mrs Ida Mae Reitz Stichnoth was still trying to find out what had happened to her son, Technical Sergeant Lawrence Edward Reitz. He was a first radio technician on a B–24 called Damfino on the raid on the Ploesti oil field on 1 August 1943. He was seen several times in Stalag 3B in 1943 and 1944. Then in the spring of 1945 he was sent to Luckenwalde. In April 1945 he and his crew disappeared with as many as 500 other Allied prisoners when the camp was taken over by the Soviets. The American government, though, said that Edward Reitz had never even been taken prisoner and insisted that he had been killed in a ball of flame on the day of his shoot down.

In her efforts to find out what had happened to her son Mrs Reitz went to see the Soviet Ambassador in Washington, Mr Novikov. At their hour-long meeting Mr Novikov told Mrs Reitz that it was only politics that America was holding some Soviet prisoners and the Soviets were holding some Americans, she said. She believed that there were some 4,000 Americans in Soviet hands and that her son was probably working in a radio factory in the Soviet Union. Mr Novikov said he would try to help find Lawrence Reitz, but she heard no more.[7]

Mrs Reitz assembled witnesses who had bunked with her son in Luckenwalde. She also found one of the German prison guards who knew him well. Men who had made it home established that Reitz was in Luckenwalde on 22 April 1945, when the Soviets took over, and later, on 3 May, when a roster of the remaining prisoners was smuggled out. She found pictures of her son in captivity in POW publications – one showed him with the rest of his crew shortly after capture – and the German Red Cross traced him through the camp records to Luckenwalde on the day the Soviets came in. German and Austrian POWs returning in the 1950s said that they had seen Reitz in Soviet labour camps along with several thousand World War II POWs in prison camps northeast of Moscow. After her story was carried in a German newspaper, she got so many reports that she could track her son from camp to camp around the Soviet Union.

He was at Vorkuta, Shaft One, from August 1952 until the spring of 1954, according to the camp's German barber who shaved Reitz twice a week and cut his hair once a month. From there, Reitz went to a camp at Vladivostok, then to Odessa where there were twenty or so smaller camps. Three Austrians saw Reitz in Odessa, along with two other American prisoners whose names appeared in the US government report 'Americans Detained in the USSR', pages of which have recently been declassified piecemeal.

But all this was not enough to convince the American government that Reitz was alive and being held in the Soviet Union. In 1957 they still denied that he had even been a prisoner of the Germans – he had 'unfortunately been killed during World War II'. Her twelve-year struggle to prove that her son was not dead eventually wore Mrs Reitz down. She became confused and erratic, and began to claim that she had seen her son, under guard. His face was burnt and she fainted. He begged her not to follow, she said.

A benign US government never told the family of missing US army officer Major Wirt Thompson that, in 1955, he had been seen alive in a Soviet labour camp. A German returnee reported to the American authorities that Thompson had told him he had been imprisoned at Budenskaya prison near Moscow, and also in the Taishet labour camp after World War II. He was one of five American citizens the US government had good information about in captivity in the Soviet Union at that time. All five cases were brought up with the Soviet authorities. Details of the other four cases were given to the press. But the United States' government felt that 'no publicity at all should be given to the Thompson case' no doubt because he had already been declared dead.[8] The result was that Thompson did not come back. Nor were the family of Major Thompson ever told.

Not only was Thompson's daughter overwhelmed when she found out early in 1991 that this information existed, but she wondered how her family could have been told by the US government in 1944 that Major Thompson had been killed in action in Burma and his body not recovered. Her father's plane had gone down in a remote jungle area, which no search team ever managed to reach. It had crashed because it was overloaded with airmen, escaping the Japanese who were about to overrun their base. This was consistent with the story the German returnee told.

Thompson would have been captured by the Japanese and spent two years, probably in a camp in Manchuria, under their tender mercies. For the rest of his life, he was a slave of the Soviets.

## CHAPTER 35

# Treatment of the Enemy

ALTHOUGH THE FAMILIES of missing prisoners rarely learned what happened to their loved ones, at the highest levels of the US government the subject of missing POWs was still discussed. In a secret State Department cable from Australia dated 16 August 1950 – soon after the beginning of the Korean War – Secretary of State Dean Acheson raised the possibility of revealing the truth:

> [The State] Department has proposed to UK, France and Australia, through Embassy here, that they join US in submitting to next General Assembly (of UN) question of failure of USSR to repatriate or otherwise account for POWs and civilian internees detained in Soviet territory. Case would consist of factual record of Soviet failure to either repatriate or account for vast number of German, Japanese and other POWs as well as civilians deported to USSR, despite repeated Allied appeals and in clear violation of Moscow Agreement, April, 1947, Potsdam Proclamation, July, 1945, SCAP–USSR Agreement 1946 and recognized standards of international conduct.

At that time the World Veterans Federation estimate that 2.5 million prisoners of war remained in captivity in the Soviet Union.

Britain, Australia and the United States duly brought up the matter in the General Assembly on 20 August 1950. The result was the establishment of the UN Ad Hoc Committee on Prisoners of War. All the interested parties – with the exception of the Soviets – turned up. And every member of the United Nations was asked about the prisoners they were holding. Despite repeated requests, the Soviet Union never replied. But their views were recorded in the minutes of the Ad Hoc Committee:

The Soviet Union, despite overwhelming evidence to the contrary, maintained that there were no longer any prisoners of war in the Soviet Union except for a few thousand persons who were being detained in connection with war crimes. The Soviet Union government has not even divulged the names of those persons or their present whereabouts, nor has it disclosed of what crimes they had been accused.

As criticism of the Soviet position at the committee grew, the Soviet reaction became more strident. In 1953 *Pravda* published an article violently attacking the committee, which the Soviet government refused to recognise as legal. But *The Times* could see a good side to this. 'One result was that prisoners of war in Russia learned from the article that the United Nations was concerning itself with their fate,' it said. 'This alone was enough to raise their spirits.'[1] However, no source has ever suggested that POWs in the Soviet Union actually had access to newspapers.

In the first session of the Ad Hoc Committee, in 1951, the Japanese claimed that about 2,726,000 Japanese had been taken in the areas occupied by the Soviet forces. Many died, some were returned. But Japanese families were crushed when, on 20 May 1949, Tass announced that only 95,000 former Japanese troops remained to be repatriated. The Japanese government and the American authorities in Tokyo listed a total of 469,041 still to be repatriated from Soviet-controlled areas. When asked to account for the 374,000 missing, a Soviet spokesman brushed aside the question and spoke scornfully of the book-keeping methods of the Japanese government and the Allied command.[2]

There had, of course, been shocking casualties. One returnee explained what they had been through: 'After surrender, we were disarmed at Hsingan, Manchuria, and taken to the coal mining town of Morodoi, Mongolia. Later an epidemic broke out among us and all the prisoners in the camp contracted it. Only 225 prisoners out of more than 600 survived.'

Another said: 'Our battalion of 350 men was detained in the 3rd PW Camp in Khabarovsk. About 200 men died from illness and malnutrition.' A death rate of around 60 per cent was not uncommon.

A 1948 repatriate explained to the widow of one of his POW comrades: 'In October 1945 we were sent to a camp west of Chita, where we felled trees. Owing to meagre food rations and severe cold, many prisoners in the camp died. At that time your husband fell ill with eruptive typhus. Owing to the shortage of medicines, he died.'

Another 1948 returnee said: 'Our group of about 1,000 was taken prisoner in Manchuria when the war ended. We were taken as far as the Ural mountains in European Russia, and interned in a camp. About 70 per cent were repatriated safely, but the rest died either from malnutrition or accidents while working.'

Smallpox and other contagious diseases scythed through the camps. A repatriate employed as a gravedigger at a POW hospital reported that 'so many died from starvation and disease that a crew of 50 men could not keep up with the job of burying the dead'.

And the casualties were not only among servicemen. Approximately 26,000 Japanese civilians were assembled in the area around Hamhung in Korea in May 1946. Seven thousand died from exposure and starvation. They were marched for about a month across the Siberian wilderness, suffering from hunger, chill and fatigue, to a camp in a mountain mining area which was otherwise totally uninhabited. Only the strongest survived.

Internees were fed only potatoes. To survive they had to scavenge from the countryside. They supplemented their diets by eating bark, frogs, snails and slugs. Only prisoners with fever temperatures of over 100 degrees and those with visible external injuries were relieved from work. Hernia, appendicitis, pneumonia, tuberculosis and other illnesses often killed prisoners. The top killer was eruptive typhus.

This was not random brutality, though. It was part of a well-thought-out plan. Those who survived the first winter were strong enough to perform hard work valuable to the Soviet economy.

In 1947, older prisoners, the injured and ill were returned to Japan. The rest were encouraged to work hard – not by coercion, but by getting camps to compete against each other for better conditions. Extra food or money was given to POWs completing more than 100 per cent of their daily quotas, though most of the money was retained as 'expenses'.

Once the older men, who would be more set in their beliefs, were dead or had returned to Japan, the propaganda was started. Younger men were turned against their officers, and against the whole imperial system.

Propaganda from a Japanese communist newspaper helped, but the decisive factor in turning many of the young Japanese was the attitude of the local Russians. They did not seem much better off than the prisoners themselves. They worked almost as hard for as little reward and did not exhibit the racist attitudes that the Japanese expected from Americans and the British, who had traditionally treated them as inferiors.

Many prisoners became communists, joined the 'Democratic Leagues', and were allowed to organise within the camps. POWs were led to understand that the date of their repatriation depended on how quickly they became indoctrinated. Standard practices of group- and self-criticism were used, along with denouncements, and symbolic 'lynchings' or 'trampling to death' were performed. Chillingly, these sometimes degenerated into the real thing.

All courses were based on the assumption that every prisoner loved and revered the Soviet Union and was reluctant to leave its shores. The prisoners were always judged as a group, which progressed at the speed of the slowest. This system put incredible peer pressure on the POWs. According to a returnee, a Soviet physician was treating a Japanese for a leg injury in the Rybstroy POW camp in April 1949. But the prisoner was not feverish, so the doctor had to place him on full-duty status. Wracked with pain, the POW had trouble working and his Japanese foreman denounced him. He was prosecuted for his 'un-democratic' attitudes by a People's Court. That night, scorned by his comrades, he hanged himself with his leggings.[3]

Those successfully indoctrinated were moved on to camps where they had better food, more classes and less work. Some were even sent to special schools in Moscow. There they were trained in subversion techniques. The Soviet Union had shared in the spoils of war in Europe, seizing East Germany, Poland, Hungary, Czechoslovakia, Bulgaria and Rumania. Only firm action by the Allies stopped them taking Austria and Greece too. But in the Far East they had gained only North Korea and a handful of Japanese islands. The communist takeover in China had deprived them of Manchuria. Meanwhile the United States had taken the industrial core of Japan and were exploiting it to the hilt. So the Japanese prisoners of war became a powerful weapon in the struggle against capitalism.

When these Japanese POWs were eventually returned home they were diehard communists. As their boats entered Japanese waters, cries went up: 'We are entering enemy territory. Don't lower your defences.'

The captain of one of the boats was tried by a kangaroo court, though history does not record what happened to him. Returning POWs refused to fill in landing cards and staged demonstrations on the dockside. They made unplanned stops on the way home to attend communist rallies and 400 ex-POWs forced their way into the Diet, Japan's parliament. The families of the returnees, and the Japanese public generally, were horrified.[4] But the Soviets had established the core of a powerful Communist Party in what was to become the most successful capitalist nation on Earth.

The Japanese complaints at the Ad Hoc Committee on Prisoners of War did not fall on deaf ears. Although the People's Republic of China did not have a seat in the United Nations, on 1 December 1952 Peking Radio admitted that some 30,000 Japanese nationals were still held in China. These prisoners had actually been captured by the advancing Soviet forces in 1945, but handed over to China when the communists took over in 1949. If the Japanese provided transport they could go home. By 11 September 1953, 22,487 had been returned. The UN reported that another 165 Japanese POWs had been returned from Australia and 108 from the Philippines. But the Japanese continued to complain that 85,045 Japanese were still being held by the Soviet Union and communist China, excluding 246,009 known to have died.

In the committee's seventh session the French finally got round to admitting that 300 or 400 French nationals from Alsace and the Moselle region still appeared to be detained in the Soviet Union and that very little was known about their fate.

Holland submitted two lists to the USSR. One contained the names of forty-six Dutchmen who had volunteered to fight for the Germans. The other contained the names of twenty-seven civilians who had been deported to do forced labour in Eastern Europe. Some were returned.

No other Allied nation made any complaint about missing men, which is surprising. Many of the Allied nations had turncoats who fought for the Germans and may well have ended up in Soviet camps. Eric Pleasants certainly was not the only example. The British knew that Frank Kelly was in a Soviet jail, and said nothing. And both Britain and America had collected a large number of live sightings of their former POWs in Soviet captivity.

The Germans, of course, had nothing to hide. In the opening sessions the German Federal Republic complained that in all there were 1,300,000 German soldiers missing – 1,200,000 from the eastern and southeastern theatres. It presented fifty volumes of information about the missing prisoners. One contained the names of 99,856 known prisoners of war not returned. Others contained live sighting reports and letters from the men in the camps.

West Germany also complained that 750,000 German civilians had been taken into the Soviet Union; 8,243 were still detained in Czechoslovakia, and 8,910, including 3,240 children, in Poland.

In the fourth session of the committee the West German delegation submitted a further nineteen volumes of evidence. One contained the names of 102,958 POWs whose presence in the Soviet Union had been established between 1945 and 1953 – whom the Soviet press said had been killed in battle. The Soviet authorities had long maintained that repatriation of German, Japanese and Italian prisoners of war was complete. Some 9,717 Germans were detained and sentenced as war criminals, and 3,815 cases were still under investigation. These figures had been given on 18 March 1947 by the Plenipotentiary Council of Ministers of the Union of Soviet Socialist Republics. They had been repeated by Tass in 1949 and 1950. And *Pravda* published them again as a statement of the Soviet government's position on 31 August 1953.

The German delegation pointed out that the figures could not be true. Between 1947 and 1953, 450 Germans had been returned. Another 125 had died in captivity, but the figures the Soviets gave had remained the same. During that period 120 Austrians had been returned from the USSR and 27 from Yugoslavia – and 286 Spaniards had been returned by the Soviets.

The Soviet Union maintained its position, and repeated the same figures, even though, between the third and fourth sessions alone, something like 40,000 to 50,000 prisoners of war – mostly Germans and Japanese, but also French, Italians, Spaniards and Dutch – had been repatriated. The commission again appealed for all governments to co-operate over unrepatriated prisoners.[5] By 19 September 1957, when the Ad Hoc Committee wound up, 22,457 Germans had returned from the Soviet Union. Others were returned from Czechoslovakia, Hungary, Poland, Rumania, Canada, Denmark, Britain, France, Norway, the United States and Yugoslavia. The Soviets maintained their position – and the figures – to the end.

In its last statement to the committee, in August 1957, the Federal German government stated that it had positive proof that seventy-eight German POWs were still in Soviet camps. It was also in possession of the names of 87,353 German POWs and 16,480 German civilians 'whose presence in captivity in the Soviet Union at one time or another had been established, but whose subsequent fate was not known'. And there were other German POWs still being held in Czechoslovakia, Poland, Rumania and Hungary.

Of course, many of the German prisoners of war in the Soviet Union died in captivity. But 22,685 German POWs also died under French control and 2,963 died in British custody. Of the 10,000 German and Austrian POWs in a camp in Kiev in September 1945, 8,000 died of starvation within two months. Others suffered terribly during their first years of captivity.

In 1972, the US Senate Judiciary Committee said that the Soviets themselves had indicated in 1946 'that more than two million prisoners of different nationalities were working as laborers on a northern link of the trans-Siberian railroad'.

With the death of Stalin in March 1953 the conditions for enemy prisoners of war improved. The most important change was the abolition of the MVD's Special Conference, which had imposed long sentences by administrative action, often without the accused being present.

The Soviets claimed that the population of corrective labour camps declined by two thirds between 1953 and 1957, through the repatriation of foreign prisoners and through a systematic review of individual cases. The slave-labour system had been as disastrous for the Soviet Union. At one point nearly one fifth of all adult males were imprisoned, with devastating demographic and economic consequences. All the camps at Vorkuta, except two, were closed or converted to free settlements by the end of 1955.

Shifts were cut from twelve hours seven days a week, to eight hours six days a week, and several million prisoners were freed as a result of six separate amnesties issued between 1953 and 1957. The last people to benefit from these amnesties were those Soviet soldiers who had surrendered to the Germans during World War II. They suffered worse even than those who had actively collaborated with the enemy. Common criminals were allowed to return home, while political prisoners were forcibly resettled in the area of their camp or allowed to choose among other restricted areas.

Many Germans found their sentences halved, making them eligible for repatriation. Those remaining in the camps were paid 456 roubles – though 200 roubles were withheld as 'reparations'. Prisoners with good records were allowed to go to and from work without a guard.

In 1954 the nationalities were segregated in separate camps. Soviet citizens accepted incarceration stoically. Foreigners did not. According to a 1958 CIA report

The foreigners created serious disciplinary problems. They were a nucleus of dissidence when thrown [in] with native prisoners; they frequently refused to work. Moreover, by 1953, the task of rebuilding war-damaged areas had been largely completed, as had several large construction projects which used prison labor. Many ex-prisoners report very high disability rates and long sojourns in camps where the prisoners did not work. The mass of reports from repatriated prisoners shows clearly that, by and large, the foreign nationals detained in the camps during 1953– 56 must have been an economic liability.

'Many of the missing prisoners have certainly died,' the Senate Judiciary Committee report concluded, 'and some of them may have reverted to a civilian existence within the Soviet Union . . . most of the prisoners who were still in the Soviet Union in the mid-1950s apparently occupied the status of laborers.'

The Senate Committee's report went on to say, finally, that captives freed by the Soviet Union had provided shocking evidence that, even in 1972, 'several hundred thousand of the missing persons [from World War II] were still being held as forced laborers or prisoners'.

In 1951, when the United Nations Ad Hoc Committee on Prisoners of War was convened, the Italian representative placed on the record nine volumes containing 63,452 names of people, some of whom had been seen in camps in the USSR by one or more sources.

The Italians complained that over 73,000 Italian prisoners had been taken on the Soviet front, only 10,000 returned home. Around 21,000 Italian soldiers and an equal number of civilians had disappeared in the Balkans.

On 2 January 1954 Associated Press reported from Rome that the Soviet Ambassador to Italy, Mikhail Kostilev, had announced that, after the repatriation of twenty-eight Italian POWs from the Soviet Union the following month 'there would remain not one single Italian prisoner of war in Russia'.[7] In fact, by the time the Ad Hoc Committee had been wound up, sixty-nine Italians had been returned in all – still not many when you were expecting over 63,000.

Then, on 11 November 1957, a strange letter appeared in *Time* magazine:

In the marshes near Sicily's town of Marsala, hunter Paolo Lamia took aim and shot down a black-plumed, white-breasted stilt plover, a breed seldom seen in Italy, which migrates each fall from Arctic Siberia to North Africa. On the bird's right leg Lamia found a glass vial containing a message, written in Italian with scrawled capital letters on both sides of an eight-inch strip of paper. On orders of the Ministry of the Interior, the paper was painstakingly analyzed, [and] determined to be of Russian manufacture. [The message read:] 'Many messages but no hope. For 12 years we have been working as slaves in the mines. These men have slit eyes. One dies like a dog. We are in the Polar Arctic. We are 300 Italian soldiers from Salara, Friuli, Verona, Padua, Rovigo. God is our hope of salvation.'

The Interior Ministry had handed the message to the Italian Foreign Ministry. The government made no comment, but officials said they considered the message authentic.[8]

On 14 March 1960 *Time*'s attention returned to Italian POWs. The magazine asked what it called the '64,000 question' – what had happened to the 64,000 Italians who had gone missing at Stalingrad?

In 1942 the Russians broke out to the west of the city on the front held by 220,000 men of Mussolini's Italian Expeditionary Force. In his memoirs Field Marshal Erich von Manstein said: 'The Italians disappeared from the battlefield.'

After six weeks of catastrophic rout and retreat, the Italians' ten divisions suffered casualties officially estimated at 115,000 men. Of these, 30,000 were wounded and 11,000 were listed as dead. Later, the Russians returned 10,000 Italian prisoners of war.

'What became of the other 64,000?' asked *Time*.

> The Russians say that they have none. But in Italy, the question dogs the Communists in every election. In the Neapolitan district of Mergellina, an association of several hundred mothers holds regular meetings and petitions Parliament for word of their sons in Russia. When Italy's President Giovanni Gronchi was in Moscow last month, his wife, Donna Carla Gronchi, demanded an official accounting on behalf of the Italian Red Cross. 'I asked for documentation for every one of the missing,' she said, 'and if any one of them is dead, I want to know how he died, why he died and where he died.'

The week before, *Komsomolskaya Pravda* offered a partial accounting. The Soviet Commission Investigating German Atrocities had taken testimony from one Nina Pietruskowna, a young Polish interpreter for the Italian command, who said that after Mussolini's fall in 1943, Nazi authorities in Lvov asked the Italian troops and officers to swear allegiance to Hitler's Germany and continue the war against the Soviet Union, and that those who refused were arrested.

'More than two thousand Italians were arrested, and the Nazis shot them all,' she testified. 'Among those shot were five generals and forty-five officers, many of whom I knew personally.'

If true, this would account for several thousand, but not the full 64,000. But *Time* reported that Italian diplomats in the USSR doubt that the Soviets are now holding many Italians against their will, despite what the Italian government said to the Ad Hoc Committee.

'Perhaps many died in slave-labor camps. But most of them probably fell in battle or died of starvation or disease in the terrible winter retreat of 1942–43. Uncounted thousands of Germans, Russians and probably Italians lie buried in shallow graves hurriedly hacked in the frozen steppes across the Ukraine,' *Time* said.

The problem was that Soviet Premier Nikita Khrushchev's own son Leonid was killed in the Battle of Stalingrad, fighting against the Italians. Khrushchev once expressed brutally what he thought on the subject: 'They write that we should answer what happened to the Italian soldiers who fought against us, invaded our country, and never returned to Italy. Don't they know what war is? War is a holocaust into which you jump, but it is hard to jump out again. You burn up. And in the war, the Italian soldiers were burned up.'[9]

However, they were not burned up completely. In 1992 a large number of bones, perhaps those of the men who sent a message from the Arctic Circle tied to a plover's leg, were returned to Italy.

And if that was not wild enough, an even more extraordinary tale appeared in the Congressional Record in 1978. On 12 June Congressman Larry McDonald of Georgia brought up the question of Allied prisoners of war in Soviet labour camps in the House of Representatives. He drew the attention of the House to the activities of Mr Ted Greeves, a private detective from Grand Rapids, Michigan. Greeves had been compiling reports about a secret forced-labour camp in the Soviet Union where foreign prisoners were held. One report he had recently come across was from a Rumanian who had escaped from a Soviet camp during a freak flash flood.

Representative McDonald laid in the Congressional Record a letter Greeves had sent to President Nicolae Ceausescu of Rumania soliciting his help. Addressed care of the Central Committee of the Rumanian Communist Party, Bucharest, the letter read:

Dear President Ceausescu,
I am writing to you after nearly three years of exhaustive private investigation and considerable financial sacrifice and many days and hours of time away from my family and profession. This letter is about a Rumanian national by the name of Gheorghe Risoiu, who was forced to fight with the German occupation army during World War II and was captured along with many of his Rumanian countrymen in the Soviet Union. He was presumed dead by his family and loved ones, not having been heard of for over thirty years, but, he was not dead, and with five of his countrymen he escaped from a special Soviet prison camp in the far eastern reaches of Russia, a result of the confusion of a flash flood that occurred at this prison camp in January of 1975. A most

incredible journey resulted during which one of the escapees died.

Allowing their hair to grow and travelling by night they lived off the land. Through a miracle, they were able to avoid detainment and apprehension until Gheorghe Risoiu returned to the village of Pitesti in his homeland of Rumania, an unbelievable six months later in June of 1975, after a journey of over 4,500 miles.

Then Greeves quotes from testimony of Avraham Shifrin, a former Soviet prisoner himself for fourteen years who now resides in Israel and, Greeves says 'is without doubt the world's foremost authority, outside the USSR, on the Soviet prison camp system'. His testimony, which covered Special Russian Camps, had been given before the ninety-third United States Congress on 1 February 1973:

Senator Gurney: How long is this railroad?
Mr Shifrin: Sixty kilometres to Barashevo, from Potma to Barashevo, it is a very little district for concentration camps, I was there and I can show you this.
Senator Gurney: How many concentration camps are on this railroad line?
Mr Shifrin: I do not know, because you see, maybe here I was in 10 or 15. But they have another here also, I explained before my testimony that here we have one place which no one except the KGB in the USSR can tell you anything. We know that there is a big concentration camp with the name Sarovo. In this concentration camp, they have not only fences and earth and guards and so on, they have a special highway around this concentration camp, with more secret police which see that no one would come into this district. Because they have this concentration camp so secret that no one knows what is in there. They bring cars with prisoners only in the night with a special guard takes them from Barashevo to this site.

Greeves' letter continues:

When Gheorghe knocked on the front door of his home, a human tragedy unfolded that is generally known only in opera, theater or literature. By this time his hair was long and his clothing extremely tattered, and after identifying the woman who answered the door by her first name, he told her that she was his wife. Of course, she denied it, so he then told her the names of their children and the church where they were married and the woman still denied it, claiming her husband had been forced to fight with the German Army and died during World War II on the Russian front and had never been heard from again. He then told her the date of their marriage, her parents' names and the dates of the birth of their children. She finally gasped, realising that this was in fact her husband, even though she had remarried, believing her first husband to have perished.

Greeves says he learned of this story a short time after the return of Mr Risoiu and he understood that Risoiu was cautioned by Rumanian government officials not to speak to anyone of his prison experiences. He was given a government pension and a home in the city of Curtea de Arges and reunited with his wife and family. Greeves' letter ends with a plea:

> My purpose in writing to you today, President Ceausescu, is one that concerns the deepest of all humanitarian endeavors, and that is that we have knowledge of the fact the secret prison camp that Mr Risoiu and his fellow countrymen escaped from holds many foreign nationals, mostly German army officers from World War II, but also citizens from the Netherlands, Belgium, France, Spain, England, Italy, and Yugoslavia, also Austrians, Japanese and of course additional Rumanians, but what concerns me most is this camp holds Americans.
>
> President Ceausescu, Mr Gheorghe Risoiu and his fellow escapees, I am informed, have an extensive list of names available identifying and describing those persons being held in this camp . . . In all sincerity I ask to be allowed to interview the remaining Soviet escapees, who are now living in your country, prior to have them testify without delay before an appropriate US Congressional Committee so that the remaining Americans now illegally imprisoned in the Soviet Union and all other foreign nationals held there can immediately be brought home to their families and loved ones.

The loss the families of these missing men had suffered, Greeves maintained, was far worse than the finality of death.[10] For American POW activists, Risoiu is a touchstone. Ceausescu shut him up. But since Ceausescu was killed, some say Risoiu has been speaking out again.

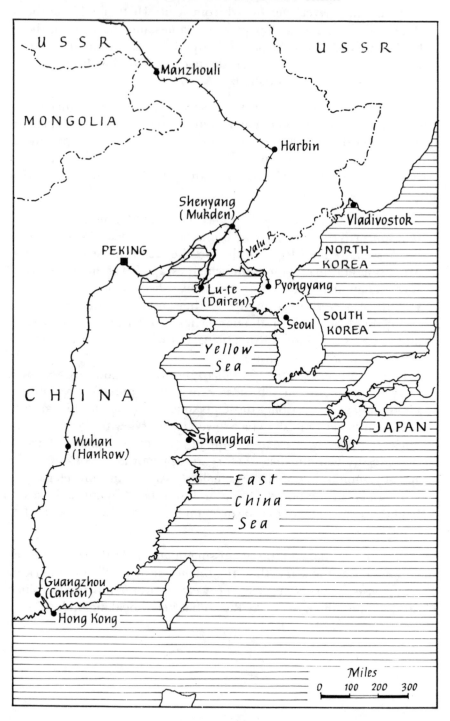

## CHAPTER 36

# Little Switch, Big Switch

✝

WITH THE SURRENDER of Japan in 1945, the peninsula of Korea was divided along the 38th parallel. The Soviet Union occupied the north and the US occupied the south. A Joint US–USSR Commission convened in Seoul in 1946 to discuss the reunification of Korea but foundered when the Soviets sought to exclude Korean groups from the discussions.

In September 1946 the United Nations called for a general election to reunite the country, to be carried out under the observation of a UN Temporary Commission. Those elected would make up a National Assembly, establish a government and arrange with the occupying powers for the withdrawal of troops from the country.

However, the Soviets barred the Temporary Commission entering North Korea. But in 1948 the elections went ahead in the south anyway and Syngman Rhee became President of the newly established republic. The UN General Assembly declared the republic, based in Seoul, the only lawful government in Korea. US forces withdrew, leaving a force of only about 500 as a US Military Advisory Group. However, President Truman began giving Rhee over $10 million a year in military and other assistance, declaring that Korea had become a testing ground in the ideological struggle between communism and democracy.

Meanwhile, in the north, a People's Republic was set up in Pyongyang under Kim Il Sung, First Secretary of the Korean Communist Party and a former Red Army major. In turn, the Soviet Union recognised the People's Republic as the only lawful government in Korea.

On 25 June 1950 the North Korean People's Army launched a full-scale invasion across the 38th parallel. The UN Security Council adopted a resolution demanding the immediate withdrawal of the invading force. The Soviet Union was unable to veto the measure as its delegate was boycotting the Council at the time in protest at the UN's refusal to admit mainland China. When the Security Council's resolution was ignored, the UN passed resolutions recommending military action under US command.

On 2 July 1950 the US 24th Infantry Division landed at Pusan, but was forced back by the invasion forces. Then on 15 September a daring amphibious landing at Inchon turned the tide. The communists were forced out of Seoul and the invading army was routed.

When North Korea rejected a surrender ultimatum issued by the UN commander, General Douglas MacArthur, he drove on, crossing the 38th parallel on 8 October. His aim was to press on to the Yalu River, North Korea's northern border, thereby toppling the communist regime and reuniting the country. On 15 October, as he pushed on northwards, MacArthur personally assured President Truman that it would all be over by Thanksgiving.

However, the Chinese 'volunteer' army was massing on the Korean border. By mid-October it was infiltrating across the Yalu, moving by night and hiding by day in the hills and gorges of the border region.

On 1 November, with elements of the American 24th Division just eighteen miles from the Yalu River, the Chinese attacked, driving back MacArthur's army. In this ferocious Chinese counter-attack countless UN soldiers vanished without a trace. Many were blown into pieces too small to identify. Some were captured, summarily executed and buried in unmarked graves. Others died of exposure – that winter, in North Korea temperatures dropped to 30 degrees below zero. Hunger, wounds and brutality on the forced marches to POW camps all took their toll. But it now appears that hundreds who survived these marches were never returned.

Although much has been made of the atrocities of the Korean War, most occurred in the first few months. They were committed largely by North Korean troops, who routinely shot prisoners they did not want to be bothered with. In contrast, the Chinese often released wounded prisoners, exhorting them to spread the word about their 'humane treatment'. And, as a general rule, those held captive were subjected to relentless indoctrination – brainwashing – rather than physical torture.

On 23 June 1951, with the combatants roughly back where they started, the Soviet delegation to the UN proposed a ceasefire. UN and communist commanders met on 10 July at Kaesong, and later at Panmunjom. The first stumbling block was the Chinese demand for the withdrawal of all foreign troops. The US refused. The second was the communists' demand for the restoration of the 38th parallel as the border between North and South. The US insisted on the existing battle line.

The third and most important was the issue of the prisoners of war. The communists demanded an all-for-all prisoner exchange. But the United States was reluctant to agree to this formula, following their experiences with forced repatriation in World War II. The UN forces held 171,000 North Korean and communist Chinese prisoners, 50,000 of them unwilling to return to their homelands. On this matter the negotiations were deadlocked and for two bloody years the two sides fought solely over the fate of the prisoners.

The battle did not just rage over the barren hills of the Korean peninsula. It also raged inside the prisoner-of-war camps. Korean POWs in UN camps unwilling to be returned to the north put together a petition consisting of bloody thumb prints and sent it to President Eisenhower. This forced the US Judge Advocate General's Office to concede that under Article 7 of the Geneva Prisoner of War Convention of 1949: 'A prisoner of war can renounce his "right" to repatriation by claiming asylum as a civilian or by enlisting in the armed forces of the detaining power.'

The communist response was to take its own ideological struggle into the camps. They organised riots and, on 7 May 1952, a group of dedicated communists in Compound 70 of Camp 1 on Kojedo island seized the camp commander, Brigadier General Francis T. Dodd, while he was making a tour of inspection. Dodd became a prisoner of war inside his own POW camp.

The leader of the communist prisoners, Pak Sang Hyong, issued four terms for Dodd's release. These were:

**1.** The UN high command admitted that bloodshed had taken place in the UN prisoner of war camps, and promised that treatment would be more humane in future.
**2.** The repatriation of prisoners would take place under the conditions demanded by the communist delegates at Panmunjom.
**3.** There would be no more screening of prisoners – separating communists from anti-communists – and no more searches.
**4.** That representatives from the North Korean People's Army and the Chinese People's Volunteer Army to visit prisoners of war.

Dodd admitted that prisoners had been killed by guards. There had been so much rioting that it was inevitable. He denied that prisoners were forcibly screened. As to conditions at the peace talks and visits by representatives of the communist armies, these things were out of his hands. Dodd was released after seventy-eight hours and sent back to the US in disgrace.[1]

The ideological war was also raging in the communist POW camps where the Chinese and North Koreans went to huge lengths to brainwash UN prisoners with Marxist-Leninist principles. In some cases they succeeded.

As part the propaganda war there was also a battle over POW numbers. Although the 1949 Geneva Convention was now in force, the People's Republic of China did not ratify it until December 1956 and North Korea until August 1957. So there was no official notification of prisoners of war as there had been in World War II. On 18 December 1951, at the peace talks, the communists handed over a list of just 11,559 names – although in March 1951 Peking and Pyongyang had claimed to be holding 65,000. The talks broke off and did not resume until after Stalin's death in March 1953. By then, the US were keen to end the war. The new American administration under Dwight D. Eisenhower was eager to balance the budget.

In April 1953 the first 6,670 communist and 684 UN prisoners were exchanged at Panmunjom in an operation known as Little Switch. Little Switch stopped almost as soon as it had started, as details of the exact arrangements for the return of prisoners – and the handling of prisoners who did not wish to be repatriated – continued to be the stumbling block. The talks were further complicated by South Korean President Syngman Rhee's opposition to any settlement that would leave Korea divided. He threatened to withdraw his army from UN Command while the US, now desperate to get out of the war, secretly prepared a plan codenamed Ever-Ready which would seize control of South Korea, holding Rhee 'in protective custody, incommunicado' until a peace treaty was signed.

Rhee realised what was coming and pulled a master stroke. On 18 June 1953 he simply released 27,000 North Korean anti-communist prisoners in defiance of the United Nations. Free to settle in the south, these men disappeared like raindrops in a pond. The communists promptly broke off negotiations.

To placate Rhee the US promised to extend economic aid and offered South Korea a mutual security pact. Talks resumed on 20 July. Rhee gave in and agreed to support the armistice, even though he would not sign it.

The armistice was signed by the other combatants on 27 July 1953. The United Nations had won most of its demands. US forces were to stay in the south and the military line became the new border. The prisoners of war who did not want to be repatriated were to be held for ninety days by a Neutral Nations Repatriations Commission – comprising Sweden, Switzerland, Poland and Czechoslovakia – during which time representatives of their own governments would have free access to them. Their future would then be discussed by a 'political conference' for another thirty days, after which they would be considered civilians and released.

The exchange of prisoners would be handled by an Indian Neutral Supervisory Commission in what was called Operation Big Switch. It took place over one month from 5 August to 6 September 1953. Under the terms of the armistice, UN Command returned 75,823 North Koreans and Chinese. A further 21,809 – 7,582 North Koreans and 14,227 Chinese – refused repatriation (plus the 27,000 North Koreans who were unwilling to return and were released earlier). The North Koreans were resettled in South Korea and the Chinese were sent to Taiwan.

In exchange the communists turned over 12,773 UN prisoners of war. Only one Briton – Royal Marine Commando Andrew Condron – and twenty-one Americans elected to stay behind with the communists and were resettled in China. Condron returned to Britain in 1970. These twenty-two defectors are not considered as unrepatriated POWs.

So in Truman's battle of ideology nearly 49,000 rejected communism, against a mere 22 who rejected democracy. Worse, three out of four Chinese POWs chose not to return to their homeland. In this inconclusive war such rejection added up to a huge propaganda defeat for China, North Korea and the Soviets. In 1953, with the eyes of the world on Panmunjom, this was a hugely publicised humiliation. Many people believe that, to even up the score, the communists forcibly held back some UN prisoners.

US government documents state that nearly one thousand known US POWs – and an undetermined number of the 8,177 still listed MIA after Operation Big Switch – were not repatriated at the end of the Korean War.

On 1 July 1953 the British Commonwealth Missing in Action and Prisoner of War Lists, Korea, carried 970 men as 'confirmed PW'. The basis of this was a list of 926 British prisoners the communists admitted holding, handed over on 19 December 1951. Added to this were the names of other men whose presence in communist prison camps was confirmed by sick and wounded POWs repatriated early. Twenty-eight sick and wounded British POWs on the list had been returned at Little Switch in April 1953, along with another twelve who were not on the communist list. So the 1951 list had been trimmed to 898, with another 72 added from the testimony supplied by returned POWs.

Along with the 970 'confirmed PW', 55 were carried as 'missing believed PW', 31 'missing believed died as PW', 91 'missing believed killed', and 163 'missing in action'. This list included Canadians, Australians, New Zealanders and South Africans. Out of the 55 'missing believed PW' were 1 navy officer, 3 British army officers and 18 British army 'other ranks'.[2]

So, in all, 1,188 British and Commonwealth officers and men were posted missing or taken prisoner. In 1953 1,036 British POWs were repatriated and 31 POWs were thought to have died – making a shortfall of 121. Some of them may have been dead. But documents in the US National Archives prove that some of these 121 were taken into captivity in China and the Soviet Union and were never returned. There may have been more. It was certainly not uncommon during the Vietnam War – another war fought without the protection of the Geneva Convention – to declare a man dead, accidentally or otherwise, when he had, in fact, been captured.

But the allegations that British, Americans and other UN POWs were not being returned did not surface until years later when people started playing with the figures. Only three days after Operation Big Switch had started, it was known there was something terribly wrong. On 8 August 1953 *The New York Times* reported: 'General James A. Van Fleet, retired commander of the United States Eighth Army in Korea, estimated tonight that a large percentage of the 8,000 American soldiers listed as missing in Korea were alive.'

Two days later, just five days into the month-long prisoner exchange, a report by the UN Combined Command for Reconnaissance Activity, Korea, (CCRAK) stated: 'Figures show that the total number of MIAs, plus known captives, less those to be US repatriated, leaves a balance of 8,000 unaccounted for.'

The report mentions numerous sightings of UN POWs who were being transferred to Manchuria, China and the Soviet Union from the beginning of hostilities in Korea.

'Many POWs transferred have been technicians and factory workers,' the report said. 'Other POWs transferred had a knowledge of Cantonese and are reportedly used for propaganda purposes.'

By the end of Operation Big Switch it was clear to the UN authorities that they had a major problem on their hands. After questioning returned POWs, military authorities figured that 3,404 UN personnel known to have been in communist custody, including 944 Americans, had been unaccounted for. It was known who these men were. Of the

944 Americans missing 610 were ground troops, 312 airmen and 22 marines and sailors.

According to the *Army Times* of 13 October 1986,

> Many of the missing had been identified as POWs by repatriated prisoners, mail received from POW camps, Communist radio broadcasts, propaganda photographs and intelligence reports . . . Still, the Communists insisted they knew nothing about the missing men – and they never have budged from that position. For instance, they denied having any information about a prisoner whose mother had received a Christmas message from him in a Chinese radio broadcast. They maintained that a US Army pilot had escaped – though repatriated prisoners reported that he had lost both legs.

Even though it was well known that prisoners had been left behind, nothing could be done about it. The American public were tired of the war. It had cost 54,000 American deaths and $18,000 million over three years. Coming so soon after World War II, it had never properly been understood or fully supported by public opinion. The public were particularly shocked by the UN's bloody retreat from North Korea in 1950 and were mystified by President Truman's dramatic dismissal of General MacArthur as commander of the UN forces in 1951, after MacArthur had advocated the extension of the war into China. Public patience was further strained by another two years of truce talks while bodies piled up as battles seesawed over barren hills. Without the will to fight, the US had no political leverage – exactly the same position they found themselves in during 1973, at the end of their involvement in the Vietnam War. Britain and the other UN allies certainly could not carry on the war alone – even if they had the political will to do so.

Diplomatic channels were also closed. China and North Korea were not members of the United Nations. America had no diplomatic relations with China at the time. Relations between the West and the Soviet Union were also strained. Forty years later, no peace treaty has been signed and there have been no direct talks between any member of the UN coalition and the North Koreans since 1953. With the armistice still in force, all enquiries have to be handled by the Military Armistice Commission which has been sitting at Panmunjom – and continuing the war on paper – ever since the truce was signed.

At the time, even raising the issue was a futile gesture. In his autobiography, *The Right Hand of Power*, US career diplomat U. Alexis Johnson, who played a key role in the Korean ceasefire talks, says: 'It is difficult nowadays, after decades of increasing warmth between Washington and Peking, to make the depth of enmity that guided our dealings with China in the 1950s come alive for someone who was not there to witness it.'

Nevertheless, something had to be done. These men simply could not remain on the POW lists for ever. But President Eisenhower, and Prime Minister Winston Churchill who had returned to power in 1951, had been through this sort of thing before. Soon the UN Command had managed to winnow the figure of 3,404 UN personnel, including 944 Americans, down to 2,233 UN personnel including 389 Americans, known to be in communist custody. For these men there was compelling evidence that they were alive, in enemy hands, before the armistice. Some of them were almost certainly British.

Although almost all the documents referring to the return of British POWs in the Public Record Office in Richmond are either closed for 75 years or 'retained by the department', the list of British Commonwealth prisoners of war and missing in action from the Korean War, prepared on 9 July 1953 and circulated on 13 July 1953 in the run-up to Big Switch, is available. This list is particularly interesting because, unlike a copy of the same document which I had obtained from Canadian archives earlier, the British list had the names of the men who had returned ticked off and the date of their return added by hand. This effectively updated the list to 14 September 1953, the date of the last handwritten return and almost a week after the end of Big Switch.

Other details of the list have also been updated. The names of some men returned have been written in. In the main, they had been captured after 9 July, when the list had been compiled. Others had had their status altered by hand. Some who had been returned had had their status changed, reasonably enough from 'missing' to 'prisoner of war' or, curiously, from 'missing' to 'missing believed prisoner of war'. If they had been handed back, there was no doubt that they had been a prisoner of war.

Others, who did not return, had had their status changed from 'missing' to 'missing believed killed' or to 'missing died as prisoner of war'. These handwritten changes of status were presumably made on the basis of new information provided by the returning prisoners.

However, some other, more interesting, handwritten changes had also been made. G. Allen of the Royal Fusiliers had had his status changed, by hand, from 'missing' to 'prisoner of war'. He had gone missing on the night of 24/25 November 1952 and, according to the list, had not been returned. Five others – Second Lieutenant P.A. StClair-Morford, Private H. Girard, Private J.P. Monnett, Private D. Smith and

Private T.W. Wright – had had their status changed from 'missing' to 'missing believed prisoner of war'. And Private R.M. Perfect of the Royal Norfolks, who had been listed as 'missing died as prisoner of war', had had the 'died as' crossed out. Presumably these men's status, too, had been changed because of new information from the returning prisoners of war. So, by the end of the prisoner-of-war exchanges, there was good reason to believe that these men were still in enemy hands.

Three other men – Second Lieutenant L.S. Adams-Action, Royal Marine R. Nicholls and Fusilier A. Pryor (leaving aside voluntary stay-behind Andrew Condron) – retained their prisoner-of-war status, even though they were not listed as returned. Six more retained their missing-believed-prisoner-of-war status.

So, according to this list, four British servicemen known to be prisoners of war and nine believed to be prisoners of war were left in communist hands. Added to this, there were seventeen other Commonwealth servicemen still listed as 'missing believed prisoner of war' after the end of Big Switch – eight Australians, eight South Africans and one Canadian soldier.[3]

## CHAPTER 37

# Slave Labourers in Communist Hands

†

ON 18 DECEMBER 1953, four months after the end of the prisoner exchange, *US News & World Report* published an important article datelined Panmunjom, Korea, which shed light on what had happened to the missing men. It said that Americans positively identified as being in North Korean prisons had been 'lost' from work parties sent from one prison to another in the weeks immediately before the ceasefire. The lost men were taken, the *Report* said, by the Chinese and moved across the Yalu River out of Korea. They were to become, the subheading of the article made clear, 'Slave laborers in Communist hands'.

The article, entitled 'Where are the 944 missing GIs?', went on to outline the delicate political position the nations who had fought under the UN Command now found themselves in.

'The United States did not win the war in Korea,' it explains. 'As a result, it cannot demand and expect to receive any reliable accounting for those still missing. America can only protest.'

The only protest so far had been an army communiqué in September 1953. American officials seemed reluctant to press the case of the GIs who were still missing. The emphasis, instead, was on finding a way to make a deal with the communist Chinese on terms of peace. The POW issue had become a political football.

'Military men, unable now to exert pressure on the Communists under terms of the truce, refer to the missing as a diplomatic problem,' said *US News & World Report*. 'State Department diplomats, in turn, say the problem of missing Americans is not yet under their jurisdiction, and won't be until a political conference with the Communists either begins or is definitely abandoned. So they are doing nothing.'

This political conference was never begun – or abandoned. The situation remains stalemated today forty years later, just as it was in December 1953.

Meanwhile, new reports about the missing continued to flow in. There was substantial evidence now that a number of Allied prisoners had been marched through the streets of Mukden (Shenyang), deep inside Manchuria, in a 'victory' parade. As far as was known, none of the men in it had been returned. No repatriated prisoner said he had been in that parade.

The article went on to report official confirmation that some Americans were sent to Manchuria. One of them, Captain Lawrence V. Bach, a twenty-nine-year-old fighter pilot from Grand Forks, North Dakota, spent four days in Manchuria, where he was questioned by the Chinese, North Koreans and Soviets. He was followed by Major General William F. Dean, commander of the US 24th Division, who spent some time in communist Manchuria. Both of these Americans were repatriated. Others who were sent there were not.

Most of the new evidence coming in was from evaluated reports from Allied prisoners repatriated during Operation Big Switch. As they were being shipped home, former prisoners were questioned intensively about men who had died or disappeared either during the lengthy forced marches northwards or while they were in the camps. During the long sea voyage, in the comparative comfort of hospital ships and transports, the ex-POWs could relax and tell coherent stories of what they saw. Trained Intelligence men checked and re-checked each report. The pattern that finally emerged out of this long and intensive probing revealed not only that the communists committed systematic atrocities on their prisoners but that they were taking POWs as slaves as well.

'The Chinese Communists did not merely want Americans to work in [the] salt beds of Stantung or the uranium mines of Sinkiang,' *US News & World Report* said. 'They primarily wanted – and got – Americans who could handle the sensitive and complex instruments of modern warfare such as radar, airborne and ground, and infrared instruments for night combat. They were particularly interested in airmen with technical training, and artillerymen who knew the secrets of intricate fuses.'

There are echoes here both of the *London Evening Standard* report of 7 August 1992 which broke the story that British POWs from World War II were taken by the Soviets for their technical skills and of the screening of American POWs in Vietnam where the brightest and the best were not repatriated but shipped off into the USSR.

The names of these technicians did not appear on any of the communist prisoner lists, so the Chinese felt no compulsion to explain what happened to them. When the UN Command asked the whereabouts of specific men known to have been alive in communist camps, the Chinese merely replied that they had no records to show that these men were ever prisoners.

Many returned prisoners said many technicians disappeared from communist camps in the final weeks of the war. This indicates that the communists could not persuade them to co-operate willingly – the Chinese could certainly not afford to turn these technicians over to the Neutral Nations Repatriations Commission and hope that they would refuse repatriation. Instead, they ceased to exist as far as the communist prisoner-of-war records were concerned.

*US News & World Report* could only speculate where they were. There had been reports from returning Japanese prisoners, repatriated from Russia in 1953, that some Allied POWs from Korea had been seen in prison not far from Moscow. War prisoners of many Western nationalities were also reported to be working on a huge underground project in Siberia. The prison compounds of Manchuria were closed to neutral inspection. So were the communist research and development centres in that part of the world.

Some of the 944 may be dead, said *US News & World Report*, victims of the torture techniques for 'persuasion' widely reported by repatriated prisoners. But US Intelligence officers believed that most of those missing POWs were probably somewhere in Manchuria. Communist bases along the Yalu River, at Port Arthur, Changchun, Mukden and Harbin were closely guarded and restricted for all but the military. And there were enough Soviets in these areas to make several hundred Westerners inconspicuous. Elsewhere in China, Westerners would be noticed and the grapevine would quickly pass on the news. But Manchuria was a closed military area and Allied POWs could live there under guard and unremarked for years, with no opportunity for escape.

The same story came up in the *Los Angeles Times* on 3 July 1992. It said: 'The Defense Department has collected evidence indicating that several dozen American servicemen who disappeared during the Korean war, were captured and sent to China, where they were subjected to psychological and medical experiments before they died in captivity.'

The *LA Times* story was based largely on information supplied by an East European military official, but it prompted the US to send a high-level American delegation to Peking to question the Chinese. But the Chinese government said there was no evidence to confirm the existence of such a facility. US Defense Secretary Dick Cheney turned the report over to the National Security Council and the CIA to investigate.

The East European Intelligence source had told investigators from the Defense Intelligence Agency that American captives were transferred directly from Korea to a facility believed to have been in the Manchurian city of Harbin. There, American prisoners were subjected to tests designed to determine how regional and racial differences affected their ability to withstand torture and interrogation. A second source said that testing might also have involved germ warfare agents.

'The ultimate fate of the American captives is unclear,' the DIA report said, 'but the DIA concluded that some were executed after their ordeals and some may have died during the course of the experiments.'

The DIA report also claimed that officials and scientists from the Soviet Union's military medical corps were present and participated in the experiments focused on distinctions between American blacks and whites, as well as differences in the pain thresholds of servicemen from the American southeast and north.

The *LA Times* stated: 'One official said that American officials were uncertain which country – Russia or China – to press for more information, given the uncertainty over the location of the alleged research facility in China and the role allegedly played in it by the Soviet Union and its East European allies.'

There is no evidence that any of the Americans who may have been held at the Chinese facility were returned at the end of the Korean War. The Chinese repeatedly declared that they had repatriated all *prisoners of war*, but the American government maintained for almost forty years that the Chinese failed to return some servicemen held as *political* prisoners.

The need for technicians in expanding communist forces accounted for the missing specialists. But other men were missing too. US military officials had long speculated that many others who had already resisted communist persuasion methods would be used for an experiment in long-term brainwashing. And there was always the opportunity for communists to enhance their bargaining position or to obtain ransom, 'as was done with American fliers forced down in Hungary', *US News & World Report* said. 'What the US will do about Communist withholding of American prisoners, in direct violation of the truce agreement in Korea, is the big question now. Families of the missing men are beginning to wonder if 944 more Americans must be added to the price of going into a war without winning it.'[1]

The answer is that the US government was going to do nothing – except lie to the American people. And the families of the missing men would soon learn that 944 more Americans *would* be added to the price of going to war. It would also have to be paid by British families, and by families from the fifteen other countries who went to war under the flag of the United Nations.

Mr Paul Bath of Marshall, Texas, read 'Where are the 944 missing GIs?' in *US News & World Report* and wrote to his senator. He was a Democrat and currently the Senate Majority Leader, though he would one day go on to be President during another Asian war. His name was Lyndon B. Johnson.

Senator Johnson wrote to the Secretary of State on 21 December 1953 to air his constituent's concern. The first reaction of the Secretary of State's office was to call Johnson and dispose of the matter by phone. However, a written reply was requested and the task of replying was given to the Assistant Secretary of State for Congressional Relations, Thruston B. Morton, who duly passed the task on to his staff. The evolution of the text of Morton's letter to Johnson – which took four rewrites to complete – shows how the United States government had learnt to tackle these delicate problems. The British Foreign Office and the Ministry of Defence were almost certainly streets ahead of them.

The four drafts of Morton's letter still exist today. They illustrate perfectly how the State Department artfully sought to mislead the most powerful leader in Congress at the time. Part of the first draft read:

> On September 9, the United Nations Command presented to the Communist representatives on the Military Armistice Commission a list of approximately 3,404 Allied personnel, including 944 Americans, about whom there was evidence that they had at one time or another been in Communist custody. The kinds of evidence from which this list was drawn included letters written home by prisoners, prisoner of war interrogations, interrogations of returnees, and Communist radio broadcasts. The United Nations Command asked the Communist side for a complete accounting of these personnel.
>
> On September 21, the Communists made a reply relative to the list of names presented to them by the United Nations Command on September 9, in which they stated that many of the men on the list had never been captured at all, while others had already been repatriated.

This entire section was crossed out by Morton, but a persistent foreign service officer sent back a second draft, with the section quoted above unchanged, as well as a new sentence at the end of the introductory paragraph which read: 'He [Mr Paul Bath of Marshall, Texas] can be assured that efforts are being made to obtain the release of all our men in Communist custody and may be interested in having the following information about this matter.'

The second draft also contained a new page which followed the paragraphs quoted above. It read:

General Clark, in a letter of September 24 [1953 – two and a half weeks after Operation Big Switch ended] to the Communist side, stated that he considered their reply [that the 944 US men were never captured or had been repatriated] wholly unacceptable, and pointed out that by signing the armistice agreement the Communists had undertaken a solemn obligation to repatriate directly or to hand over to the custody of the Neutral Nations Repatriation Commission all of the captured persons held by them at the time the armistice was signed. He pointed out that this obligation was binding upon them and applied to all United Nations Command persons regardless of where captured or held in custody. I am enclosing a copy of General Clark's letter of September 24 which you may wish to send to your constituent.

On November 21, the United Nations Command provided the Communist side with a revision of its original list of unaccounted for Allied personnel which it had presented to the Communists on September 9. The revised list contained a total of 3,400 names, and the figure for United States prisoners of war unaccounted for was increased by eight to a total of 952.

On November 21, the United Nations Command protested in the Military Armistice Commission to the Communists that they had still failed to give a satisfactory reply concerning the list of unaccounted for United Nations Command personnel, and pointed out that additional evidence provided by three Korean prisoners of war who recently defected to the United Nations side corroborated the United Nations Command statements that the Communists were withholding prisoners of war. The United Nations Command demanded that the Communists 'hand over to the custody of the Custodian Forces of India all those prisoners that your side still retains.'

Ambassador Arthur Dean has also referred to this problem in the course of his negotiations with the Communists at Panmunjom.

Your constituent may be assured that it continues to be our determined purpose to obtain the return of all personnel in Communist custody and the United Nations Command will make every effort to accomplish the objective.

Assistant Secretary Morton rejected all the proposed changes in the second draft by crossing them out. The third draft of the letter to Johnson was so disagreeable to Morton that he typed out two sentences and attached it to the draft, crossing out everything else. As a result, the final letter read:

My dear Senator Johnson:

I refer to your letter of December 21, acknowledged by telephone on December 30, with which you enclose a letter from Mr. Paul Bath of Marshall, Texas concerning an article in the December 18 issue of U.S. News and World Report. It is believed that Mr. Bath refers to the article 'Where are 944 Missing GIs?' on page 27 of this publication.

I am enclosing copies of a statement recounting the efforts being made to secure the return of American prisoners of war who *might* still be in Communist custody which I believe will be of assistance to you in replying to your constituent. As the statement points out, it continues to be our determined purpose to obtain the return of all personnel in Communist custody and we will do everything possible to accomplish this objective.

With regard to questions as to whether there are military personnel or other United States citizens in the custody of the Soviet Government, a few of the prisoners-of-war of other nationalities recently released by the Soviet Government have made reports alleging that American citizens are imprisoned in the Soviet Union. All of these reports are being investigated by this Department with the cooperation of other agencies of the Government.

You are probably aware that representations which the United States Government recently made to the Soviet Government resulted in the release in Berlin on December 29 of Homer H. Cox and Leland Towers, two Americans reported by returning [German] prisoner-of-war as being in Soviet custody. The Department will investigate, as it has done in the past, every report indicating that American citizens are held in the custody of foreign governments.

Sincerely Yours,
    For the Secretary of State,
    Thruston B. Morton[2]

Morton's final draft contained no specific or accurate information, in contrast to the three drafts he had rejected earlier. The rhetoric of the State Department could not go beyond the word 'might' to describe the possibility of US servicemen being held by communist forces. While the State Department was taking credit for having released two Americans from the Soviet Gulag and for investigating 'every report indicating that American citizens are held in the custody of foreign governments', it was dismissing any real possibility that there could be more POWs in communist prisons.

CHAPTER 38

# Prior Knowledge

THAT ALL THE prisoners of war from Korea were not returned should
have surprised no one. Early in the Korean War British and American
prisoners had already turned up deep inside China – belying the
Chinese claim that the war was being fought by a 'volunteer' force
rather than the People's Republic of China itself. None of these men
were returned. A CIA report dated 27 June 1951 says:

> In early April American prisoners of war from Korea began
> arriving in Hankow, where they were turned over to the Chinese
> Communist Central and Southern Military Command. By 15
> April approximately 500 had arrived in Hankow, and on 18 April
> some of these prisoners were paraded through the streets of
> Hankow under heavy guard.
> 2. In mid-April 60 prisoners of war, most of them American and
> the rest British, arrived in Canton via the Canton–Hankow rail-
> way. In early May, they were being detained in a foreign-style
> compound at the corner of Tunghua Road, East, and Kheinichao
> in Tungshan, Canton. There were barbed wire barricades around
> the compounds, and a Public Security division mounted a heavy
> guard around the area. No one was allowed to enter without
> permission from high Communist authorities. The prisoners
> were treated fairly well, and were given good food and billets.
> 3. In mid-June 52 American prisoners of war from Korea were
> incarcerated in the Baptist church on Tunghua Road, Canton.
> These prisoners were sent to Canton because the Chinese Com-
> munist authorities hoped to obtain military and medical supplies
> from the United States government in return for their release.
> They planned to demand US $100,000 worth of supplies for each
> prisoner released. The British and Indian governments would be
> used as intermediaries.

The source of the information in this CIA report is believed to be 'fairly reliable', though the accuracy of the information could not be judged.[1]

The CIA Intelligence analyst commented that according to another informant, as of 24 May there was no indication of American prisoners being held in Canton and there were no barbed wire barricades at the end of Tunghua Road, East, Canton. However, the analyst also mentioned that 'casual informants have stated that as of 20 April American prisoners of war who had arrived in Canton were being held in three foreign style houses at the end of Tunghua Road, East'. And another report said that these prisoners were transferred to Kweilin on 2 May.

Although Chinese newsmen in Hong Kong could not confirm the presence of United States or United Nations troops in Canton as of mid-June, the Hong Kong newspaper *Haing Tao Jih Pao* had reported them there in late April. The reporter probably based his information on the statement of a traveller from Canton who said he had seen prisoners in Tunghua Road, the CIA analyst said. However, he added: 'The *Haing Tao Jih Pao* would print any news embarrassing to the United States.'[2]

According to another CIA report in late July, US prisoners were again seen in Canton. They were in the central part of the Baptist Church compound in the Tungshan area, heavily guarded by rings of armed guards.

Then 'on 2 August fifty-two US prisoners of war from Korea, who had been held in the Baptist church on Tunghua Road, Canton, left by train for Peiping via Hankow under guard of Chinese Communist soldiers'.

The informant was judged to be fairly reliable and the information 'possibly true'. The report also gave references for two other reports of sightings of US prisoners in Canton.[3]

More American prisoners of war were seen at a camp on the Yuyuan Road, Shanghai, on 15 August 1951. Their names were given by a usually reliable informant to the CIA. Unfortunately, they had been transliterated into Chinese characters, then back into English. The resulting garbled list of names is Fa-hsing – a major and adviser to 30 Regiment, 9 Division; K'o-lin-asu, an air liaison officer to the Chinese division [sic]; Pei-k'o – a captain with 29 Regiment; Shih-lai-te – a major; and Ta-erh-ti – an air force lieutenant. However, some of these names could be linked to names on POW/MIA lists.

The CIA analyst also noted that there was a supplementary report on Allied prisoners of war being held at number 35, Lane 1136, Yuyuan Road, Shanghai.[4]

A CIA report of 22 August 1951 explained why these men were constantly being moved around:

> The Chinese Communists have been using numbers of UN prisoners of war captured in Korea for propaganda tours throughout China. The tours are to demonstrate to the Chinese people Communist political achievements and the success of the 'volunteer' forces, as well as to encourage youths to join the army and aid in fund raising.
>
> The arrival of the above prisoners in the South China area was co-ordinated with the Delegation for Comfort of Troops in Korea and by Kwangtung Youth and the Delegation of Air to Korea Volunteers.
>
> In Canton some 40 UN prisoners participated in street demonstrations. Most were former residents of South China or Hong Kong and among the group were British and American officers and enlisted men selected for their knowledge of Cantonese dialect. Although detained in a local concentration camp, they have been allowed to write to friends and relatives in order to capitalise on their propaganda value. Broadcasts have also been planned.[5]

Another usually reliable informant told the CIA on 6 September 1951 about American prisoners of war in Canton:

> As of mid-July about 60 American prisoners of war were being held in the former villa of Ch'en Chi't'ang at Plum Blossom Village in Canton. They were given two meals daily of the same food Chinese Communist soldiers receive and were being given daily political and ideological training. Their guards were drawn from the garrison regiment of 15 Army Group Command Headquarters.[6]

Another informant confirmed that the Chinese were selecting Chinese speakers from among the UN prisoners:

> The Chinese Communist 4 Field Army under the command of Lin Piao has selected a group of United Nations prisoners of war who can speak Mandarin or Cantonese and sent them to Canton. About 108 such prisoners have arrived in Canton, including 13 Americans, 8 British, and 103 South Koreans. More than 40 were in the first group of arrivals, and the remainder came later in another group. The American and British prisoners were confirmed in the former USIS office in Shaneen, Canton. They are

restricted to the building, but are receiving good treatment. The South Koreans are not treated as well as the British and Americans. No official or unofficial information concerning the prisoners has been disclosed by the Chinese Communist authorities, but it is believed that they are to be used for propaganda purposes.

The CIA analyst pooh-poohed this idea. Although he noted that a similar report mentions Chinese-speaking prisoners being used in street demonstrations, he commented 'that it is most unlikely that United Nations' prisoners could be used without reports of such activity appearing in the [strictly censored] Chinese press'. Besides, another informant stationed at Shinach'i reported there were no UN prisoners in Canton as of mid-July.

However, he noted, an informant with contacts in Mukden had reported that thirty American prisoners of war were sent by train from Mukden south to Hankow on 8 May 1951. Other CIA reports from June took them on from Hankow to Canton. 'The prisoners seen in Mukden were reported to be in good spirits and tidily dressed,' the analyst noted.[7]

Whatever these British and American prisoners of war were going to be used for, their presence attracted some interest. According to another CIA report: 'On 13 September, Chao Erh-lu, a staff member of the Central and South China Military Area headquarters, after inspecting a camp for American and British prisoners of war at 52 Fu Hsing Road, Shaneen, Canton, issued an order prohibiting prisoners from speaking to people outside the compound.'

The informant said that the British were from the Gloucesters and Argylls. Their names were given, but again they had been transliterated into Chinese and back again into English, so came out extremely garbled.[8]

Again, it was reported on 23 October 1951 that

On 3 October, about 170 United Nations prisoners of war arrived at Canton by train from Hankow. They were taken to the former American consulate building on Shaneen. Two squads of Public Security guards were posted around the building, and no pedestrian was permitted to approach closer than 50 metres.

The source was usually reliable and the information judged to be 'possibly true'.[9]

A three-page CIA Intelligence report, consolidating information gathered in January to May 1952, mentioned large numbers of Black troops being held in Manchuria. It was clear to the CIA that these men would not be returned either. The report read:

*War Prisoner Administrative Office and Camp Classification*
**1.** In May 1952 the War Prisoner Administrative Office (Chan Fu Kuan Li ch'u) . . . in P'yongyang, under Colonel No-man-ch'i-fu . . . an intelligence officer attached to the general head-quarters of the Soviet Far Eastern Military District, controlled prisoner of war camps in Manchuria and North Korea. The office, formerly in Mukden, employed 30 persons, several of whom were English-speaking Soviets. LIN MAI . . . and NAM IL . . . were deputy chairmen of the office.
**2.** The office had developed three types of prisoner-of-war camps. Camps termed 'peace camps,' detaining persons who exhibited pro-Communist learning, were characterized by considerate treatment of the prisoners and the staging within the camps of Communist rallies and meetings. The largest peace camp, which held two thousand prisoners, was at Changchun. Peace camps were also at K'aiyuan Ksien . . . and Pench'i . . .
**3.** Reform camps, all of which were in Manchuria, detained anti-Communist prisoners possessing certain technical skills. Emphasis at these camps was on reindoctrination of the prisoners.
**4.** Normal prisoner-of-war camps, all of which were in North Korea, detained prisoners whom the Communists will exchange. *Prisoners in peace and reform camps will not be exchanged.* [Emphasis added.]
**5.** Officials of North Korean prisoners of war camps sent reports on individual prisoners to the War Prisoners Administrative Office. Cooperative prisoners were being transferred to peace camps. ROK [South Korean] officers were being shot; ROK army soldiers were being reindoctrinated and assimilated into the North Korean army.

The report also detailed the camps at Kangdong, Suan, Sariwon, and camp 106 at Mirim. At Kangdong there were 100 English, 840 American, 60 Turkish and 200 French, Dutch and Canadian prisoners. The compound was divided into four with barbed wire and mud embankments, separating the British, American, Turkish and prisoners of other nationalities. The Americans there were from the First Cavalry and the 24th Infantry Division. In all 10 per cent of the prisoners at

Kangdong were black. General William Dean was moved to this camp in 1951 after being held at Harbin and Mukden in Manchuria, the report noted.

A massive amount of detail was also supplied. At Kangdong prisoners received 600 grams of cereal and salt every day. They were not required to work and spent only two hours a day outside the caves where they were held. Three guards armed with submachine guns and rifles were stationed outside each cave. An average of two prisoners a day were dying from malnutrition and typhus. The prisoners were extremely anti-communist, despite being forced to study for three hours a day and discuss political problems for another two.

The South Korean prisoners at camp 106, Mirim, had passed through five ideological screenings and were being assimilated into the North Korean army. They were paid 50 won monthly and received 1 kilogram of grain and 45 grams of soy bean oil, vegetables, salt and soy bean paste daily. Organised into ten-man squads they worked ten hours a day constructing air-raid shelters at the nearby airfield and were given two hours of indoctrination lectures.

On 5 May 1952 there were 110 United Nations prisoners, including 80 Blacks, at Suan. The name of the camp commander is given. The prisoners received only rice balls for food, but several UN prisoners bought wheat paste from local villagers with their watches and other personal belongings.

In late April approximately 800 UN prisoners were seen being held in a series of underground shelters. They received 600 grams of cereal and pork soup three times a day, plus one pack of cigarettes a day. They worked one hour daily and attended indoctrination meetings for two hours a day.

The report also gave details of local transportation, the topography of the surrounding countryside, the organisation of the camps, their exact locations and the numbers and armaments of the guards. The informant was believed to be fairly reliable and the information 'possibly true'.

The last paragraph of the report described a camp across the border at Mukden (Shenyang) in China:

On 6 January four hundred United States prisoners, including three hundred negroes, were being detained in two buildings at Nsiao Nan Kuan Chaih, at the southeast corner of the intersection, in Mukden. One building, used as the police headquarters in Nsiso Nan Knan during the Japanese occupation, was a two-story

concrete structure, 30 meters long and 20 meters wide. The other
building, one story high and constructed of gray brick, was behind
the two-story buildings. Both buildings had tile roofs. All
prisoners held here, with the exception of three second lieutenants, were enlisted personnel. The prisoners, dressed in Chinese
Communist army uniforms, with a red arm band on the left arm,
were not required to work. Two hours of indoctrination were
conducted daily by staff members of the Northeast Army Command. Prisoners were permitted to play basketball in the courtyard. The attempt of three white prisoners to escape caused the
withdrawal of permission for white prisoners to walk alone
through streets in the vicinity of the camp. Two Chinese Communist soldiers guarded groups of white prisoners when such groups
left the buildings. Negroes, however, could move outside the
compound area freely and individually. Rice, noodles, and one
vegetable were served daily to the prisoners in groups of 10 to 15
men. One platoon of Chinese Communist soldiers guarded the
compound.[10]

Given the 'considerate treatment of the prisoners', this latter was
plainly a peace camp and its occupants not returned. Interestingly,
Mukden, where these men were seen, was a railhead for the line that
ran into Siberia. Later, several witnesses would say that they saw UN
POWs, including a large number of Blacks, at Manchouli where the rail
line from Mukden crosses the border into the USSR.

It is also interesting to note that this form of segregation of prisoners
seems to have been used again during the Vietnam War. Only those
destined to be used as propaganda tools before being returned home
were maltreated.

Although these reports can be dismissed individually, taken together
they clearly indicate that British and American POWs were deep inside
China. Their presence did not come up at the peace talks. So, as early as
28 December 1951, a new policy on the handling of prisoners of war
was developed by the Americans. It looked back to the failure of the
Yalta Agreement and the forced repatriations.

'Repetition of our previous policy would discourage defections by
Chinese communist forces in any future conflict,' says a policy document in the Truman Library. 'It would therefore in the long run cost us
more American lives than are involved in the exchange of prisoners.'
In other words, the fate of POWs must take second place to casualties
on the battlefield.

The authors of that report – Gordon Gray, later National Security Advisor to President Eisenhower, and Wallace Carrol – recognised that there were more than just these psychological factors to consider, but they understood that Truman was now deeply opposed to forced repatriations.[11]

# CHAPTER 39

# Usable Human Material

†

ON 17 FEBRUARY 1953, with the Korean War coming to an end, the British government again asked the Soviets to help secure the release of nine British subjects interned in North Korea. On 19 March 1953 Molotov replied that the Soviet Foreign Ministry would take up the matter with the North Koreans. The British then asked the French to postpone their plans to speak in the United Nations about French civilians interned in North Korea, awaiting further developments.[1] Meanwhile, the Foreign Office tried to discourage press speculation on the matter, to ease East–West tensions.[2]

The nine British internees included Captain Holt, British Minister in Seoul and two of this staff; the Bishop of Seoul, the Right Reverend A.C. Cooper; Commissioner Lord of the Salvation Army and Mr Deane, correspondent for the *Observer*. These six were returned via Moscow. Two other British missionaries died in captivity. Nothing was known of the fate of a third.[3] When the six returnees reached Berlin on 21 April 1953 they made short statements which were obviously cleared in advance by British officials, who also took the unusual step of isolating the group from the press.[4] American Intelligence officers in Berlin watched with interest.

On 24 February 1953 Combined Command for Reconnaissance Activity in Korea (CCRAK) reported:

> This office has received sporadic reports of PsW being moved to the USSR since the very inception of the hostilities in Korea. These reports came in great volume through the earlier months of the war, then tapered off to a standstill in early 1951, being revived by a report from January of this year. It is definitely possible that such action is being taken as evidenced by past experience with Soviet authorities. All previous reports state PsW who are moved to the USSR are technical specialists who are

242

employed in mines, factories etc. This is the first report that they are being used as espionage agents . . .[5]

One prisoner was certainly used as an espionage agent. British diplomat George Blake was captured in Seoul, interned and later became a Soviet spy.

Zygmunt Nagorski of the Foreign News Service, an organisation that specialised in gathering news from behind the Iron Curtain, reported in May 1953 that some United Nations troops captured in Korea were turning up in the Soviet Union. Up to April 1951 he had received many indirect reports from Koreans and Chinese who had witnessed mass shootings of captured UN troops.

'Up to that time the Chinese and North Korean forces were harsh and brutal in their treatment of POWs,' he said. 'Then the orders – from Peking or from Moscow – changed. From that time onwards GIs were treated as usable human material.'

According to official statistics the number of American soldiers missing in action in Korea was 13,012 in December 1952, Nagorski said. He did not know how many of them were still alive, how many were prisoners in Korea, how many were in China or Russia. But his best information was that large numbers of UN POWs were then living in camps scattered in the various republics of the Soviet Union.

The co-ordinating centre for these camps seems to have been the city of Molotov, which has now reverted to its ancient name of Perm. An industrial centre, it lies west of the Ural Mountains. In Molotov, the Headquarters of the Soviet political police was a large building also used as a prison, where UN POWs were kept for screening and interrogation. Northeast of the city, in the area known as Northwest Siberia, Western prisoners had been seen in at least six camps, and other POWs had been reported from camps situated on the Pacific coast of Siberia, in Khabarovsk and in the towns of Chita and Omsk, both on the Trans-Siberian railway. Some 200 were assigned to a camp where they worked building a railway. Others gave lectures on the latest weapons and tactics to selected Soviet officers.[6]

South Korean POWs were handled separately. After their first interrogation, officers, technicians and cases of special interest were separated and sent to the nearest outpost of the Soviet Military Mission in China. It was widely rumoured in China at the time that a secret agreement had been concluded between Peking and Moscow regarding these prisoners. The existence of this agreement has recently been confirmed by President Yeltsin's POW spokesman General Dmitri Volkogonov. A plan to withhold one fifth of all UN prisoners of war –

even after all POWs were ostensibly released – was discussed in correspondence between Stalin, China's Mao Tsetung and North Korea's Kim Il Sung.[7]

Certain cases were to be automatically transferred by the Chinese to the Soviet authorities. Such cases included all high-ranking South Korean officers, who were accused of deliberate and active co-operation with the enemy, branded war criminals and treated accordingly. Active anti-communists and men unwilling to talk were also turned over to the Soviets.

Men who failed the Soviet Military Mission screening were sent to isolated camps in the Yakutsk Autonomous Soviet Republic. At 1,169,000 square miles it was the largest of the Soviet republics, but had one of the smallest populations – only 420,000. The region had no railways and few roads, and escape was all but impossible. The Central Commission for Korean POWs operated from the Ministry of State Security Building in Yakutsk.

'Colonel Ivan Achsagnyrov, a police officer who heads the Central Commission, recently sentenced a number of South Korean officers to 15 to 25 years in labour camps,' Nagorski reported. 'Although Russia officially is not at war with the United Nations forces defending Korea, these men were all accused of co-operating with the enemy.'

Only Asians were sent to Yakutsk. All other UN prisoners were taken to camps along the Yalu River where they were interrogated by Chinese and Soviet officers who spoke perfect English. American air force officers, artillerymen, tank specialists and other technicians were separated from the rest and sent to special camps.

Some of these specialists, those considered particularly valuable, were flown directly to the Soviet Union. Their first stop was usually at Poset, a naval station at Poset Bay on the Chinese–Soviet frontier.

The special camps were scattered along the Chinese side of the Yalu River. In June 1952, Nagorski said, about 900 non-Korean POWs, mostly Americans but also some British and Turks, were housed there in two camps. Each camp had about 450 men divided into units of 50 or 60. The communists tried to make their captives feel at ease: food was decent, the daily routine was light and there was plenty of recreation. Books and magazines were available in English, French, Russian and German. And propaganda films, usually showing cities and villages being bombed by American planes, were screened.[8]

POWs stayed there for only a couple of weeks before being taken on into the Soviet Union. They were taught the rudiments of Russian and given political lectures. Those who reacted well to indoctrination were marked as dead on the official POW list. Later, as they graduated up through the Soviet prison system, they were informed that they had been declared dead. The choice then was simple: co-operate and enjoy a reasonable standard of living, refuse and be sent to the labour camps. There was no going back.

The Chinese were getting their prisoners too.

'In late May, 1,500 United Nations prisoners of war were confined in a camp at Tungchutan . . . [south of Peking],' a CIA report of 15 July 1953 said. 'The majority of these prisoners of war were American marine officers and men who were sent to this camp after recovering from wounds.' The CIA analyst commented: 'A POW camp once tentatively accepted in Tientsin was dropped from available listings in January 1953 because of a lack of recent reports concerning it. Available information fails to indicate the positive presence of any POW camp in China outside of Manchuria.'[9]

On 10 August 1953, during Operation Big Switch, CCRAK confirmed that POWs had been transferred from North Korea into Manchuria, China and Siberia. 'Many POWs transferred have been technicians and factory workers,' the report said. 'Other POW transferred have had a knowledge of Cantonese and are reportedly used for propaganda purposes.'[10]

The men returned in Little Switch or Big Switch said that they had been held in North Korea – except for a few who had been, briefly, into Manchuria. Camps outside North Korea do not appear on the official maps and men who were transferred into China and Siberia did not return.

## CHAPTER 40

# Panmunjom

IT WAS NOT just General James A. Van Fleet who was concerned about prisoners of war not being returned. On 11 August 1953, just eight days into Big Switch, *The Times* correspondent in Tokyo was already expressing the Allies' fears. Few officers had been returned – half a dozen Americans, one British and one South African. There were also 'unsubstantiated reports' that British and American POWs had been sentenced by the communists for alleged disciplinary offences to terms of imprisonment of from three months to a year:

> Such sentences are said to have taken effect even after the announcement of the armistice. The Americans calculate that they have a total of 8,700 missing. Assuming that 60 per cent were killed in action, that should leave 3,200 in Communist hands, over and above the 3,300 Americans listed as returnable by the Communists. Peking radio said to-day that 1,050 United Nations prisoners died in captivity in Communist camps, which leaves 2,000 unaccounted for. This tallies with General Clark's estimate that the Chinese are 'holding back between 2,000 and 3,000 prisoners'.

*The Times* admitted that some of these had surrendered to communist blandishments. Returning prisoners were reporting that as many as 180 Americans and 51 Britons had refused to come back. But only 21 Americans and 1 Briton were reported to have voluntarily stayed in communist hands. Were more retained secretly? Two British ex-prisoners of war demanded an investigation, alleging that 'about 5 per cent' of the total number of British prisoners in enemy hands were 'stool pigeons or worse'.[1] Even so, there was a discrepancy. The British authorities in the Far East had estimated that about 1,000 Britons were in prison camps. The communists had undertaken to return 922 Britons.[2]

However, little credence can be given to the statements of the British military during wartime. It was only on 13 August 1953, ten days after the armistice was signed, that it was revealed that the Royal Navy had been involved in the Korean War. Four aircraft carriers, 1 ferry carrier, 6 cruisers, 7 destroyers and 14 frigates had been deployed. Commonwealth naval forces included 1 aircraft carrier, 4 destroyers and 4 frigates from Australia, 8 destroyers from Canada and 6 frigates from New Zealand.[3] Up to the end of the war, none of this was admitted.

By 16 August 1953, twelve days into Operation Big Switch, some 500 Commonwealth prisoners had been repatriated.[4] Despite this, the next day the United Nations Command demanded a 'more complete accounting' of 2,840 United Nations prisoners captured during the Korean War who were still in communist hands.

Rear Admiral T.B. Brittain, chief United Nations delegate to the Military Armistice Commission, handed over a revised list to the communists at Panmunjom. It included the names of 526 American soldiers, 19 British, 9 Europeans, 3 Canadians, 8 South Africans, 3 men from Belgium and Luxembourg, and 2,265 South Koreans.

Admiral Brittain told the chief communist delegate: 'We are convinced the prisoners are in your hands and we still consider they have not been accounted for in a satisfactory manner.'

The number had been reduced from an earlier estimate of 3,405 prisoners, revised because the United Nations had received information that 565 men had either died or been repatriated. Admiral Brittain demanded details of where the prisoners were being held, and when they would be released. If any had died, he wanted information on the cause of death, place of burial, and when their remains would be returned. Admiral Brittain said the United Nations would provide the communists with available information on the prisoners and demanded that 'the exchange should be reciprocal and instantaneous'.

The chief communist delegate, Lieutenant General Lee Cho, refused even to pick up the revised list. He said that all persons had been repatriated in accordance with the armistice agreement. The UN's list, he insisted, was a 'fabricated roster'.[5]

On 25 August 1953, with two thirds of the UN prisoners returned and ten days of the prisoner-of-war exchanges left, *The Times* reported from Tokyo:

The British Commonwealth has already received back 850 out of a total of 957 prisoners listed by the communists, but so far only two officers, of an estimated total of about 50, have returned.

The Canadians to-day got back another eight, all hitherto unaccounted for, which brings their total to 24 returned already, or 10 more than the original figure of 14 Canadians reported held by the Chinese and North Koreans. This gives ground for hope that other Commonwealth countries, including Britain, may yet receive more repatriates than were included in the Communist lists. To-morrow a further 17 Britons are among the total of 400 repatriates expected.

Peking Radio had claimed the day before, for the first time, that about 400 prisoners held by the communists had refused to be repatriated, but the broadcast gave no details of their nationalities.[6]

By 27 August 1953, well before the end of the repatriations, the United Nations Command was already planning how to protest about the 'non-return of UNC personnel whom there is reason to believe are, or were, in Communist custody but for whom no accounting has been made'. Part of the UNC plan was retaliatory action, including holding communist hostages as bargaining chips to be exchanged for UNC prisoners the communists were withholding. General Mark Clark, the US general commanding, justified this action by saying 'our experience with the Communists to date clearly indicates they will agree to any action only if it is to their advantage'.[7]

On 29 August 1953 the UN made another complaint to the communists. In reply they accused the UN of holding *their* men hostage.[8]

By 9 September the United Nations' negotiators had revised the list of missing prisoners up to 3,404 again. It contained the names of people who had been heard on communist radio or whose names had been broadcast, who had – earlier – been listed by the communists as captive, who wrote letters from the prison camps or who had been seen in captivity. The communists' response was predictable. They again accused the UNC of withholding their prisoners.[9]

On 10 September Peking Radio angrily rejected the United Nations contention that 3,400 Allied prisoners remained in communist hands. It asserted that the UN's list was faked; it was obviously aimed at diverting attention from the fact that a large number of Chinese and North Koreans who desired repatriation were still being forcibly detained by the Americans.

That same day a twenty-eight-year-old Polish interpreter, Jan Haj-dukiewicz, sought asylum with the American air force in Seoul, just before he was due to return to North Korea. Although he feared reprisals against his family in Poland, he told correspondents: 'There is no freedom in Poland – we cannot discuss anything. There is only preparation for war.'[10]

He was right. The whole period of the armistice talks at Panmunjom had been marked with a new chill in Cold War tensions in Europe. Thwarted in the East, the pressure was on in the West again. On 24 February 1953 the provincial committee of the Socialist Party of Lower Austria in the Soviet zone had passed a resolution 'strongly protesting against fresh attempts by the Russian occupying authorities to interfere in local Austrian affairs'.[11]

As the repatriations grew to a close, the frost nipped in Panmunjom too. On 21 September *The Times* reported from Tokyo:

At Panmunjom to-day a Communist spokesman told the joint military armistice commission that the Communists denied the authenticity of a list of 3,404 names which the United Nations had submitted on September 9 as being Allied prisoners still held by the Communists and about whom the United Nations had demanded account. The Communist spokesman said that of this total 579 had already been returned to the United Nations, another 380 had been 'released at the front', several more had refused to be repatriated, and that 'most of them had never been captured at all'.

The implication was that most of the names on the Allied list were those of persons who had been killed in action although listed by the United Nations as 'missing believed prisoners of war' or even 'confirmed POW'.

At the same time the communist spokesman demanded an account from the United Nations of 98,000 North Koreans and Chinese who, he claimed, were captured by the United Nations but never accounted for.[12]

All Major General Bryan, senior Allied delegate to the military armistice commission, could do was bluster. He said that the communist reply to the demand for an accounting of the 3,400 men was 'totally unsatisfactory and unacceptable'. All the men listed had been in communist custody at some time. None had been repatriated or reported by the communists to have died or escaped.[13]

Big Switch was over, and the Cold War became chillier than ever. Nothing could be done about the unrepatriated UN POWs. In November 1953 a newspaper in Taiwan reported that British and American POWs were being moved deeper into China. The paper failed to mention the fact that 'officially' they had all been returned home.[14]

Eisenhower, Churchill and his successor, Eden, were Cold Warriors, but they were also insiders. They knew what had happened to British and American POWs after the end of World War II. They knew that nothing could be done about prisoners the communists had taken, and if everyone kept quiet about it, the problem would go away. But there was one Cold Warrior who would not shut up. Backed by information from J. Edgar Hoover – who was still fighting a rearguard action to smother the CIA at birth and take over the FBI's Intelligence role – Senator Joe McCarthy spoke up. On 26 November 1953 *The Times* reported from Washington that McCarthy was savaging his own party, fearing that the Republicans were falling victims to the same evil that beset the Democrats. What, he asked, was the country going to do about the 900 young Americans who were unaccounted for and those others who were shot down over Manchuria during the Korean War and were still being held by the Chinese?

'Are we going to continue to send perfumed notes,' McCarthy demanded,

> following the style of the Truman–Acheson regime? Or are we going to take the only position that an honourable nation can take – namely, that every uniformed American packs the honour and pride and power of this entire nation on his shoulders? . . . How brave are we when we do not use all the power of this nation to rescue these airmen and the 900 other military men who have been unaccounted for all these months?

He also denounced Britain for trading with the enemy, referring to published figures that British trade with communist China had increased by 1,500 per cent between January 1952 and January 1953.

Senator McCarthy was not alone in his criticism. A 1954 Senate report on 'Korean War Atrocities' listed among its findings and conclusions: 'Communist forces violated the "Little Switch" Agreement by failing to repatriate the sick and wounded in accordance with the Panmunjom truce' and 'several thousand American soldiers who have not been repatriated were victims of war crimes, died in action, or are presently confined behind the Iron Curtain'.

General Mark Clark, last American commander in Korea, said in public speeches in 1954, long after the POW exchanges: 'In Korea we found the most despicable foe I had yet encountered, one who conformed to none of the recognised rules of warfare, one who murdered our wounded as they lay on the fields of battle, one who tortured our prisoners of war and who now, in my opinion, still holds 3,000 of our men behind the Iron Curtain.'[15]

## CHAPTER 41

# The Border Crossing

✝

WITH THE ARMISTICE in place and the diplomatic channels closed, there was nothing left to do but whinge. On 15 January 1954 the State Departmentdeclared that neutral India's decision to release the remaining prisoners who did not want to be repatriated just three days early 'will destroy the Korean truce'.[1] When the 22,000 unrepatriated Chinese and North Korean prisoners of war were released, just one day early, the Soviet press blamed the United States for an 'illegal transfer' of prisoners.[2]

The other tactic that had been tried with some limited success after World War II was to narrow down the focus. On 5 December 1954 Dr van Kleffens, President of the United Nations, called a special meeting to take up the United States' request that the UN act 'promptly and decisively' to bring about the release of eleven American airmen held prisoner by China.

US permanent representative to the United Nations Henry Cabot Lodge had sent a memorandum called 'Complaint of detention and imprisonment of United Nations military personnel in violation of the Korean armistice agreement' to UN Secretary-General Dag Hammarskjöld. It complained that a United States air force B–29, on a mission of the United Nations command in Korea, was attacked fifteen miles south of the Yalu River near the North Korean town of Sunchon and shot down on 12 January 1953. The men on board were captured. More than a year and a half later, long after the end of Big Switch, eleven officers and men from that aircraft were brought before a Chinese military tribunal and sentenced to long terms of imprisonment. This action, the memo said, was a clear-cut viola-tion of the armistice agreement. The sixteen other nations who took part in the Korean conflict backed the American move, although some seemed to have reservations about the 'strong language used in the memorandum'.[3]

China's response was to protest about the United States signing of a mutual security treaty with Nationalist China, on the island of Formosa (Taiwan), on 2 December 1954, and about Britain's support of the Americans' action. The Chinese people 'will never stop till Taiwan is liberated, and will never forget the date December 2 on which the United States aggressors openly occupied Taiwan'.[4] Again Britain and America found themselves in a diplomatic impasse.

In 1954 Soviet Intelligence agent Yuri Rastvorov defected to the Americans in Japan. He said that UN POWs have been taken into Siberia, where they had been forced to renounce their citizenship.[5]

On 5 January 1954 *The New York Times* drew attention to the whole problem of missing prisoners of war in a piece under the headline 'The Other Prisoners':

> While world attention has been focussed on the Korean war prisoners comparatively little heed has been paid to many other prisoners from many nations who languish in Communist jails or are being worked to death in Communist slave labour camps. Their plight has been brought into the news by the experiences of two Americans, Homer H. Cox and Leland Towers, who have just been freed by the Soviets, and of Arnold M. Kiehn, the American businessman released from a Shanghai prison suffering from partial paralysis and beriberi.[6]

Cox and Towers had been released because they had been identified by returning Austrian prisoners. All three confirmed that the Soviet bloc and the Chinese communists were holding many foreigners, including soldiers and civilians. Cox and Towers had identified at least four more Americans and reported six others.

According to the State Department, at that time, the total number of Americans held by the Soviets and their European satellites exceeded 5,000, with several times that number of possible claimants to American citizenship. The Chinese communists were known to hold about 100 Americans, excluding any prisoners of the Korean War deported to China.

Many West Europeans were also in communist custody, the *New York Times* said. They had been 'caught by the Communist tide', taken from German war prisoner camps, or, like Homer Cox, kidnapped by the Soviets. On 25 January 1954 Senator John Marshall Butler complained in the US Senate about the missing UNC prisoners held by the communists. And on 2 February 1954 he wrote to the Secretary of Defense, Charles E. Wilson. American Legion Post 343 complained on

24 May 1954, citing the case of a Sergeant Glasser who had been seen in captivity and had not been returned.

By January 1954 the US army had increased the number of men known to be in communist captivity, over and above 21 November's 'revised list', by another two. In a secret memorandum to the Secretary of the Army, dated 16 January 1954, under the heading 'The Unaccounted-for Americans Believed to Be Still Held Illegally by the Communists', Assistant Secretary of the Army Hugh M. Milton II wrote:

> There are approximately 954 United States personnel falling in this group. What the Department of the Army and other interested agencies is doing about their recovery falls into two parts. First, the direct efforts of the UNC Military Armistice Commission to obtain an accurate accounting, and second, efforts by G2 [military Intelligence] of the Army, both overt and covert, to locate, identify, and recover these individuals. G2 is making an intensive effort through its information collection system worldwide, to obtain information on these people and has a plan for clandestine action to obtain the recovery of one or more to establish the case positively that prisoners are still being held by the Communists. No results have been obtained yet in this effort. The direct efforts of the UNC are being held in abeyance pending further study of the problem by the State Department . . . A further complicating factor in the situation is that to continue to carry this personnel in a missing status is costing over one million dollars annually. It may become necessary at some future date to drop them from our records as 'missing and presumed dead.'

But Assistant Secretary Milton did not have to worry about this 'million dollars annually' for long. The Department of Defense were already busy 'dropping them' from DoD records as 'missing and presumed dead'. In three months, 336 of them mysteriously disappeared.

By April, there were only 618 of these 954 'illegally held' American POWs still officially alive and Major General Robert Young, the Assistant Chief of Staff, G1 (personnel department) of the US army, was about to deal with those.

In a secret memorandum dated 29 April 1954, Young updated Assistant Secretary Milton on his progress:

> Under the provisions of Public Law 490 (77th Congress), the Department of the Army, after careful review of each case and

interrogation of returning prisoners of war, has placed 618 soldiers, known to have been in enemy hands and unaccounted for by the Communist Forces in the following categories:

313 – Finding of Death – Administratively determined, under the provisions of Public Law 490, by Department of the Army.

275 – Report of Death – reported on good authority by returning prisoners.

21 – Dishonorable Discharge [the stay-behinds].

4 – Under investigation, prognosis undecided. Missing in Action over one year.

2 – returned to Military Control.

The Americans were also using presumed findings of death to whittle down the number of US soldiers listed as MIA. According to the 'Interim Report of U.S. Casualties' prepared by the Office of the Secretary of Defense, as of 31 December 1953 the total number of US soldiers who had been listed as Missing in Action from the Korean War was 13,325. During Operation Big Switch 5,131 MIAs had been repatriated, cutting that number to just over 8,000. But by 1 January 1954 only 2,953 were listed MIA. The figure for the dead, or presumed dead, had climbed to 5,140, while 101 were listed as 'Current captured'.

What makes General Young's 29 April memorandum fiddling the figures doubly despicable is that, in the very same memorandum, he refers to an Intelligence report showing that hundreds of these men he was happily writing off had actually ended up in the Soviet Union. While dropping over 900 from DoD records for administrative reasons, as requested by Assistant Secretary Milton, General Young used the same memo to respond to another request from Milton: to 'consolidate information on prisoners of war which may remain in Communist hands'.

In his classified reply, Young refers to a report from Hong Kong that

> . . . corroborates previous indications UNC POWs might have been shipped to Siberia during Korean hostilities . . . reports have now come [to the] attention [of the] U.S. Government which support earlier indications that American prisoners of war from Korea had been transported into Soviet Union and are now in Soviet custody. Request fullest possible information these POWs and their repatriation earliest possible time.

The report referred to was a Foreign Service Despatch sent by Air Pouch and dated 23 March 1954, from the American Consul General in Hong Kong to the State Department in Washington:

American POWs reported en route to Siberia
A recently arrived Greek refugee from Manchuria has reported
seeing several hundred American prisoners of war being transferred from Chinese trains to Russian trains at Manchouli [Manz-
houli] near the border of Manchuria and Siberia. The POWs were
seen late in 1951 and in the spring of 1952 by the informant and a
Russian friend of his.

The informant was interrogated on two occasions by the Assistant Air
Liaison Officer and the Consul General agreed with his evaluation of
the information as probably true and the evaluation of the source as of
unknown reliability. The full text of the initial Air Liaison Office
report, Despatch 1716 which was also sent to US diplomatic posts in
Taipei, Moscow, Paris and London by American Consul General Julian
F. Harrington, read:

First report dated March 16, 1954, from Air Liaison Office, Hong
Kong, to USAF, Washington, G2.
    This office had interviewed refugee source who states that he
observed hundreds of prisoners of war in American uniforms
being sent into Siberia in late 1951 and 1952. Observations were
made at Manchouli (Lupin) . . . on USSR–Manchurian border.
Source observed POWs on railway station platform loading into
trains for movement into Siberia. In railway restaurant source
closely observed three POWs who were under guard and were
conversing in English. POWs wore sleeve insignia which indicated
POWS were Air Force noncommissioned officers. Source states
that there were a great number of Negroes among POW shipments and also states that at no time later were any POWs
observed returning from Siberia. Source does not wish to be
identified for fear of reprisals against friends in Manchuria . . .

When the USAF in Washington received this despatch, it requested
elaboration of the following points:

**1.** Descriptions of uniforms or clothing worn by POWs including ornaments.
**2.** Physical condition of POWs.
**3.** Nationality of guards.
**4.** Specific dates of observation.
**5.** Destination in Siberia.
**6.** Presence of Russians in uniform or civilian clothing accompanying movement of POWs.
**7.** Complete description of three POWs specifically mentioned.

Sergeant Lackey at the Air Liaison Office cabled back:

**(1)** POW wore OD outer clothing described as not heavy inasmuch as weather considered early spring. Source identified from pictures service jacket, field M1943. No belongings except canteen. No ornaments observed.

**(2)** Condition appeared good, no wounded, all ambulatory.

**(3)** Station divided into two sections with tracks on each side of loading platform. On Chinese side POWs accompanied by Chinese guards. POWs passed through gate bisecting platform to Russian train manned and operated by Russians. Russian trainmen wore dark blue or black tunic with silver colored shoulder boards. Source says this regular train uniform but he knows the trainmen are military wearing regular train uniforms.

**(4)** Interrogation with aid of more fluent interpreter reveals source first observed POWs in railroad station in spring 1951. Second observation was outside city of Manchouli about three months later with POW train headed towards station where he observed POW transfer. Source was impressed with second observation because of large number of Negroes among POWs. Source states job was numbering railroad cars at Manchouli every time subsequent POW shipments passed through Manchouli. Source says these shipments were reported often and occurred when United Nations forces in Korea were on the offensive.

**(5)** Unknown.

**(6)** Three POWs observed in station restaurant appeared to be 30 or 35. Source identified Air Force non-commissioned officer sleeve insignia of Staff Sergeant rank, stated that several inches above insignia there was a propeller but says that all three did not have propeller. Three POWs accompanied by Chinese guard. POWs appeared thin but in good health and spirits, were being given what source described as good food. POWs were talking in English but did not converse with guard. Further information as to number of POWs observed source states that first observation filled a seven passenger car train and second observation about the same. Source continues to emphasise the number of Negro troops, which evidently impressed him because he had seen so few Negroes before.

Sergeant Lackey also included a comment by the Reporting Officer:

Source is very careful not to exaggerate information and is

positive of identification of American POWs. In view of information contained in Charity Interrogation Report No. 619 dated 5
February 54, Reporting Officer gives above information rating of
F-2. Source departing Hong Kong today by ship. Future address
on file this office.

Charity Interrogation Report No. 619 had been forwarded to the
Department under cover of a letter dated 1 March 1954, to Mr A. Sabin
Chase, DRF. It was another sighting of servicemen being taken across
the Siberian border at Manchouli and said: 'On another occasion
source saw several coaches full of Europeans who were taken to USSR.
They were not Russians. Source passed the coaches several times and
heard them talk in a language unknown to him.'

A third report saying roughly the same thing originated from US air
force Intelligence officer Colonel 'Delk' Simpson who is now retired
and living in North Palm Beach, California. He remembers sending a
'top secret' report to the Pentagon in 1955, when he was Air Attaché in
Hong Kong. He had interrogated a Polish émigré in his early twenties
on his way to Australia.

The man told Simpson he had been a railway worker at Manchouli
on the Manchurian–Siberian border. Around the time of the ceasefire,
a train heading north into Siberia stopped at Manchouli so workers
could change the undercarriage (to make the change between different
gauges of track). The man saw about 700 prisoners get off on to the
platform. Although he overheard them talking, he could not recognise
English. But many of the prisoners were Black, and the only Blacks
there would have been Americans, Simpson told the *Wall Street Journal*.

Indeed, a disproportionate number of Blacks had been captured. A
CIA Intelligence report, consolidating information from the period
October 1950–February 1951, read:

> One Republic of Korea soldier who was captured by the
> Communists on 29 October 1950 was sent to a war prison camp at
> Pyoktong . . . in North Pyonman. This camp in early November
> had about 1,000 American war prisoners, of whom about 700
> were negroes, approximately 1,500 ROK [Republic of Korea]
> prisoners, and about 300 civilian employees of the United Nations
> forces.

'I was convinced that [the railway worker's story] was true,' Simpson
told the *Journal*. But, 'as far as I know', US Intelligence officials never
followed up on the report, Simpson said. 'I think the Pentagon sent it to
the State Department, who sent it to our UN ambassador, who asked

the Russian ambassador if it was true. You can imagine the answer.'

For years Simpson tried to get someone in Washington to listen to his story. 'It's like trying to punch holes in Jell-O,' he says.

These were not the only reports of UN POWs being moved into Siberia. One report of sixty-three POWs being shipped across the border into the Soviet Union was considered so reliable that the air force was ordered not to bomb the train, according to retired army Intelligence officer Mel Gile.[7]

The State Department also took the report of the Greek refugee very seriously indeed. On 5 April 1954 E. O'Shaughnessy at the US Embassy in Moscow wrote to the Soviet Foreign Ministry:

> The Embassy of the United States of America presents its compliments to the Ministry of Foreign Affairs of the Union of Soviet Socialist Republics and has the honor to request the Ministry's assistance in the following matter. The United States Government has recently received reports which support earlier indications that American prisoners of war who had seen action in Korea have been transported to the Union of Soviet Socialist Republics and that they are now in Soviet custody. The United States Government desires to receive urgently all information available to the Soviet Government concerning these American personnel and to arrange their repatriation at the earliest possible time.

However, the Soviets were slow in responding and the State Department were impatient to discover what had happened to these men and any still held in China. They asked the British Foreign Office to make a similar request about UNC to the Chinese government.[8] The British had an embassy in Peking at the time, the Americans did not.

US Secretary of State John Foster Dulles handled the correspondence himself. In secret cable number 666 to the US Embassy in Moscow, marked 'Action Copy' and dated 19 April 1954, Dulles wrote:

> According Despatch 1716 from Hong Kong airpouched you, a recently arrived Greek refugee from Manchuria reported seeing several hundred American POWs being transferred Chinese trains to Russian trains Manchouli late 1951 and early 1952. Some POWs wore sleeve insignia indicating they were Air Force noncoms. Great number Negro troops also observed. This report corroborates previous indications UNC POWs might have been shipped to Siberia during Korean hostilities.

United States has been greatly concerned general subject UNC personnel who may still be Communist custody. Department has just accepted British offer make representations Peiping behalf UNC personnel who may be Chinese Communist custody. The US had no embassy in Peking at this time. Question raising this matter informally Geneva under careful consideration.

Unless you perceive objection, request you approach highest available level Foreign Ministry and leave Aide Memoire indicating reports have now come attention United States Government which support earlier indications that American Prisoners of War Korea had been transported into Soviet Union and are now Soviet custody. Request fullest possible information these POWs and their reparation earliest possible time.

In your discussion with Foreign Office, you may desire inform Soviets without revealing source that we have reliable accounts transfers POWs Manchouli.

The offer to approach the Chinese came from the British government – implying, perhaps, that the British were already asking for information about their missing servicemen.

On 5 May 1954 the American Embassy in Moscow wrote to the Soviet Ministry of Foreign Affairs again. On 12 May the Soviets replied:

The United States assertion . . . that American prisoners of war who participated in military actions in Korea have allegedly been transferred to the Soviet Union and at the present time are being kept under Soviet guard is devoid of any foundation whatsoever and is clearly far-fetched, since there are not and have not been any such persons in the Soviet Union.

The US request – and the Soviet response – hinges around the key wording: 'American prisoners of war who participated in military actions in Korea'. Communist forces in Korea and Vietnam often denied their captives the status of 'prisoner of war'. As no war was declared, these claims have a specious validity. In the aftermath of World War II, the Soviets denied Allied captives their citizenship, unless they had documentary proof of their nationality, their passport perhaps, which plainly servicemen and civilians emerging from German camps were unlikely to be carrying. In Vietnam the communists regularly stripped captured Americans of their citizenship and made them honorary Vietnamese, so they could be tried and sentenced under common law.

What's more they were only being asked about 'American prisoners of war who participated in military actions in Korea' – so they were not even questioned, at this time, about American prisoners of war still being held from World War II.

America was getting nowhere on its own, so on 15 May 1954 the United Nations asked the communists to account for 3,405 UN prisoners of war.[9] But it did no good. It did not matter who asked; they got no answer.

# CHAPTER 42

# Breaking the Silence

&#8224;

IN 1955 PRESIDENT EISENHOWER was briefed about the shipment of prisoners of war across the border into the Soviet Union by White House Intelligence aide Lieutenant Colonel Philip J. Corso. A White House staffer from 1953 to 1957, Corso was considered a POW/MIA expert. He retired as a full colonel in 1963, and broke his silence on the fate of UN POWs in 1992 when he spoke to investigators for the Senate Select Committee on POW/MIA Affairs.

Corso had been tasked to look at the question of missing prisoners from the Korean War in 1954, after a career in military Intelligence in Korea and Japan. During the course of his investigation he interviewed Soviet defector Yuri Rastvorov who, in early 1955, was in the hands of the CIA. Rastvorov confirmed that United Nations prisoners captured in Korea had been taken into the Soviet Union.[1]

That, together with other information Corso had unearthed in US files, led him to the certain conclusion that some 800–900 UN POWs were taken into Siberia – though he believes the total number taken could be over 1,200. The men were shipped by train. At least three trainloads were sent, each carrying up to 450 men.

Accompanied by senior National Security Adviser C.D. Jackson, Colonel Corso took the information to Eisenhower. He believed the Soviet penal system was so harsh that none of these men would ever return home. So he recommended to Eisenhower that his report should never be made public. Eisenhower accepted his recommendation and the matter was never mentioned again.

Even though Colonel Corso has now spoken up, he still believes that the decision Eisenhower took was right. The Soviets always denied taking these men and seemed unlikely to return them voluntarily. And with the Cold War at its height, Eisenhower's policy was to avoid putting pressure on the Kremlin.

In an interview with Mark Sauter of *The Morning News Tribune* in 1992, Corso said: 'Those poor souls would never come back, and there was nothing we could do . . . I did my job, I did my duty, and I moved on to other things.'[2]

Corso's report, entitled 're US POWs in USSR' and dated 31 January 1955, is still classified. In 1991 the then National Security Adviser Brent Scowcroft ordered the National Archives not to release the document after an application to see it was filed under the Freedom of Information Act. Writing on White House headed notepaper, Scowcroft said that the 1955 report was still 'secret and should be properly secured'. Scowcroft later rejected a request from Congressman John Miller to declassify the memo.

Corso believes that the White House can never own up to the truth of these POW transfers, nor can the Soviet Intelligence agencies, whose agents may still be using the POWs or their identities.[3]

While the American government was keeping quiet about the missing men, China was quite open about the prisoners it was holding – at least some of them. At the Geneva Convention of 1954–5 – the first international conference in which the People's Republic of China participated – the Chinese openly used seventy-six American captives, most of them 'civilians', as bargaining chips. Eleven of them were US airmen whose B–29 bomber had been shot down near the Chinese–Korean border. All but thirteen of them were released by 1957, but the last was not freed until after President Nixon's visit to China in 1972.

At Geneva, US co-ordinator U. Alexis Johnson repeatedly tried to get his Chinese counterpart to address the issue of POWs from the Korean War. But the Chinese Ambassador always insisted that was a matter for the Military Armistice Commission at Panmunjom.

One of the men released as a result of the Geneva Convention was Steve Kiba. He was one of the eleven flyers whose plane had been shot down just south of the Chinese–North Korean border and held prisoner by the Chinese for two years after the Korean War. He now lives in Camden, South Carolina. He vividly remembers another member of the crew who did not return home even after the Geneva Convention – the radar man on his ill-fated flight, Paul van Voorhies.

The US lists Mr van Voorhies as killed in action. Kiba says he saw van Voorhies at least a dozen times after the crash, including after the ceasefire, walking in the exercise yard of the prison they were in near Peking.

'He walked to within six feet of my prison cell,' Kiba recalls. 'He was in good physical condition.' Yet when Kiba told American Intelligence officers about van Voorhies, he says: 'They told me to forget about him and not to mention having seen him to anyone else.'

These words are reminiscent of those spoken by late returnees after World War II – and those who reported seeing other men in captivity when they returned from Hanoi in 1973.

But one thing still puzzles Kiba: why would the Chinese have released everyone but van Voorhies and the other radar man on the flight? *US News & World Report* gave the answer to that in December 1953. Citing 'U.S. intelligence officials', it said the communists 'primarily wanted – and got – Americans who could handle the sensitive and complex instruments of modern warfare such as radar, airborne and ground, and infrared instruments for night combat'. But then, Steve Kiba would not have read that article – it was printed while he was still in captivity.

On 13 August 1987 allegations that the Allies had left prisoners of war in communist hands in World War II, Korea, the Cold War and Vietnam appeared in the *Wall Street Journal* in an article entitled: 'POWs: Four Decades of Abandonment'. The US Department of Defense responsed in a press release:

> Since 1954 the UNC Military Commission (UNCMAC) has annually called for the Korean People's Army/Chinese People's Volunteers (KPA/CPV) to account for UNC POWs. The UNC has requested the repatriation of United Nations war dead numerous times beginning in 1982. In August 1986 the UNC passed new information to the North which included maps/charts of 13 POW camps and a POW hospital, 291 air crash sites (total of 301 personnel unaccounted for), and the list of 2,233 UNC POWs and 18 foreign nationals never repatriated. So far, the other side has yet to give a reasonable response to the UN appeal to account for the UNC POWs and return the remains of men who fought in defense of freedom in Korea. However, in 1988, the North Korean Government announced holding the remains of two Americans, declining thus far to repatriate them. This lack of humanitarian cooperation will not blunt our determination to pursue the issue.[4]

The British followed the American lead. On 4 November 1990 Alfred Lee in the *Sunday Express* reported: 'A senior Army officer says that North Korea may be holding up to 15 British soldiers as prisoners of war – 34 years after the fighting stopped.'

This amazing claim was made by the then British Military Attaché in Seoul, South Korea, Brigadier Timothy Hackworth. He had asked North Korea to supply information about fifteen men whose fate had never been satisfactorily explained.

Brigadier Hackworth told Lee: 'We know that these soldiers were alive and apparently well in different POW camps in North Korea when the armistice was signed. Their names were given to us by British prisoners who were returned. Time has of course passed – but it would be wrong to assume that they are dead. The truth is that we just do not know what happened to these fifteen.'

Hackworth was adamant: 'We have to face the extraordinary possibility that some of them at least are still alive, and being held prisoners.'

The Ministry of Defence confirmed that there was a list of fifteen British soldiers 'with a question mark about their fate'. But the Ministry refused to issue a list of the names, saying: 'We have made this decision out of consideration for the families concerned.'

On the list were a major, two subalterns and a lance corporal. The rest were privates.

The MoD admitted that originally there were sixteen names, but they had been able to confirm that one of the men had died in captivity. This list had plainly been updated from the thirteen still listed as 'prisoner of war' or 'missing believed prisoner of war' after Operation Big Switch. On that list there are indeed a major and two subalterns, but no lance corporal. However, there are four lance corporals among the sixty-four names listed as just plain 'missing'. One of them, along with another private, must have made it on to the 'prisoner of war' or 'missing believed prisoner of war' list.[5]

'Efforts to find out what happened to the other fifteen are continuing. The names, serial numbers and ranks of the men have been given to the North Koreans, but to date they have given no information whatever about them,' the MoD said.

Brigadier Hackworth said that he had taken this step because of films, like the Rambo movies, about POWs missing in Vietnam. They had stirred a lot of interest in America. Korean War veterans had forced the US military representatives on the United Nations Military Armistice Commission at Panmunjom to ask the North Koreans about the American POWs still unaccounted for. Britain joined in, asking about our fifteen missing POWs.

If they had stayed behind voluntarily, they were certainly unknown to the one British stay-behind, Andrew Condron. Condron, who returned after twelve years in Red China with a French-Chinese wife, told the *Sunday Express* that he knew nothing about the missing POWs.

'I am certain I was the only British POW who stayed behind voluntarily,' he said. 'There were 21 American POWs who did not want to be repatriated and we were all kept together for a time.'

The author of the piece, Alfred Lee, went on to point out that: 'Dozens of British troops taken prisoner during the Korean war may still be alive in the Soviet Union and Communist China.'[6]

In 1992 the International Red Cross in Geneva was belatedly sorting through hundreds of files for details of 56 Britons thought to have been secretly imprisoned in Russia after the Korean War. Mrs Georgia Hanbury, sister of missing serviceman Lieutenant Edmund Radcliffe of the Durham Light Infantry told the *Evening Standard*, on 11 August 1992, that she was 'disgusted' that the government did not investigate the claims made by the Senate Foreign Relations Committee 18 months before. 'The Government has got to investigate these new claims. I have felt that for so long they have tried to suppress information,' she said. Sadly, in Radcliffe's case there is no indication that he was ever captured. He was known to have been wounded when he went missing.

The British promised to bring up the matter of the missing POWs again at cross-table talks. And there may be some cause for hope. Again in 1992 the State Department revealed that North Korea wants tripartite talks with the US and South Korea to negotiate a peace treaty to replace the armistice that has existed since the 1953 ceasefire. Officially the US maintains that the armistice agreement prohibits such direct negotiations. Unresolved issues are still supposed to be handled by the Military Armistice Commission, whose UN component represents South Korea and the sixteen nations that came to its defence.

## CHAPTER 43

# In Plain Sight

THE WORDS WHITEWASH and cover-up are used far too frequently. Often things are best hidden in plain sight. Films like *Rambo II* have given the issue of missing POWs a high profile in the US. The activist group Homecoming II raised $200,000 to fund research into missing prisoners from World War II and Korea. The questions this research raises have to be answered by the US government.

According to a press advisory note issued by the State Department of 15 April 1991, the United States once again requested that Moscow 'provide us with any additional information on any other US citizens who may have been detained as a result of World War II, the Korean conflict or the Vietnam War'. This request simply 'repeated the mistake of asking for information only about US citizens that the State Department had made 37 years earlier,' says the report of the Senate Foreign Relations Committee who were investigating US policy towards prisoners of war in 1991.

> The State Department also made a point of including in its recent press advisory the government's usual statement that [they acted] 'in the interest of following every credible lead in providing families of US service members with information about their loved ones'. Furthermore, according to the press advisory, the State Department specifically asked the Soviets only about 'two US planes shot down in the early 1950s', and did not ask the Soviets any specific questions about any non-repatriated POWs from World War II, the Korean War, and the Vietnam War. It seems apparent that if the Department of State had expected to get solid information from the Soviet government, then the State Department would have sent a much more comprehensive and appropriately phrased request.

The sincerity of the State Department's declared intention to follow 'every credible lead in providing families of US service members with information about their loved ones' is, therefore, suspect. One US government document dated 21 January 1980, a memorandum from Michael Oksenberg to Zbigniew Brzezinski, the National Security Adviser to President Carter, reveals the cynical policy still adopted by at least one recent administration. Oksenberg advises Brzezinski that 'a letter from you is important to indicate that you take recent refugee reports of sightings of live Americans "seriously." This is simply good politics; DIA and State are playing this game, and you should not be the whistle blower. The idea is to say that the President [Carter] is determined to pursue any lead concerning possible live MIAs.'

But the 1991 US Senate Foreign Relations Committee report states:

> At the conclusion of Operation Big Switch, the United States Government failed to pursue vigorously credible reports and left U.S. citizens, held against their will, in custody of the North Koreans, the mainland Chinese, and the USSR. Whether any of these men are still alive is – tragically – unclear. The fate of the more than 8,000 men listed as MIA who were administratively found to be 'presumed dead' is a mystery. No rebuttal was ever made to General Van Fleet, who stated in the fall of 1953 his belief that a large percentage of the 8,000 American soldiers listed as missing in Korea were alive. 'A large percentage' translates into thousands of U.S. soldiers who were never repatriated by the Communist forces after the Korean war.

Army Major General (retd) John Singlaub, who fought in Korea and later served as chief of staff of US forces there – and also fought in Europe and Manchuria during World War II, ran the murderous Phoenix Program in Vietnam and later ran the CIA's China desk – had come to this same shocking conclusion years earlier. Four years after being relieved of his position in Korea for publicly criticising the Carter administration's plan to gradually withdraw US forces from South Korea, Singlaub wrote:

> I was reluctant to accept the idea that our government would abandon any prisoners of war. However . . . there is now what I consider to be adequate evidence from a variety of sources that we did in fact 'write off' some of the men . . . All those ex-POWs who through the years have remained silent on the subject, on the advice of the State Department, should be asked to come forward now and to give the information that they know . . .

Has there been a 'cover-up'? I only know that there are just too many instances of former POWs being told to 'cool it' and to stop talking about prisoners left behind.

While Singlaub follows his own eccentric career, and says no more, the staff of the Senate Foreign Relations Committee who brought the whole question of missing British and American POWs into the open were sacked, at the behest of President Bush's National Security Adviser Brent Scowcroft.

It did not still the lobby, though. On 4 January 1992 the *New York Times* carried an Associated Press story datelined Washington, 3 January:

The Bush administration has given several former Soviet republics the names of more than 50 Americans listed as missing in action from World War II and the Korean and Vietnam Wars who might have been moved to the Soviet Union, officials said today.

The names included those of Americans who fought in Asia in World War II, crew members of warplanes that were downed near Soviet territory in the Korean War and prisoners of war taken in Vietnam, officials said.

The British government are luckier. They do not have a vocal lobby to deal with. But the matter does surface occasionally.

Under the headline 'British POWs are still held in Siberia', the London *Evening Standard* of 5 November 1990 reported: 'Pressure is to be put on the Foreign Office this week after startling claims that 151 British prisoners of war who disappeared without trace after the Korean War are being held in China and the Soviet Union.'

The question was even raised in the House of Commons. Sir Anthony Beaumont-Dark, Conservative MP for Selly Oak, told the *Evening Standard*:

This is going to rouse in people who lost relatives in Korea tremendous pain thinking that their loved ones might have suffered for all these years in appalling conditions. The matter needs to be resolved quickly and I will be asking the Foreign Office to act on this news fast . . . I will also be raising questions in the House to put people's minds at rest about this living nightmare. If it is true, the Foreign Office has a duty to repatriate these people at once by putting pressure on the Chinese and Soviet governments.

The *Evening Standard* story continues:

268

US Senate investigators said they have 'convincing and over-whelming evidence' that thousands of captured United Nations Command prisoners were sent by train to camps in Siberia and China, confounding commonly-held beliefs that North Korean POWs were immediately repatriated.

Chief Investigator Mr Tracy Usry said: 'We believe dozens of British, Commonwealth and American troops are still alive.' One confidential CIA document marked 'Do Not Circulate' says four captured members of the Gloucestershire Regiment were held at a prison camp in Fu Hsing Road, Canton.

Usry had delivered a list of the names of unrepatriated British soldiers, their regiments and the locations of the camps where they were being held to the First Secretary at the British Embassy in Washington early in 1990, expecting their help. Instead, the British government hampered any further investigation of the matter, Usry says.

Slowly the truth has begun to come out though. Senator Bob Smith, vice chairman of the Senate Committee on POW–MIA Affairs, recently released a list of 125 American servicemen in the Korean War who, he said, 'appeared to have been "interrogated by the former Soviet Union and possibly transferred to China". Everyone of those names is presumed to be dead.'[1]

Britain was barely scathed by the Vietnam War. Although the British army did not fight there, two British 'engineers' seem to have been captured. One of them is a so-called 'discrepancy case' which the US authorities bring up regularly with the Vietnamese.

Some British fought as Australians. The Australian government maintain that, after ten years of fighting in Vietnam, no Australians were taken prisoners, though Intelligence documents from the war report numbers of Australians being held by the Viet Cong, the North Vietnamese army and the Pathet Lao, in neighbouring Laos.

Churchill, Attlee, Truman, Eisenhower, Eden, Macmillan and Home long retained positions at the height of power. Harriman would later play a key role in negotiations over Laos, that would affect the outcome of the Vietnam War, and in the 1968 peace negotiations with the North Vietnamese in Paris. Kennan went on to hold key positions in the State Department. He achieved fame as the author of the 'Containment Doctrine' (in the July 1947 issue of *Foreign Affairs*, Kennan wrote an article, signed 'X', weighing the policy of appeasement versus confrontation with the Soviet Union. He suggested 'long-term, patient but firm and viligant containment of Russian expansive tendencies' in the hope that the communist regime would eventually mellow or collapse) and now holds an honoured position as an elder statesman of the American foreign policy establishment. OSS figures in Europe – Dulles, Colby and Casey – became directors of the CIA. The future American Chairman of the Joint Chiefs of Staff, General Lyman Lemnitzer, served on Alexander's staff. General Mark Clark, later commander in Korea, also served under Alexander and both played roles in the POW repatriations.

Future US commanders in Vietnam were also involved in the repatriation of POWs. General Paul Harkins was a deputy chief of staff to General Patton at the US 3rd Army. And he was William Westmoreland's chief of staff at the 9th Infantry Division on the Elbe River and, later, on the Danube. Vernon Walters, an army translator for Roosevelt and Truman, rose to become an army general, a deputy director of the CIA and ambassador to the UN. He was to play a crucial role in playing down the problem of unrepatriated POWs after the Vietnam War.

It should be remembered that, since 1945, all decisions made concerning missing Allied POWs have been made at the highest levels and they concern the only country that the West has seen as a deadly foe. So information about this issue would be guarded by the sort of security it would be very difficult for anyone in government service to defy.

But why would the Soviets hold our men? In 1991 the US Senate Committee on Foreign Relations Republican Staff came up with five possible explanations.

Firstly, they may have held them for economic concessions, or as Major Vershenko stated, for 'credits'.

Secondly, they may have wanted to satisfy the Soviet view – as described by Molotov – that it 'was dangerous' merely to disarm an adversary, but necessary to 'make them work'.

Thirdly, in 1945 the Soviet Union desperately needed a source of slave labour to rebuild its industrial base.

Fourthly, as a British cable stated, the Soviets could have made use of them 'to blackmail us into dealing with Warsaw authorities' and for other political concessions.

And fifthly, the Soviets wanted to ensure that the Allies forcibly repatriated Soviet and other Eastern European citizens who did not wish to return to their countries then under Soviet control.

Whatever the Soviet motives were, the Russians have different motives now. George Bush's implication in the cover-up of the abandoning of American POWs in Vietnam in 1973 has slowed progress in the Joint US–Russian Commission. But after a landmark article in *Nezavisimaya Gazeta* in September 1991, Russian journalists are investigating this issue to test the limits of their new freedoms. Safely historical, they can attack the military and the communist old guard while at the same time eliciting foreign support. In August 1992, the Russian Security Ministry admitted that more than 2,000 people from 31 countries – including two British servicemen – had been imprisoned in Stalin's camps. Lieutenant Michael McKay ended up in a KGB prison in the northern part of Archangel. He was thought to have been a pilot on a wartime convoy carrying planes to Murmansk and found himself a prisoner of the KGB after being invited to celebrate a successful run aboard a Soviet ship. Later, he was moved to the Unzhlag complex in Mordovia, Russia, where he is believed to have died in 1954. The other British serviceman the KGB admitted to holding was a reconnaissance officer named Gerald Phillips, who was spoken to by Yuri Vidovsky, a Russian prisoner who spent twenty years in the camps. He said he saw Phillips in Novocherkassk in southern Russia.[2]

Individuals are speaking up too, despite their fear that the current thaw may be another Prague Spring. One former Gulag inmate wrote to the BBC. He had spent twenty-three years in the camps at Vorkuta. He was a Ukrainian living in Germany and enclosed in his letter a statement from his father, who was still in the Ukraine. It read: 'I, Kravchenko, Pyotr Yakovlevich, was born in 1925. I was arrested in 1948 and was imprisoned in Stalinist camps from 1949–1956. In the period between 1949 and 1952, in a settlement village called Abez in the Komi Autonomous Republic, I have met an American called Trishchenko who said he was a New Yorker and either worked or lived on Fifth Avenue. He was my closest friend in the camps for over two years. Also in the settlement Abez, I have met an American called Yuri Puzyrev, although I think his name had been changed and in America he was called John Aldridge. In 1949, at the railway station at Lvov in the Ukraine where the prisoners were transported to different destinations, I met Lieutenant Colonel Cherny.'

Another man wrote to say that he had spent twenty-three years in the camps at Vorkuta, just up the railway line from Abez. With him, he said, there were British.

## CHAPTER 44

# Journey to Vorkuta

✝

RESEARCHING THIS BOOK has not been easy. Even before I had signed the contract with the publishers, questions had been asked in Parliament. While I was out being interviewed on ITN News, British Telecom dropped round for what they told my girlfriend was a 'routine inspection' of my phone. And a shadowy character from MI6 contacted me.

I went to the Public Record Office in Richmond and discovered, as I expected, that almost all the documents I wanted to see were closed to me. Normally, government records are closed for thirty years. In the case of politically sensitive material, this limit is sometimes extended to fifty years. Most of the documents I wanted to see from the Korean War were closed for seventy-five years and the POW and repatriation records I needed from World War II were not even lodged at the Public Record Office. They were 'retained by the department', according to the PRO's catalogue. This is supposed to mean the records are in day-to-day use by the department, but what use the Ministry of Defence can find for debriefs of ex-POWs returning from Odessa in 1945 I cannot imagine. So I put myself on a plane to Washington D.C. and the US National Archives. The material for this book comes almost exclusively from that source.

Curiously, neither the Public Record Office nor the US National Archives – nor the Red Cross nor the Order of St John – could find the lists of names of the registered British prisoners of war in German prison camps in 1945 – the total number of whom consolidated sources put at 199,592 – though the British government, the International Red Cross, the British Red Cross and the Order of St John *must* all have had them. A list purporting to give the names of the British servicemen held by the Germans during World War II has been published, but that is a list of the 168,476 who returned. Neither the Public Record Office nor the US National Archives could turn up the camp records captured by General Patton's Third Army. Captured Nazi records were micro-filmed and shared by America and Britain. One would keep the originals, the other would have the microfilm. In this case, neither side can find their copy, though researchers at the US National Archives are convinced that is 'in there somewhere'.

At one stage I was summoned to Whitehall by the Army Historical Branch which is based there. They wanted to know everything I knew. However, they said that they were only interested in individuals whose service files they could pull up. I gave them a few names and they helped me resolve a few cases. However, they would not discuss figures with me – not even to confirm how many British there were in German prisoner-of-war camps during World War II. Mr John Harding of the Army Historical Branch also asked me why, if what I alleged was true, there had not been a deluge of letters from the missing men's families. I pointed out that a huge petition had been gathered in America after the war. In secretive Britain, it was unlikely there would have been a similar reaction – after all, if you were a mother who received a telegram in 1945, after the war was over, saying that your son had not been captured, as they thought at first, but had been killed in action, you would not know that someone else was getting a similar telegram just a few streets away. You would be unlikely to question it – and, if you did, you would get nowhere. Later Mr Harding tried to dissuade me from repeating my allegations (although, at that time, I was only repeating the US Senate's allegations) because it was upsetting the families. In apparent contradiction of what he had said earlier, he now seemed to be deluged with enquiries and complaints that had not surfaced in 1945.

Some time after my visit to Whitehall, MP Tam Dalyell passed me a letter from Viscount Cranborne, Parliamentary Under-Secretary for Defence. It accused me of not co-operating with the Ministry of Defence's investigation – even though I had. The letter also said that the status of the files I had requested at the Public Record Office had been reviewed and they were now open – as I well knew. But when I went to check, they were still closed for seventy-five years or 'retained by the department'. Surely the government had made some mistake.

Viscount Cranborne also expressed his concern that I was doing what they had most hoped to avoid – reopening wounds they had sought to heal and raising hopes which would almost certainly be false in every case. I could sympathise with this point of view. However, the allegations had not been brought up by me, but by the US Senate. In my reply, I pointed out that if Viscount Cranborne wanted to end speculation about this matter once and for all, all he had to do was find the full list of the prisoners of war held by Germans during World War II. If it was substantially the same as the list of the 168,476 men who had returned, there was no story. If it was different, then there should be a full investigation. No list has yet been forthcoming.

Meanwhile the Americans are actively looking into the fate of their missing men through the joint US–Russian Commission. ABC TV has also aired a programme about the missing prisoners of war and a number of American citizens trapped in the former Soviet Union since the 1930s have been uncovered.

The French are also investigating similar allegations about missing French prisoners of war. Several documentaries about the foreign prisoners who were taken to Tambov have already been aired in France. Two Frenchmen have even been found alive in the former Soviet Union. One, Paul Catrain, returned to France on 14 February 1993, after having been captured by the Germans during World War II. He had been found in the Ukraine.

French film-maker Georges Drion found another former French POW living in Estonia. He had been captured on the Maginot Line in 1940 and taken to a German POW camp in Poland. He escaped and went east into Russia. In 1945, he expected to be sent home. Instead, he was sent to the labour camps at Vorkuta. When he was released, he was told that he must settle in the area of Vorkuta. However, in the mid-1960s, he managed to make his way to Moscow and slipped past the guards to enter the French Embassy. Inside, he begged diplomats to send him home. But French officials told him that they were not prepared to create a diplomatic incident over one man. They kicked him out. Now in his mid-eighties, he has lived out the rest of his life in the former Soviet Union and no longer has any desire to return to France.

The Italians too have been looking into the fate of their missing prisoners of war. Project Ark, an organisation that researches those who disappeared in the Gulags, told me that a large number of bones have already been returned to the Italian government.

It seems to me that if these other countries are looking into the fate of their missing POWs, the British should be looking too. The British tax-payer maintains an expensive embassy in Moscow, but they plainly have much more important things to do than discover what happened to British subjects who disappeared while serving their country. It seemed I would have to go to Russia myself.

I went in June 1993 with two young TV journalists, Richard Parry and Richard Pendry. They were working for Frontline News and making short documentary items for BBC TV's *Newsnight* and *Channel Four News*, among others. Since a mutual friend had told them about my work, they too had become interested in the fate of the missing British POWs.

In Moscow, we discovered that American, French, Italian, German, Austrian, Japanese, even Korean researchers were looking for traces of their citizens. A former KGB colonel now working for the Institute of Oriental Studies in Moscow claimed to have found seventy former Japanese prisoners of war alive in the republics of the former Soviet Union. Yet although a British Embassy official had visited the KGB Special Archives, no one from the Embassy had been to the Archives of the October Revolution, where the records of the repatriations are lodged.

I travelled on to Syktyvkar, 600 miles northeast of Moscow and the capital of the Komi Autonomous Republic which stretches up towards the Arctic Ocean. Komi had long been a place of exile and imprisonment for enemies of the regime. In Czarist times, it had been known as the 'prison without bars'. One of the suburbs of Syktyvkar is called Paris. One hundred and fifty prisoners of war from Napoleon's ill-fated invasion of Russia in 1812 were held there, according to local archives. Their wives had joined them there and their descendants had lived in Paris, Komi, until 1941. Komi men with French-sounding names who joined the Red Army's tank corps proudly told the Soviet press that they were 'French'.

During the Stalinist era, Komi had been full of labour camps. Gulag expert Mikhail Rogatchov of Syktyvkar State University confirmed that, although foreigners had spread throughout the prison population, there had also been special camps for foreigners. Little was known about them. They did not appear on the maps of the Gulag and were only known by post office box numbers. Two of them, camps 222 and 224, were at Ukhta in the Komi republic, Rogatchov thought. We were also told that more foreigners had been held at Abez on the railway from Ukhta to Vorkuta, where Pyotr Kravchenko had been imprisoned with an American (see p. 271). A stoker from the local heating plant spends his spare time tending the graves at Abez and trying to discover who was buried in them.

There was a large German presence in Syktyvkar – many of whom were aiming to return to Germany – and Rogatchov had spent his time looking into the fate of Poles who had been imprisoned in the area. However, he agreed to look into the fate of British prisoners in Komi for us. He, like a local KGB officer sacked for his revelations about the

Gulag, expressed no surprise that British POWs had ended up in Russia. No one we met in Russia did. The Gulag had had an open-door policy, it seemed. Its gates were open to anyone – on the way in, that is.

From Syktyvkar, we travelled on to Vorkuta – a name that has come up repeatedly in this book. Let me tell you, if you ever want to take a holiday in hell, go to Vorkuta. Situated at the northernmost tip of the Urals, it is the most desolate and chilling place on earth. From 1943 until the late 1950s it was a penal colony.

There is no road to Vorkuta. The railway which runs up from Ukhta was begun in 1941 and built by prisoners. The train journey takes twelve hours and it is said that there is one corpse for every sleeper. The dead could not be buried in the frozen ground so their bodies were stacked at the side of the tracks until the brief summer thaw came. Then a thin layer of soil was sprinkled over them. After a time, their bones would poke white through the earth. They were left that way because at the time, the local people believed that those who had died were 'enemies of the people'. Recently though, local villagers have gone out and buried the remains.

We flew into Vorkuta, over miles of barren tundra. The bleak landscape is cut by rivers and puddled and stained by ponds and marshes. From the air, it looks like a Rorschach ink-blot test that spread as far as the horizon, a sewage farm on the moon. This vast expanse of scrub and marshland had been patrolled by native people who were given food and ammunition in exchange for the heads of runaway prisoners. For most of the year it was frozen and impassable. Even in June there were still huge banks of snow, though the sun did not set, day or night. During Vorkuta's years as a penal colony, not a single person successfully escaped. The dead bodies of runaways were displayed at the watch posts for three days as a warning to others.

My companions agreed that Vorkuta was the most terrifying place we had ever seen. It was the mother of all housing projects. Even the apartment blocks looked as though they had been plucked direct from Alcatraz. The town's main square, Victory Park, was a swamp of mud and garbage, though there were fresh flowers on the statue of Lenin. The road, which ran 60km in a closed loop around the coal mines, was cracked and potholed. Palls of black smoke belched from the heating-plant chimneys, forming black ribbons of soot that stretched out to the horizon.

Vorkuta is reputed to be the toughest town in Russia. Since the collapse of the Soviet system, the mafia has taken over. While we were there, a family of four were murdered for their TV set and stereo. There are running battles between youth gangs on the street. The town's only hotel is a mecca for crime. The soundman with a German

TV crew had been stabbed there. One of the rooms was burnt out, the black hole where the window was and the scorch marks on the concrete scarring an already ugly building.

There were no picture postcards of Vorkuta in the hotel lobby. Postcard photographers are usually an inventive lot, somehow injecting old world charm into the grimiest of Northern industrial towns. But the unremitting ugliness of Vorkuta would defy even the most talented airbrush artist. A sturdy Russian girl posing in a bikini and a process-blue sky would have made no difference. No matter how you cropped the shot, there were no pleasant views. Vorkuta was where all rundown 1960s housing estates came to die.

Around the town were the remnants of the sixty camps that had supplied labour for the mines there. Officially each camp held between 1,800 and 2,400 prisoners – though they often accommodated four to five times that number. At the height of the Stalinist era, there had been just 7,000 free men in Vorkuta – people who had completed their sentence but remained in exile there, plus guards and railway workers.

At the exhibition dedicated to the camps at the local town hall, the cheery hostess announced that twenty million people had died in Vorkuta. The town was just fifty years old. The local representative of Memorial – the organisation for the Gulag survivors – thought this was something of an over-estimate. Some sixty million people had died in the Gulag altogether and Vorkuta was by no means the biggest of the penal colonies. Only two to three million had died in Vorkuta, he thought, including those who had died during the construction of the railway. We put the hostess's figure of twenty million down to civic pride – 'our town is badder' than anywhere else in the old Soviet Union. But a death-toll of two to three million was grim enough. It put Vorkuta in the same league as Auschwitz.

We were told that 190 different nationalities had passed through Vorkuta. Some former German POWs still lived there, but they did not come forward when German TV crews came to town. After a lifetime of tyranny and isolation, they were afraid to identify themselves. The town had only been open for two years and people were still unused to foreigners. A French TV crew had also been in Vorkuta recently. They brought with them a Frenchman who had served time there.

Along with the mining camps, there were two women's camps. One was at the brickworks, where the Polish women were kept. The other, which was now the fire station, had supplied labour to build the railway line northwards to the furthest flung camps at a place known as the 'Valley of Death'.

In Memorial's offices, women who had been released from the camps in the mid-1950s were filling in forms to have themselves 'rehabilitated'. This would officially declare that they were innocent of all crimes, restore their pension rights and give them some small compensation for the years they had spent in forced labour. Rehabilitation also meant that they would be given the train fare to visit their place of birth. This was no earthly good to some residents of Vorkuta, though; many had been born in the camps.

The town was ringed with the remnants of the camps. Many of them were nestled in the crook of a fast-running river that, even in June, had ice in it. The far bank was steep and exposed, posing further formidable obstacle to escape.

Some of the prison barracks were still inhabited. Barracks designed for seventy men had been restyled into charming terraced cottages made of plaster-covered wooden slats and painted pink. These must have been desirable residences when they had been freshly converted – provided it did not trouble you sleeping there. Others had been left to decay, the earth insulation spilling from their walls.

Iron cages, where prisoners may have been left to die of exposure, were still intact. And under the stone-built guard houses you could still see the tiny, unheated punishment cells. These were so small you could neither stand up nor lie down. Prisoners were left to squat in the freezing cold for days on end for committing such heinous crimes as trying to draw a picture on a torn piece of canvas with a lump of coal.

The watch-towers still stood at the corners of the work compounds, with their four concentric barbed wire fences. The wire was strung from birch poles – at least the Soviets had found some use for the silver birch trees that spread for mile after mile across sub-Arctic Russia. But we could not figure out why they bothered with such elaborate security precautions. Even if you got through the wire, there was nowhere to run to.

It was difficult to comprehend the enormity of what had gone on there. The sheer scale of the camps, the mines and the consequent human suffering was numbing. Only the most banal events had any impact. Swallows singing high above the ruined camps at midnight, in the full daylight of the Arctic summer sounded full of despair. Suddenly it was only too easy to imagine yourself a prisoner in this evil and terrifying place. That same twittering song must have reminded the poor souls who ended up there that the birds would soon by flying south while you would remain through the dark depths of winter when there is only a glimmer of light in the sky for an hour and twenty minutes each day. Even the thought of the next summer and the next visit of the swallows would not raise your spirits. You would be destined to stay there until, more than likely, they worked you to death.

Outside the remains of the German camp was a settlement called Berlin II, where freed German prisoners of war settled. There were also distinctive, high-gabled Alpine-style houses built by the Germans. German and Lithuanian cemeteries were now marked by large monuments to the dead, but the same old anonymous grave markers were still in place. Their cross-pieces carry simply a letter and two digits – A46, R87. When the gravediggers reached V99, they would start again at A00. This helped minimise the scale of the deaths in the minds of the people who worked there. One wonders why they bothered. Why didn't they just throw all the dead into a mass grave? The answer is that giving the dead individual graves legitimised the whole process. The Soviets were not butchers like the Nazis, the official thinking went. The men worked to death in Soviet labour camps had been tried and sentenced individually as enemies of the people. What's more, someone, somewhere, in the depths of the KGB or MVD archives, has a list of which person lies under which grave marker, probably with their photograph, date of birth, place of birth and numerous other snippets of information. In the Soviet system you can guarantee that the paperwork on each victim was done meticulously. It was not uncommon for an execution to be postponed until all the forms had been filled in properly. Sadly, no one has yet come forward with the list of the dead from Vorkuta. When they do, people from Memorial will undoubtedly start identifying the graves and erecting proper gravestones with the names of the deceased.

When *The Gulag Archipelago* was first published in the West and copies were smuggled into the then Soviet Union, people were shocked – except, it is said, in Vorkuta. They were not in the least surprised by the brutality Solzhenitsyn describes. They had lived with it all their lives. One man who found *The Gulag Archipelago* no surprise whatsoever was Pavel Negretov. He had been arrested as a student in Leningrad in 1945, for criticising Soviet science too strongly. He spent ten years in Vorkuta. He wept as he described the utter despair he felt there. 'All you wanted was to have a full belly and to die,' he said. Like many other prisoners, he stayed on in Vorkuta after being released, rather than return to the Ukraine. After being branded an 'enemy of the people', he would have been shunned by his own people. He did not think they would have permitted him to register to live back there. In Vorkuta, he was among others who had served their time. Even after the camps closed, some sixty per cent of the miners were former prisoners who had stayed on.

Negretov is now a camp historian and he told me that he had met foreigners in the camps, including Germans from both East and West Germany. He also said that in Mine Number Four, where he worked in 1952–3, he had also met an Englishman who had said, stoically, that he did not judge all Russians by those who had imprisoned him there. Negretov had also met a Frenchman called Louis, who had been captured by the Vietnamese during the French Indo-China war. A prisoner of war, he had been handed over to the Soviet authorities, who sent him to Vorkuta.

In 1954, a Japanese prisoner had turned up there too. According to Negretov, he did not know a single European language, but explained in sign language that he was a fisherman, detained for fishing in Soviet territorial waters.

A former nurse at one of the camp hospitals told us another intriguing tale that is so far off the wall that there might be some truth to it. She said that in 1948 she nursed an Austrian count who claimed he was a major in the British army. His name was Count Alfred von Butller and he had begun the war with the Abwehr, German counter-intelligence. As an Austrian aristocrat, he did not get on very well with the Nazis and in 1942, she said, he escaped to London, where his mother and sister were living. There he joined the British army. In 1948, she continued, he was with the British army in West Germany when he was kidnapped by SMERSH and sent to Vorkuta. He was not strong enough to work and in 1949 he was conscripted into a Soviet special military unit. She never saw him again.

She was absolutely sure that von Butller had changed sides in 1942, but she had no idea how he had got from Austria to London. She said that she sensed that he was not telling her everything, besides they had 'other concerns'. Plainly, they had been in love. Von Butller had maintained throughout their short affair that he had British citizenship, and he was always confident that the British would find some way to get him out. Not surprisingly, there is no von Butller in the Army Lists for the period 1942–1948.

Who or what von Butller was, is destined to remain a mystery, I fear. But the fate of other people who disappeared into the Gulags is now being unravelled. Investigators from many other countries are looking into the histories of their prisoners of war.

I have put out appeals in the Russian media, asking for information. Former KGB officers and members of Memorial have pledged their support in trying to uncover the fate of British prisoners of war who fell into Uncle Joe's merciless hands. These people are all too keenly aware of the obstacles that stand in the path of this sort of research. It is going to take a very long time to unearth more hard information – or find any men still alive – if it is possible at all.

However, I think we owe it to the missing men at least to try.

# *Endnotes*

**CHAPTER 1**
1 *As Far As My Feet Will Carry Me*, M. Bauer
2 *The Guardian*, 18 June 1992

**CHAPTER 3**
1 An Examination of Policy Toward POW/MIA, Senate Foreign Relations Committee Minority Staff, 23 May 1991
2 Report by 1st Lieutenants Dwight Fistler and Albert May
3 US War Department telegram 221, 14 April 1919, to Military Intelligence
4 Letter from US Secretary of War to Acting Secretary of State, 12 May 1919
5 Telegram 2045–297, 4 February 1919, from Archangel to Military Intelligence
6 *The New York Times*, 18 April 1921
7 Herbert Hoover, *An American Epic*
8 John Silverman, *The Victors' Dilemma*, Barrie & Jenkins, 1970
9 War Department cable 1272, Military Intelligence, 'Russian Prisoners Arriving in France from Germany', 17 December 1918
10 'Alleged Confinement of American Officers and Soldiers in Russian Prisons', memo to Acting Assistant Chief of Staff C-2, 12 November 1930
11 ibid.
12 US government letter to Mr Huckleberry evaluating the affidavit taken by the US Justice Department, 8 November 1930

**CHAPTER 4**
1 *No Citation*, James Allan, 1955
2 *Novoje Vremja* (*New Times*) Feb.–April 1992

**CHAPTER 5**
1 *Red Web*, Tom Bower
2 *Toronto Sunday Star*, 29 October 1989
3 WO32/11139

4 Cipher telegram, from 30MM to War Office, 1 November 1944, marked Most Secret

5 Scotty Young, *Descent in Danger*

## CHAPTER 6

1 RAMPs: The Recovery and Repatriation of Liberated Prisoners of War

2 ibid.

3 Washington National Archives RG 107, Office of the Secretary of War, top secret correspondence of Secretary of War Stimson, 'Safe File', July 1940–September 1945

## CHAPTER 7

1 *Witness to History, 1929–1969*, Chip Bohlen

2 *I Was There*, William D. Leahy, 1950, Whittlesay House

3 SHAEF S65 R61 33 Entry 1 Box 87

4 Department of State telegram EFM-852, 15 February 1945

5 Memorandum from Arthur Robinson, Special Representative of the American Red Cross

6 Cable MX-22867 from US Military Mission in Moscow, 23 February 1945

7 Cable from US Military Mission in Moscow to the War Department in Washington, 1 March 1945

8 *The Strange Alliance,* John R. Deane

9 SHAEF MX-22792

10 Sir James Grigg, House of Commons 20 February 1945

11 State Department cable JH-983

12 Directorate of Prisoners of War, Imperial Prisoners of War Committee, Subcommittee A, 22 February 1945

13 SHAEF Main S-83110

## CHAPTER 8

1 Roosevelt-Stalin cable 276

2 Roosevelt-Stalin cable 277

3 State Department cable M-23119

4 WO32/11139, Report of Activities of PW Contact Team 1st to 19th March 1945

5 Cipher telegram Mil 2724, marked secret, 30 March 1945.

6 Daily Report on Position of British Prisoners of War in Germany, number 52, 25 April 1945

7 Cipher telegram 864, from Moscow to Foreign Office, 19 March 1945

8 Sir James Grigg, House of Commons 6 March 1945

9 Letter from Lublin to Major Croft in Odessa, 7 March 1945, WO32/11139

10 Cable classified Urgent, Top Secret, 'A Personal Message for the President, from US Ambassador to Russia, W. Averell Harriman,' 8 March 1945

11 SWP 711.94114 A/6-2145

## CHAPTER 9

1 *US Veteran News & Report*, 29 May 1989
2 Major D.P. Constable and Flying Officer David Floyd report, 21 March 1945
3 Foreign Office cable 1397 to Moscow
4 PREM3 364/17/762
5 State Department cable PH–1449/738, 14 March 1945
6 FO to Moscow cable 805
7 FO 916/1427

## CHAPTER 10

1 FO 916/1427
2 Cipher telegram 835, from Moscow to Foreign Office, 16 March 1945
3 Mil 255 from 30 MM 'for Chiefs of Staff'
4 Roosevelt-Stalin cable 278
5 Cable 1325 from Moscow to Foreign Office
6 Foreign Office cable 1396
7 Prime Minister's personal minutes M.246/5, 24 March 1945, Churchill Papers 20/209
8 PM's personal telegram T.312/5, marked 'Personal, Private and Top Secret', 21 March 1945, Churchill Papers 20/213
9 *Yalta Betrayed, Road to Victory*, Winston S. Churchill
10 Foreign Office cable 1397
11 Roosevelt-Stalin cable 279
12 Foreign Office cable 1434
13 Prime Minister's personal telegram T.346/5
14 State Department cable CLB-955, Top Secret, Kirk to Secretary of State
15 Cipher cable from AMSSO to 30MM
16 Cipher telegram Mil2780, marked Secret, 6 April 1945
17 Draft of memorandum by the War Office, Chief of Staff Committee, Top Secret, 'Treatment of British Commonwealth Prisoners of War Recovered by the Soviet Forces'
18 Report from Costello and Floyd, 21 March 1945, WO32/11139
19 American Red Cross 'Prisoners of War Bulletin', April issue, Volume III, Number Four
20 Foreign Office cable 602

## CHAPTER 11

1 RAMPs: The Recovery and Repatriation of Liberated Prisoners of War
2 AGWAR Washington WARX-58751
3 Suggested Plan for General Younger, marked Secret, 6 April 1945
4 Memo 30 Military Mission, 3 April 1945
5 Special Report number 755, signed Albert A. Fadler
6 SHAEF Main BAX-25586
7 SHAEF 'Evacuation of British and American Released Prisoners of War', 4 April 1945

8 Cipher telegram Mil 2780, marked Secret, 6 April 1945
9 Memorandum entitled Prisoners of War – Points of Interest 7.4.45 by Colonel R.N. Brinckman
10 Memo from PWX Branch to Sir Archibald Clark Kerr, 18 April 1945
11 War Office telegram 81543
12 FO 916/1202

## CHAPTER 12

1 Foreign Office telegrams 1663, 8 April 1945 and 3923, 20 April 1945
2 Cipher telegram Mil 2792, marked Secret, 8 April 1945
3 Letter from Napoleon Brinckman to General Younger, 9 April 1945
4 Letter from General Golubev to Admiral Archer, 12 April 1945
5 WO 32/11139
6 Cipher cable KW2 2/117 from Foreign Office to Moscow
7 WO 224/227/135
8 Foreign Office telegram 1439
9 Memorandum to the Commissioner for the USSR
10 Report by Lieutenant Colonel Hundall, Head of PWX Branch, 30 British Military Mission, Moscow, 16 April 1945
11 Cipher telegram 0/70 from Britmiss Odessa to Troopers
12 Cipher telegram Air 300 from 30 Mission to HQMAAFSSO (R) HQTC, 25 April 1945
13 Secret cable from AFHQ Caserta 5324
14 Letter from Archer to Golubev, 12 April 1945
15 State Department telegram No. ASB 1304, 13 April 1945, 'To: Secretary of State'
16 Cipher telegram 230, From Moscow to Washington, War Cabinet Distribution
17 PREM3 364/14/797
18 Telegram from Britmiss Odessa to Britmiss Moscow, 18 April 1945

## CHAPTER 13

1 Associated Press, Paris, 19 April 1945
2 *The New York Times* 20 April 1945
3 Foreign Office cable to Washington number 3935, 20 April 1945
4 Order to Commanding General, Mediterranean Theater, and Headquarters Communication Zone European Theater signed Major General J.E. Hull, Assistant Chief of Staff, CPD
5 Cipher telegram 3936, from Acting Secretary of State to Lord Halifax
6 Foreign Office telegram 3936 of 20 April 1945
7 Cipher telegram 3924
8 Memorandum by the Red Cross Commission, 6 May 1945
9 State Department MES-40, Kirk to Secretary of State, 21 April 1945
10 FO 916/1201

11 SHGAP S85822
12 SHGAP FWD-19726
13 Foreign Office cipher telegram KW2/129
14 *Toronto Sunday Star* 29 October 1989
15 *Soldiers of Misfortune*, James Sanders, Mark Sauter, Cort Kirkwood
16 Imperial War Museum, Rolf collection, statement by D.B. Palmer
17 David Rolf, *Prisoners of the Reich*, Cooper, Coronet, 1989
18 See for example *Piece of Cake*, Geoff Taylor, Corgi, 1980

## CHAPTER 14

1 Statements taken at Odessa by Squadron Leader Harris on 11 April 1945
2 Sworn statement given by Rifleman Miles and Lance Corporal Lewis to Major J.S. Buitt, 11 April 1945
3 Statement made at Odessa 11 April 1945
4 Telegram 3910, from Foreign Office to Moscow, 10 June 1945
5 PRO FO 916/1202 XC 14935
6 Letter from Archer to Golubev, 29 April 1945
7 SHAEF routine secret cable MX-24072
8 State Department telegram RS-710/1423
9 *Moscow News*, 1 May 1945

## CHAPTER 15

1 Washington National Archives 226/19/461
2 Memo from Admiral Archer to General Golubev, 2 May 1945
3 Cipher telegram RAC 1158/4641 from BMM Rumania to Troopers marked Top Secret
4 FO 916/1201
5 Cipher telegram number 1658 from Moscow to the Foreign Office, repeat to Washington
6 House of Commons Hansard, 2 May 1945, Oral Answers
7 Cipher telegram 90386 from Troopers to SHAEF Forward
8 SHAEF Forward PWX cipher telegram 90386, marked Top Secret
9 SHAEF cipher telegram number 91432, marked Top Secret
10 Cipher telegram 91432, marked Top Secret, from Troopers to SHAEF Forward
11 Letter from W. St C. Roberts to Lieutenant Colonel H. Phillimore, 7 May 1945
12 Memo from Archer to Golubev, 3 May 1945
13 Letter to 'H.M. Minister' from J.E.T. Younger, 11 May 1945
14 Cipher Telegram X/147 020930, June
15 State Department telegram DRM-283 (Secret)
16 Cipher cable number 2440 from Foreign Office to Moscow
17 Letter from Younger to Kolesnikov, 30 May 1945
18 SHAEF Mission to Belgium, Psychological Warfare Division, Intelligence Section memo from Captain G.C. Curtis to Major I.R. Deacon, 7 May 1945

19 SHAEF FWD KX-21203

20 Official Report, House of Commons, 9 May 1945

21 House of Commons Hansard, 9 May 1945

22 Washington National Archives 383.6/8

23 SHAEF FWD 147/10 KX-21205

24 SHAEF FWD M-24293

25 SHAEF FWD S-87705

26 US Military Mission communication number 942

27 Letter from Colonel Hurndall to General Younger, 10 May 1945, ref. PWX 22

28 Cipher telegram Mil 2995 from 30 Mission to Troopers

29 Memos from Archer to Golubev, 11 May 1945

30 Memo marked Secret from Basilov to Archer, 2 June 1945

## CHAPTER 16

1 *Sunday Star*, Washington DC, 13 May 1945

2 *The New York Times*, 15 May 1945

3 *Sunday Times*, 6 January 1974

4 Memorandum, 'To: the United States Political Advisor for Germany (Murphy), From: Mr. Parker W. Buhrman, Munich', 28 January 1946

5 *My Three Years in Moscow*, Walter Bedell Smith

6 See Nicholas Bethell, *The Last Secret*, Deutsch, 1974, and Nikolai Tolstoy, *The Victims of Yalta*, Hodder, 1977, for further reading on this

7 *Forced Labor in the Soviet Union*, David Dallin and Boris I. Nicolaevsky, Yale University Press

## CHAPTER 17

1 Department of State telegram 2625

2 Washington National Archives 383.6/10

3 Report 'From: Major General R.W. Barker, Subject: Report of Conference with Russian Officials Relative to the Repatriation of Prisoners of War and Displaced Persons, To: The Chief of Staff', SHAEF, 23 May 1945

4 SHAEF MAIN 8-89142

5 Memorandum, classified secret, 'To: Secretary of State, From: Heath, Deputy to Robert Murphy, Subject: Overland Exchange of Ex-Prisoners of War and Displaced Persons Liberated by all Allied Expeditionary Force and the Red Army', 1 June 1945

6 Report 'From: Major General R.W. Barker, Subject: Report of Conference with Russian Officials Relative to the Repatriation of Prisoners of War and Displaced Persons, To: The Chief of Staff, SHAEF', 23 May 1945

7 SHAEF File Number (4) 383.6/11

8 FO 916/1202

9 RAMPs: The Recovery and Repatriation of Liberated Prisoners of War

## CHAPTER 18

1 Letter from Archer to Golubev, 16 May 1945
2 Letter from Basilov to Archer, 18 May 1945, marked Secret
3 Letter from Archer to Basilov, 20 May 1945
4 Letter from Basilov to Archer, 18 May 1945
5 SHAEF FWD CA-1739
6 SHAEF FWD KX-21617
7 'An Examination of US Policy Toward POW/MIA by the US Senate Committee on Foreign Relations Republican Staff' 23 May 1991
8 FO 916/1202
9 *The Times*, 19 May 1945
10 RAMPs
11 PREM3 364/17/721
12 *New York Times*, 22 May 1945
13 SHGAP S-89283 secret priority
14 FO 916/1198

## CHAPTER 19

1 SHAEF FWD FX-44670
2 Macmillan's War Diaries
3 SHAEF FWD FX-76272
4 SHAEF FX-80335
5 Notes on Conference Held at Linz, Austria, on 23 May 1945, Washington National Archives 383.6/10
6 *Macmillan at War*, BBC1, 21 December 1984
7 *The Minister and the Massacres*, Count Nikolai Tolstoy
8 SHAEF FX-82606
9 NARA document copied from PRO WO32:13749
10 WO 204/10126 and FO 1020/39, 11, 20
11 Tolstoy, op. cit.

## CHAPTER 20

1 SHAEF FX-84965
2 Draft of telegram from Younger to Chetwode, not sent after discussion with Archer
3 WO204/10126
4 Telegram Younger to Chetwode, 29 May 1945
5 SHAEF WX-90429
6 WO 224/227

## CHAPTER 21

1 SHAEF MAIN S-89142
2 SHAEF FWD AG-3700

3 Daily Report of British Prisoners of War, number 76, marked Secret, 28 May 1945

4 House of Commons Hansard, 29 May 1945

5 House of Commons Hansard, 15 May 1945

6 Letter from Archer to Basilov, 31 May 1945

7 WO32/11139

8 SHGAP FWD-22796

9 Cable classified Secret Routine, 'To: SHAEF FORWARD, From: SHAEF MISSION FRANCE, to SHAEF FORWARD G5', Ref. No.: MF-14427, 30 May 1945

10 SHAEF FWD 22790

11 SHAEF 383.6-2 MED

12 SHGAP FWD-23059

## CHAPTER 22

1 SHAEF FWD 225/24

2 Department of State telegram DSH-1522

3 FO.371/48819, 78–9

4 WO2OH/10126

5 State Department cable 2433

6 Secret memo from The Directorate of Repatriation to Admiral Archer, 2 June 1945

7 Cipher telegram 2225 from Moscow to Foreign Office, Cabinet Distribution

8 Copy filed at the American Embassy, Moscow, 8 June 1945

9 Cipher telegram 2226 from Moscow to Foreign Office, Cabinet Distribution

10 Cipher cable 3342 from Foreign Office to Moscow, Cabinet Distribution

11 *Chicago Daily Times*, 5 June 1945

12 Quoted in *The Minister and the Massacres*, Nikolai Tolstoy

13 ibid.

## CHAPTER 23

1 FO 916/1202

2 Letter to Basilov signed lieutenant general ref PWX, 5 June 1945

3 FO 916/1427

4 Foreign Office to Moscow cable 3107

5 *US Veteran News and Report*, 29 May 1989

6 Department of State telegram MJK-1962

7 Department of State telegram PEM-1103

8 *I Survived*, Godfrey Lias

9 *In the Name of Humanity*, Alexander Thomsen, Longmans, 1963

10 PRO FO 916

**CHAPTER 24**

1 'An Examination of US Policy Toward POW/MIAs' by the US Senate Foreign Relations Republican Staff, 23 May 1991

2 Document from PW5 (b) marked Depute Assistant Adjutant General, 8 June 1945

3 RAMPs, Office of the Chief Historian – European Command, 1947

4 Document from PW5 (b) marked Depute Assistant Adjutant General, 8 June 1945

5 RAMPs, Office of the Chief Historian – European Command, 1947

6 *The New York Times*, 13 June 1945

7 House of Commons Hansard, 12 June 1945

8 Cable 2477 from Moscow to Foreign Office

9 Cipher cable 2436 from Moscow to Foreign Office

**CHAPTER 25**

1 *US Veteran News and Report*, 29 May 1989

2 ibid.

3 ibid.

4 *The New York Times*, 2 July 1945

5 SHAEF S-92930

6 SHAEF MAIN M-24981

7 *Strange Alliance*, Viking, NY, 1947

8 SHGAP S-94080, S-92030

9 PREM3 364/17/715

**CHAPTER 26**

1 *The Times*, 2 July 1945

2 FO 916/1202

3 PREM3 364/17/712

4 *The Last Secret*, Nicholas Bethell, p. 50

5 Cipher telegram 4050 from Foreign Office to Moscow, 21 July 1945

6 Cipher telegram 26, from Hankey to Foreign Office, 20 July 1945

7 FO 916/1201 telegram 57

8 *Victims of Yalta*, Nikolai Tolstoy

9 *Diplomat Among Warriors*, Robert Murphy, Collins, London, 1964

**CHAPTER 27**

1 Foreign Office telegram 4417

2 FO 916/1201

3 FO 916/1427

4 FO 916/1202

5 *The Times*, 22 August 1945

**CHAPTER 28**

1 FO 916/1201

2 Cipher telegram 69505 from WO to 30 MM No. 276
3 Cipher telegram 69506 from WO to 30 MM No. 275
4 Cipher telegram 28 August 1945 from 30 MM to WO
5 FO 916/1201
6 FO 916/1201
7 FO 916/1202
8 *Speaking Frankly*, James F. Byrnes, Harpers, 1947
9 *Witness to History, 1929–1969*, Chip Bohlen
10 *Forced Labor in the Soviet Union*, David J. Dalkin and Boris I. Nicolaevsky, Yale University Press, 1947

## CHAPTER 29

1 *The New York Times*, 30 November 1945

## CHAPTER 30

1 Cipher telegram Mil 2709, 29 March 1945
2 FO 916/1427
3 *Soldiers of Misfortune*, James Sanders, Mark Sauter, Cort Kirkwood

## CHAPTER 31

1 State Department telegram 13cd kz Intl Nl
2 *Political Science Quarterly* Volume 88, number 2, June 1973
3 Counter Intelligence Corps Region 1 File Nr. I-G-820

## CHAPTER 32

1 *The Times*, 16 September 1946
2 Private correspondence, 26 October 1992
3 Department of State letter 777 from the American legation in Bucharest
4 Memo from the International Committee of the Red Cross to the American National Red Cross, 1 December 1948
5 Memo Office of European Affairs, Department of State, 3 November 1948
6 *The Times*, 22 April 1949
7 State Department memo 183 from the American Consul General in Hamburg, 23 April 1949
8 Despatch BB-021 from Robertson in Baden-Baden to the Commander in Chief US Forces in Europe, for action
9 *Soldiers of Misfortune*, James Sanders, Mark Sauter, Cort Kirkwood
10 Foreign Service Despatch from the Political Adviser, Heidelberg, Number 43, 2 February 1954
11 EUCOM report RS-112–50

## CHAPTER 33

1 *Private Kelly, By Himself*, Frank Kelly
2 Alexandr Solzhenitsyn, *The Gulag Archipelago*

3 *The Times*, 13 November 1953

4 *The Times*, 17 November 1953

5 *The Times*, 18 November 1953

6 *The Times*, 23 November 1953

7 *The Times*, 4 December 1953

8 *The Times*, 17 December 1953

9 *The Bamboo Cage*, Nigel Cawthorne

10 *I Killed To Live*, Eric Pleasants and Eddie Chapman, Cassell & Co, London, 1957

11 *The New York Times*, 5 January 1954

12 *If This is a Man*, Primo Levi

13 *Alexander Dolgun's Story*, Patrick Watson and Alexander Dolgun

14 *I Survived*, Godfrey Lias

15 *I Was a Slave in the Soviet Union*, John Noble

16 *Toronto Sunday Star*, 29 October 1989


## CHAPTER 34

1 *Soldiers of Misfortune*, James Sanders, Mark Sauter, Cort Kirkwood

2 *Français au Goulag*, Pierre Rigoulot

3 Correspondence with Pierre Rigoulot, 17 September 1992

4 Letter from J. Harding, Army Historical Branch, 26 November 1992

5 *A Hidden World*, Raphael Rupert, World, 1963

6 UP, 26 October 1953, datelined Berlin

7 Washington National Archives 611.6124/9–1252

8 USG Bureau of Security and Consular Affairs memo, 1 July 1955


## CHAPTER 35

1 *The Times*, 6 April 1954

2 FW 740.00114 PW/11–1949

3 General Headquarters Far East Command, Military Intelligence Section, General Staff, Special Report 'Japanese Prisoners of War, Life and Death in Soviet PW Camps'

4 *Nippon Times*, 5 August 1949

5 *The Times*, 6 April 1954

6 CIA Economic Intelligence Report 'Forced Labor in the USSR, 1953–57' CIA/RR148, 12 September 1958

7 *The New York Times*, 3 January 1954

8 *Time*, 11 November 1957

9 *Time*, 14 March 1960

10 Congressional Record, 12 June 1978, E3173


## CHAPTER 36

1 *POW – The Uncivil Face of War*, Richard Garrett

2 Canadian archives 112.3M2.003 (D28) British Commonwealth Missing in Action and Prisoner of War Lists, Korea, 13 July 1953

3 Public Record Office WO208/3999

## CHAPTER 37
1 *US News & World Report*, 18 December 1953
2 Correspondence 'To: Senator Johnson. From: Assistant Secretary of State for Congressional Relations, Thruston B. Morton', SEV 611.61241/12–2153, 20 January 1954

## CHAPTER 38
1 CIA report: 'American prisoners of war in South China', 27 June 1951
2 CIA Information Report SO 66740
3 CIA Information Report SO 69870
4 CIA Information Report SO 71388
5 CIA Information Report SO 70338
6 CIA Information Report SO 71388
7 CIA Information Report SO 71388
8 CIA Information Report SO 74807
9 CIA Information Report SO 74469
10 CIA Information Report SO 91634
11 Papers of Harry S. Truman, Psychological Strategy Board, Box 32

## CHAPTER 39
1 State Department memo 'British Subjects Interned in North Korea', 19 March 1953
2 State Department cable 5200, 20 March 1953
3 State Department cable 5406, 2 April 1953
4 Foreign Service Despatch from HICOG Berlin, 25 April 1953
5 CCRAK H-101
6 *Soldiers of Misfortune*, Sanders et al.
7 *Washington Post*, 24 September 1992
8 *Esquire*, May 1953
9 CIA Information Report CS 14835
10 CCRAK Specific Request 66–53

## CHAPTER 40
1 *The Times*, 13 August 1953
2 *The Times*, 12 August 1953
3 *The Times*, 13 August 1953
4 *The Times*, 17 August 1953
5 *The Times*, 18 August 1953
6 *The Times*, 25 August 1953
7 Cable CX 64657 from Clark at CINCUNC Tokyo to UNCMAC Korea
8 Cable 237570 from CINCUNC Tokyo to DEPTAR Washington DC for the Joint Chiefs of Staff
9 *Soldiers of Misfortune*, Sanders et al.

10 *The Times*, 11 September 1953
11 *The Times*, 24 February 1954
12 *The Times*, 22 September 1953
13 *The Times*, 22 September 1953
14 *Soldiers of Misfortune*, Sanders et al.
15 Tighe Report Epilogue, Lt. Gen. Eugene Tighe, 27 May 1986

**CHAPTER 41**

1 *The Times*, 16 January 1954
2 *The Times*, 23 January 1954
3 *The Times*, 6 December 1954
4 *The Times*, 6 December 1954
5 *Soldiers of Misfortune*, Sanders et al.
6 *The New York Times*, 5 January 1954
7 *The Morning News Tribune*, 23 July 1992
8 State Department telegram 666 from Dulles to Moscow
9 *The Times*, 15 May 1954

**CHAPTER 42**

1 *Soldiers of Misfortune*, James Sanders, Mark Sauter, Cort Kirkwood
2 *The Morning News Tribune*, 23 July 1992
3 ibid.
4 Department of Defense memo 'DoD Response to Unfounded Allegations that the US Government Abandoned POWs in World War II and Korea'
5 Public Record Office WO208/3999
6 *Sunday Express*, 4 November 1990

**CHAPTER 43**

1 *Los Angeles Times*, 3 July 1992
2 *Daily Telegraph*, 1 September 1992

# Index of Prisoners

Australia
 WW1
 Cox, Gunner Vivian 145
Austria
 WW1
 Messmer, Leopold 6
 WW2
 'Germanovitch, Erwin' 195
 Ludwig, Richard 199
 Pauer, Karl 199
 von Butller, Count Alfred 280

Britain
 WW2
 Albert (Harajzti), Pilot Officer
  173
 Alexander, Private Donald 75
 Allan, James 18–23
 Ashmore, Private 149
 Bainbridge, Corporal Robert
  18–19, 20
 Barnes, Petty Officer
  Maurice    19
 Barratt, Warrant Officer R.H.
  128, 171–3
 Bateman, Fusilier Kenneth 'Bill'
  20–1
 Boughton, Fusilier Eddie 20–1
 Briggs, Sergeant Major George
  19, 20–1
 Cartwright, Peter 200
 Chambers, Lance Corporal 87,
  123
 Chapman 193
 Clarke, Sergeant 158

Clements (Vajda), Lieutenant
 John 173
Clough, Private Fraser 75
Dimmock, Private Harry 153,
 154–6
Everrett, Private 72
Godden, Rifleman 172
Hales 156
Hanson, Otto 49
Hasdell, Private F. 86
Hayhurst, George 156
Heslington, Corporal 79
Hubert, Flight Lieutenant 106
Kavin, Thomas 156
Keating, Harry 200
Kelly, Private Frank 9, 187–90,
 195, 208
Larwrence, Mark 106
Lester(s), Major Mony 200
Livett, Lance Corporal R.E. 50
Lovegrove, Private Hubert
 20–2
Lythgoe, Private 159
Mackay, Lance Corporal R.S.
 116
MaKay, Lieutenant Michael 271
McLean, H.G. 72–3
MacLennan, Company Sergeant
 Major 67
Manzie, Company Sergeant
 Major 123
Matthews 49
Nesbitt, Private 153
Oaks, Sergeant John 106
Pegg, Private James 154–6

# Index